PRODUCTIVE THINKING

Max Wertheimer

LATE PROFESSOR OF PSYCHOLOGY AND
PHILOSOPHY IN THE GRADUATE FACULTY
OF POLITICAL AND SOCIAL SCIENCE, THE
NEW SCHOOL FOR SOCIAL RESEARCH

PRODUCTIVE
THINKING

ENLARGED EDITION, 1959 ─────────────

Edited by Michael Wertheimer

HARPER & ROW, PUBLISHERS

New York and Evanston

CONTENTS

ACKNOWLEDGMENTS   xi

NOTE BY THE EDITORS OF THE FIRST EDITION   xiii

NOTE BY THE EDITOR OF THE ENLARGED
    EDITION, 1959   xv

INTRODUCTION   1

The two traditional approaches
Crucial difficulties
Modern developments

Chapter One.   THE AREA OF THE PARALLELOGRAM   13

I. Pupils learn the solution; do the assigned tasks
        excellently
    Did they really understand? The psychologist puts
        a question
    Other tasks with A- and B-responses
    The method of A-B pairs
    An extreme case is considered
    What is the crucial issue?
II. The psychologist introduces ugly procedures
    With the parallelogram
        A boy's induction plus proof
        A structurally blind hypothesis
        A crude example
    With the rectangle
        Confusion of area and perimeter

A fantastic machine is considered
A queer procedure with proof
Essential characteristics of the ugly procedures
Certain objections are considered

III. Productive processes
Finding the area of the rectangle
Character of the operations
Remark on traditional view
Remark on relations
Remark on means-end formulations
On the meaning of multiplication
Finding the area of the parallelogram
Genuine productive processes in children
Character of the operations and of the processes
A remark on drill
Graphs of the sensible processes
Items involved. Dramatic transitions in thinking
as in perception
What is needed

IV. An easier way out? The role of past experience
A question left unanswered above
Remark of a logician; with an answer
And the goal itself?

Chapter Two. THE BRIDGE PROBLEM*   79

Chapter Three. THE PROBLEM OF THE VERTICAL
ANGLES   97
Difficulties in seeing the sense of the question
I. Reciting the proof—foolish mistakes and sensible
procedures
A- and B-tasks
II. Processes in finding the proof
III. Structural issues: structure of a pair of equations
Remark on a theoretical misformulation
Why the problem is so difficult
The line of thinking
IV. Remarks on a basically misleading traditional
assumption about the nature of human thinking

* All material marked with an asterisk appears for the first time in this edition.

Chapter Four. **THE FAMOUS STORY OF YOUNG GAUSS**   **108**

I. A problem for the reader
   The story of young Gauss
   Three types of productive processes in children
   Differences and common features in the three types

II. The psychologist comes to grips with the issues
    Several structural issues

III. Why is the task so difficult for many?
     Factors working for and against productive solutions
     Structural hiddenness
     Structural simplification
     Remark on doing and undoing
     Digression on work and dance
     The structural study goes on
     Sensible tendencies in grouping
     The square set in numbers and figures
     Perception and reasonableness
     Tasks with angles

IV. The psychologist has strange experiences with structurally simplified tasks. Structural blindness
    Remarks on the role of drill
    Comments of a famous psychologist
    Comments of a mathematician
    Remarks of another psychologist

V. Deepening the issue
   A protocol of a thought process
   First part
   Second part
   Remarks on whole-qualities
   Third part
   Problem with its solution only a part
   A remark on exactness

Chapter Five. **PLUS THREE, MINUS THREE***   **143**

Chapter Six. **THE SQUARE OF A BINOMIAL; LEARNING ARITHMETIC***   **151**

Chapter Seven. TWO BOYS PLAY BADMINTON; A
GIRL DESCRIBES HER OFFICE   169

    Brief review
 I. Story of the badminton game
      Types of reaction to the problem
      Continuation of the story: the boy's solution
      Characterization of the steps and operations
        On centering
        On attitude
        On transformation
      A brief remark on great issues
 II. A girl describes her office. The Ego in the
      description
      Discussion of the structure of the description
        Relational networks
        The source of the arrows
        The hunch

Chapter Eight. FINDING THE SUM OF THE ANGLES
OF A POLYGON   193

    The process starts
    First hunch
    The "intuition"
    Remark on the usual formula
    A queer idea
    The internal angles. The hole
    Solids?
    Character of the process

Chapter Nine. A DISCOVERY BY GALILEO   205

    Introduction
    The simplified situation
 I. What happens to the speed of moving bodies?
      The order of accelerations
 II. The other half of the picture
 III. The gap. The discovery
      Structural requirements vs. familiarity
      The structural changes

Chapter Ten. EINSTEIN: THE THINKING THAT LED
TO THE THEORY OF RELATIVITY   213

  I. Act   I. The beginning of the problem
     Act   II. Light determines a state of absolute
              rest?
     Act III. Work on the one alternative
     Act   IV. Michelson's result and Einstein
     Act   V. The Lorentz solution
     Act   VI. Re-examination of the theoretical
              situation
     Act VII. Positive steps toward clarification
              Discovery of a gap
              Consequences
     Act VIII. Invariants and transformation
     Act   IX. On movement, on space, a thought
              experiment
     Act   X. Questions for observation and
              experiment
 II. What were the decisive features in the thought
    process?
    A remark on traditional interpretations
    On the role of axioms
    Survey of the line of thinking
    The structural changes

Conclusion: DYNAMICS AND LOGIC OF
PRODUCTIVE THINKING   234

    Résumé
    Table of operations as envisaged by gestalt theory
    Three groups of problems
    Dynamic theory of thinking
    Two other types of processes
      Their relation as to theory
    Ambiguity in the operations of the traditional
      approaches
    On gestalt logic
      Remarks on "class" and on several basic
        operations of logic
    Direction in the process of thinking

Appendix 1. ON THE PROBLEM OF THE DISTINC-
TION BETWEEN ARBITRARY COMPONENT AND
NECESSARY PART*   260

Appendix 2. THE ALTAR WINDOW*   266

Appendix 3. THE SCHOOL INSPECTOR*   269

Appendix 4. SUGGESTIONS FOR TEACHING
ABOUT AREA*   272

Appendix 5. THE BALANCING STICK*   286

Appendix 6. THE SUM OF A SERIES   289

Appendix 7. MAX WERTHEIMER: A BIBLIOGRAPHY*   294

Index   297

Acknowledgments

THIS book owes much to Clara W. Mayer, Dean of the School of Philosophy and Liberal Arts in the New School for Social Research. But for her untiring effort the manuscript would not have reached its final form; she was intensely interested in its subject matter and deeply devoted to its aims. That she never failed to find time for it notwithstanding her full time activities at the School, was a source of inspiration.

I am very grateful to Dr. S. E. Asch for his fine help in preparing the manuscript; to Mr. and Mrs. Benno Elkan for untiring friendly encouragement; to Mrs. Clara Mond and Mrs. Maria Di Piazza for indefatigable secretarial assistance.

Special thanks are due Dr. Alvin Johnson and my Faculty. I regret that this book, which is limited to some elementary problems, does not fully express the spirit of co-operation in the social sciences which is so alive in our Faculty and which owes so much to Alvin Johnson. Only briefly and occasionally could I touch upon these issues, which mean so much to all of us. I am likewise indebted to my friends whose work is connected with the problems of this book.

To the subjects of my experiments, the adults and the children, I am thankful for having learned so much. And I am very grateful to the distinguished men of science—Einstein above all—who made it possible for me to study intimately, in many conversations, how some of their great achievements in thinking developed.

The book contains only a small portion of the studies and material I have given to students in lectures and seminars. I have reported on parts of it in single lectures at Harvard, Chicago, Bloomington, Ann Arbor, Smith College, Swarthmore, Bryn Mawr, et al.

It is a kind of prolegomena; I hope I shall be able to finish two other books to which this is a mere introduction. In spite of its limitations I hope it may be of use.

MAX WERTHEIMER

New Rochelle, N. Y.
September 23, 1943

Note by the Editors of the First Edition

THE manuscript of *Productive Thinking*, upon which Max Wertheimer had worked during the last seven years, was completed shortly before his death. In preparing the work for publication we found that certain linguistic revisions were necessary. Mere difficulties of expression, it seemed to us, should not be allowed to obscure the meaning which Wertheimer clearly had in mind. The reader may be assured, however, that changes have been made only where the purpose of clarity could not otherwise have been attained. The content and the form of the discussion have not been altered in any place.

All remaining notes and papers of Wertheimer will be deposited with the Graduate Faculty of Political and Social Science, where qualified scholars will have the opportunity to study them.

Valentin Wertheimer assisted his father in some of the final revisions of the manuscript and has been helpful to us in many ways.

We are grateful to Mrs. Ray Borne for the painstaking care with which she saw the manuscript through the press.

S. E. Asch

W. Köhler

C. W. Mayer

1945

Note by the Editor of the Enlarged Edition

THIS edition contains, in addition to the contents of the previous edition, various chapters and fragments that were found among Max Wertheimer's notes and papers. An early version of the Table of Contents, also found among his papers, indicated that he had at one time planned to include the three chapters (Two, Five, and Six) that have been added. Although the finished manuscript of the original book did not make use of them, they and six new appendices are presented here because it seemed to many people that this material should be more widely known.

The manuscripts of the additions seemed less finished than the manuscript of the original edition. Hence some changes in organization and expression were required, but these editorial changes were kept to a minimum. Notes by the present editor are indicated by "— M.W." These persons have read the new portions of this volume, and made many helpful suggestions: Rudolf Arnheim, Solomon E. Asch, Mary Henle, Clara W. Mayer, Lise Wertheimer, and Valentin Wertheimer.

The following note, found among Max Wertheimer's papers, suggests the further work he had intended and may serve as an introduction to some of the additions.

I had limited this book mostly to subject matters which contain summative features as, e.g., the size of an area, the sum of a series, in order to focus the reader on just the gestalt in the thinking process itself; I have discussed only some formally elementary cases of gestalt features in the subject matter. In a second book I will have to deal also with the subject matters that are themselves real gestalten. Whereas methods and tools for piecemeal or structure-blind operations are highly developed, this by comparison is not the case for problems in gestalten, problems characteristic for the development of gestalt theory.

Two books must follow: one on the broader aspects of the psychology of thinking, the other on the problem of gestalt logic in which the traditional issues appear as the Euclidean special case. Here also the features of productive gestalt heuristics will have to be treated.

Boulder, Colorado   Michael Wertheimer
April 15, 1958

PRODUCTIVE THINKING

Introduction

WHAT occurs when, now and then, thinking really works productively? What happens when, now and then, thinking forges ahead? What is really going on in such a process?

If we look for answers in books, we often find apparently easy ones. But confronted by actual processes of this kind—when one has just had a creative idea, however modest the issue, when one has begun really to grasp an issue, when one has enjoyed a clean, productive process of thought—those answers often seem to cover up the real problems rather than to face them squarely. The flesh and blood of what has happened seem to be lacking in those answers.

Surely in the course of your life you have been curious about a lot of things, sometimes seriously. Have you been equally serious about what this thing called thinking may be? There are, in this world of ours, eating, thunderstorms, blossoms, crystals. Various sciences deal with them; they attempt by great effort to get real understanding, to grasp what these things really are. Are we equally serious when we ask what productive thinking is?

There are fine cases. You can find them often, even in daily life. If you have had your eyes open, you have probably encountered somewhere in your life—if nowhere else, then in children—this surprising event, the birth of a genuine idea, of a productive development, the transition from a blind attitude to understanding in a productive process. If you have not been fortunate enough to experience it yourself, you may have encountered it in others; or you may —fascinated—have glimpsed it when reading good books.

Many are of the opinion that men do not like to think; that they will do much to avoid it; that they prefer to repeat instead. But in spite of many factors that are inimical to real thinking, that suffo-

cate it, here and there it emerges and flourishes. And often one gets
the strong impression that men, even children, long for it.

What really takes place in such processes? What happens if one
really thinks, and thinks productively? What may be the decisive
features and the steps? How do they come about? Whence the flash,
the spark? What are the conditions, the attitudes, favorable or unfavorable to such remarkable events? What is the real difference
between good and bad thinking? And in connection with all these
questions: how improve thinking? your thinking? thinking itself?
Suppose we were to make an inventory of basic operations in thinking
—how would it look? What, basically, is at hand? Could the basic
operations themselves be enlarged and improved, and thus be made
more productive?

For more than two thousand years some of the best brains in
philosophy, in logic, in psychology, in education, have worked hard
to find real answers to these questions. The history of these efforts,
the brilliant ideas brought forward, the hard work done in research
and in theoretical discussion, present on the whole a rich, dramatic
picture. Much has been achieved. In a large number of special questions solid contributions to understanding have been made. At the
same time there is something tragic in the history of these efforts.
Again and again when great thinkers compared the ready answers
with actual, fine thinking, they were troubled and deeply dissatisfied
—they felt that what had been done had merits, but that in fact it
had perhaps not touched the core of the problem at all.

The situation is still somewhat of this kind. To be sure, many books
deal with these questions as if, fundamentally, everything were settled
—in one way or another. For there are basically different ideas about
what thinking is, each with serious consequences for behavior, for
education. When observing a teacher we may often realize how serious the consequences of such ideas about thinking can be.

Although there are good teachers, with a natural feeling for what
genuine thinking means, the situation in schools is often not good.
How teachers act, how a subject matter is taught, how textbooks are
written, all this is widely determined by two traditional views about
the nature of thinking: the view of traditional logic and the view of
association theory. These two views have their merits. To a degree

they seem adequate to certain types of thought processes, to certain jobs in thinking; but it is at least an open question whether the way in which they interpret thinking does not cause serious hindrance, an actual impairment of genuine abilities.

This book has been written because the traditional views have ignored important characteristics of thought processes, because in many other books those views are taken for granted without real investigation, because in such books the discussion of thinking runs largely in mere generalities, and because, for the most part, the gestalt view is only superficially known. Much is at stake and it seems proper to bring these neglected issues to the fore, to examine the traditional views, to discuss the crucial problems in concrete instances of fine, productive thought, and in doing so, to give the gestalt interpretation of thinking.

In a number of chapters (One-Six) elementary, seemingly obvious examples will be used for the discussion. We shall face the basic theoretical issues in direct contact with the concrete material. Several methods of experimental discussion will contribute to clarification. We shall study how thinking actually proceeds and what the nature of the process is as a whole, as well as in its parts, steps, and operations. In contrast to poorer ways of thinking the reader may enjoy the way in which fine, though modest, productive processes occur in children.

We shall see that what is going on in these processes is far from being adequately handled by the tools and views of the two traditional approaches. We shall recognize characteristics and operations that have been ignored because they are intrinsically foreign to the customary conceptions. We shall see how such factors work in the achievement of thinking.

In Chapter Seven we shall describe a modest example from human life, which seems to touch the essence of profound human issues.

We shall also give in Chapters Four, Eight, Nine, and Ten several descriptions and interpretations of greater thought processes, concluding with the story of the thought process that led Einstein to the discovery of the relativity theory. In the final chapter we shall formulate our general conclusions.

The expert knows how many conditions must be met in a careful investigation. I shall have to omit the report of many technical points that are important in research, because they would make the report too cumbersome. In an investigation one often encounters things one is at first disposed to understand in some traditional way. Closer scrutiny then shows that the matter is not so easily settled. As a consequence one looks for ways, for methods that may yield deeper clarification. The scientific reader would be interested in such specific methods and techniques, the nature of the steps taken in the theoretical and experimental discussion. But the first need is for careful observation and investigation in qualitative experimentation. To be sure, in many cases, it was easy to change the qualitative into a quantitative method, which for many problems is needed as a second step; however, I shall not report on them in this book.

To the scientific psychologist, to the logician, to the educator this book is offered primarily as an invitation to reconsider basic issues. I have chosen a terminology which seemed closest to the nature of the actual processes. Although much of what I am going to say comes, I think, very near genuine common sense, it is difficult to express in scientific terms, and the terms which I use may often seem strange to the reader because they are at odds with his customary ways of viewing the problems. My terms should not give the impression that the problems are settled; they are themselves loaded with—I think—productive problems. The terms and the theses are rather to be understood as arrows, pointing first of all to the concrete steps and characteristics that actually occur in the examples. Much of what I shall say could be expressed in other terminology. Many of the problems and theses are to a degree neutral to expressions of one sort or another. The terminology itself does not matter. What does matter are the problems and the nature of the theses as they vividly appear in the discussion of the concrete cases. Currently some of the terms and theses are being used in a superficial way—the concreteness of the discussion may help to clear up misunderstandings which might otherwise follow.

Notwithstanding the possibility of expressing the facts in other language, including the language of other approaches, let me caution the scientific reader: the trend indicated by this research leads to a view that is basically in contrast with many current views. I hope the reader will not rest content with storing that view in some drawer in which he classifies psychological or philosophical opinions. More is at stake. We have to face these issues in a concrete and productive fashion.

As a kind of background for the following discussions, I present first a very short characterization of the two traditional approaches. They surpass all others in the rigor and completeness with which they consider operations and establish basic concepts, standards, criteria, laws and rules. Other approaches—even if they seem at first in strong opposition to these two—often still contain as their very meat, in one way or another, precisely the operations, the rules of these two. Modern research in thinking is largely determined by one or the other, or both at the same time. I shall indicate their main lines, but shall omit some points which appear as additions of another nature and which, besides, are not clear in themselves.

I. Traditional logic attacked the problems in an ingenious fashion: how are we to find the main issues in the vast variety of the topics of thinking? As follows: thinking is concerned with truth. Being true or false is a quality of assertions, propositions, and only of these. The elementary form of proposition asserts or denies some predicate of a subject, in the form "all S are P," or "no S is P," or "some are," or "some are not." Propositions involve general concepts—class concepts. These are basic to all thinking. For the correctness of a proposition it is decisive that its "intension" or "extension" be dealt with correctly. On the basis of assertions inferences are drawn. Logic studies formal conditions under which inferences are or are not correct. Certain combinations of propositions make it possible to derive "new," correct propositions. Such syllogisms, with their premises and their conclusions, are the crown, the very heart of traditional logic. Logic establishes the various forms of syllogism which guarantee correctness of the conclusion.

Although most of the textbook syllogisms seem barren, a kind of circle, like the classical example—

> All men are mortal
> Socrates is a man
>   therefore, Socrates is mortal—

there are examples of real discoveries which can in a first approach be regarded as syllogisms, as for example the discovery of the planet Neptune. But formally, basically, there seems to be no real difference between the two kinds of syllogism.[1] The decisive characteristics and the rules are identical for both—the somewhat silly and the really sensible ones.

Traditional logic is concerned with the criteria that guarantee exactness, validity, consistency of general concepts, propositions, inferences and syllogisms. The main chapters of classical logic refer to these topics. To be sure, sometimes the rules of traditional logic remind one of an efficient police manual for regulating traffic.

If we disregard differences of terminology, controversies of a subtle nature, we may list as characteristic the following operations of traditional logic:

TABLE I

definition
comparison and discrimination
analysis
abstraction
generalization
forming class concepts
subsumption, etc.
forming propositions
forming inferences
forming syllogisms, etc.[2]

These operations as conceived, defined, and utilized by the logician have been and are being taken by psychologists as subjects for investigation. As a result, we have many experimental investigations on abstraction, generalization, definition, drawing conclusions, etc.

Some psychologists would hold that a person is able to think, is intelligent, when he can carry out the operations of traditional logic correctly and easily. The inability to form general concepts,

[1] See M. Wertheimer, "Über Schlussprozesse im produktiven Denken," in *Drei Abhandlungen zur Gestalttheorie* (Erlangen: Philosophische Akademie, 1925) pp. 164-184; see also W. D. Ellis, *A source book of gestalt psychology*, selection 23. New York: Harcourt, Brace, 1939.

[2] The nature of these operations has been minutely discussed. For our purposes it does not matter much whether they are defined in mentalistic, behavioristic, pragmatic, or other language, although philosophically there are great differences among these various views.

to abstract, to draw conclusions in syllogisms of certain formal types
is viewed as a mental deficiency, which is determined and measured
in experiments.[3]

However one may view classical logic, it had and has great merits:

in the decisiveness of its will to truth;

in the concentration on the basic difference between a mere
assertion, a belief and an exact judgment;

in its emphasis on the difference between hazy concepts, hazy
generalizations, and exact formulations;

in the development of a host of formal criteria which are suited
to testing for, and discovering mistakes, haziness in thinking
such as unjustified generalization, jumping at conclusions;

in its emphasis on proof;

in the seriousness of the rules of discussion;

in the insistence on stringency and rigor in each individual step
in thinking.

The system of traditional logic, as envisaged in its main lines in
the *Organon* of Aristotle, was recognized as final through the centuries; elaborations were added here and there, but these did not
change its main character. A new branch started at the time of the
Renaissance, a development that was essential to the growth of
modern science. The central point was the introduction, as fundamental, of a procedure which until then had been regarded as of
minor value because of lack of complete conclusiveness. This is the
procedure of induction, with its emphasis on experience and experimentation, a methodological concept which reached its greatest
perfection in John Stuart Mill's famous canon of rules of induction.

Ia. The emphasis here is not on rational deduction from general
propositions but on gathering facts, on studying the empirically
constant connections of facts, of changes, and on observing the consequences of changes introduced into factual situations, procedures
which culminate in general assumptions.[4] Syllogisms are viewed

[3] Some students nowadays think that traditional logic has no connection with
actual *behavior*. This is a mistake. For application to behavior merely presupposes
a connecting axiom, approximately as follows: behavior will be unreasonable, will
fail of achievement, will run into trouble, if it is determined by factors parallel
to mistakes in the sense of traditional logic.

[4] The main point was the study of the correlation of two series of varying items,
with resulting laws of function instead of mere classifications.

as tools by which one can draw consequences from such hypothetical assumptions in order to test them.

It is widely believed that inductive logic adds to the classical rules and operations the emphasis on:

TABLE 1a

empirical observations
careful gathering of facts
studying problems empirically
introducing experimental methods
correlating facts
developing crucial tests

II. The second great theory of thinking is centered in the classical theory of associationism. Thinking is a chain of ideas (or, in more modern terms, a chain of stimuli and responses, or a chain of behavior elements). The way to understand thinking is clear: we have to study the laws governing the succession of ideas (or, in modern terms, of behavioral items). An "idea" in classical association theory is some remnant of perception, a copy, in more modern terms, a trace of stimulations. What is the fundamental law of the succession, of the connection of these items? Answer—very elegant in its theoretical simplicity: if two items, a and b, have often occurred together, a subsequent occurrence of a will call forth b in the subject.[5] Basically the items are connected in the way in which my friend's telephone number is connected with his name, in which nonsense syllables become reproducible when learned in a series of such syllables, or in which a dog is conditioned to respond with salivation to a certain musical sound.

Habit, past experience, in the sense of items repeated in contiguity—inertia rather than reason, are the essential factors, just as David Hume had maintained. As compared with classical associationism, this theory is now being developed in a most intricate way; but the old idea of repetition, in contiguity, is still the central feature. A leading exponent of this approach stated explicitly not long ago that the modern theory of the conditioned reflex is essentially *of the same nature* as classical associationism.

[5] In later scientific developments the law had to be qualified in certain details.

The list of operations here looks about as follows:

TABLE II

association, acquiring connections—bonds on the basis of repetitions
role of frequency, of recency
recall from past experience
trial and error, with chance success
learning on the basis of repeated success
acting in line with conditioned responses, and with habit

These operations and processes are now being widely studied with highly developed methods.

Many psychologists would say: ability to think is the working of associative bonds; it can be measured by the number of associations a subject has acquired, by the ease and correctness with which he learns and recalls them.[6]

No doubt there are merits in this approach also, with regard to the subtle features at work in this kind of learning and behaving.

[6] Cf., e.g., E. L. Thorndike, *Psychology of arithmetic* (New York: Macmillan, 1922): "The pedagogy of the past made two notable errors in practice based on two errors about the psychology of reasoning. It considered reasoning as a somewhat magical power or essence which acted to counteract and overrule the ordinary laws of habit in man; and it separated too sharply the 'understanding of principles' by reasoning from the 'mechanical' work of computation . . . , remembering facts and the like, done by 'mere' habit and memory.

"Reasoning or selective, inferential thinking is not at all opposed to, or independent of, the laws of habit, but really is their necessary result under the conditions imposed by man's nature and training. A closer examination of selective thinking will show that no principles beyond the laws of readiness, exercise, and effect, are needed to explain it; that it is only an extreme case of what goes on in associative learning as described under the 'piecemeal' activity of situations. . . ." (p. 190). (See Chapter Six—M. W.)

Similarly, W. B. Pillsbury, in "Recent naturalistic theories of reasoning" (*Scientia*, 1924): "The animal solves a problem by a series of chance trials . . . A scientific problem is solved in very much the same way by a number of chance thoughts" (p. 25). "One never can predict when a fruitful suggestion is to be made. Usually a number of inadequate suggestions will be made before the right one comes. They may be suggested by another person, even by a child or person ignorant of the problem. During the solution of the problem the thinker merely stands ready to pass upon the solutions offered. His attitude is very much like that which we may assume the animal to have as he works by trial and error. It is just as little controlled. It is, in fact, a trial and error process different from the other only in that the trials are made in imagination, not in real movements . . . to find a way of obviating the difficulty. This is always by a series of trial and error processes, by a number of suggestions offered by association" (p. 30). It is only fair to add that in more recent publications Pillsbury saw the situation quite differently.

Both approaches had difficulties with regard to sensible, productive processes of thinking.

Consider first traditional logic. In the course of the centuries there arose again and again a deep-felt dissatisfaction with the manner in which traditional logic handles such processes.[7] In comparison with actual, sensible, and productive processes, the topics as well as the customary examples of traditional logic often look dull, insipid, lifeless. To be sure, the treatment is rigorous enough, yet often it seems barren, boring, empty, unproductive. If one tries to describe processes of genuine thinking in terms of formal traditional logic, the result is often unsatisfactory: one has, then, a series of correct operations, but the sense of the process and what was vital, forceful, creative in it seems somehow to have evaporated in the formulations. On the other hand it is possible to have a chain of logical operations, each perfectly correct in itself, which does not form a sensible train of thought. Indeed there are people with logical training who in certain situations produce series of correct operations which, viewed as a whole, nevertheless form something akin to a flight of ideas. Training in traditional logic is not to be disparaged: it leads to stringency and rigor in each step, it contributes to critical-mindedness; but it does not, in itself, seem to give rise to productive thinking.[8] In short, there is the danger of being empty and senseless, though exact; and there is always the difficulty with regard to real productiveness.

Realization of the latter point—among others—led in fact to the emphatic declaration by some logicians that logic, interested in correctness and validity, has nothing at all to do with factual thinking or with questions of productivity. A reason was also given for this: logic, it was said, has timeless implications and is, therefore, in principle, divorced from questions of actual thought processes which are merely factual and, of necessity, processes in time. This separation

---

[7] Cf., for instance, certain movements against traditional logic at the end of the Middle Ages, or the marvelous fragment of young Spinoza, "Improvement of the understanding." Tragic movements these were, prompted by a feeling of some basic inadequacy, but at the same time unable to achieve a really positive approach.

[8] The discussions of methodology in traditional logic, though meritorious in various respects, do not give real help at this point. Cf. the heuristic ideas (or also, veritable logical machines) of Buridanus, of Raimundus Lullus, of Jevons.

was certainly meritorious for certain problems; from a broader view, however, such assertions often look somehow like the declaration of the fox that the grapes were sour.

Similar difficulties arose in association theory: the fact that we have to distinguish between sensible thought and senseless combinations, and the difficulty in dealing with the *productive* side of thinking.[9]

If a problem is solved by recall, by mechanical repetition of what has been drilled, by sheer chance discovery in a succession of blind trials, one would hesitate to call such a process sensible thinking; and it seems doubtful whether the piling up of such factors only, even in large numbers, can lead to an adequate picture of sensible processes. In order to deal somehow with processes which reach new solutions, a number of auxiliary hypotheses were proposed (for instance, Selz's constellation theory, or the concept of the habit-family-hierarchy) which, by their very nature, do not seem to give decisive help.

In the past decades other views originated which brought new conceptions, new directions in the theory of thinking: e.g., the approach of Hegelian and Marxist dialectics which emphasize dynamic development in their doctrine of "inherent contradictions" with the three steps of thesis, antithesis, and synthesis; the broad development of logistics or mathematical logic (Whitehead, Russell *et al.*) which enriches the topics and operations of traditional logic by the study of the logic of relations, of relational networks, considers forms of conclusion other than syllogisms; phenomenology (Husserl) which stresses the viewing of essentials in "phenomenological reduction"; pragmatism (especially John Dewey) with its emphasis on doing and acting, instead of mere ghostlike thinking, on future

---

[9] Characteristic in the former respect was the brilliant book of Hugo Liepmann on the flight of ideas (*Über Ideenflucht*, 1904). Discussing concrete examples of flight of ideas in mental patients, he found that the criteria offered by association theory do not really suffice to discriminate even between certain kinds of flight of ideas and reasonable talk.

A recent formulation exhibits the basic character of the modern form of association theory in a nutshell. I am referring to Clark Hull's paper on "Mind, mechanism and adaptive behavior," *Psychological Review*, 1937, Vol. 44, pp. 1-32: "A *correct* or 'right' reaction is a behavior sequence which results in reenforcement. An *incorrect* or 'wrong' reaction is a behavior sequence which results in experimental extinction" (p. 15). One sees that the question of repetition is *the* issue. These basic definitions are no doubt in line with the spirit of association theory.

and on actual progress; also in psychology—starting about the same time as the approach developed in this book—the "Denkpsychologie" of the Würzburg school (Kuelpe, Ach, Buehler, Selz, *et al.*), with the emphasis on "Aufgabe"—the role of a given task, on "thoughts" as "unanschauliche Vorstellungen," on relations, schemes etc.; the "naturalistic approach" (J. Dewey, Pillsbury, *et al.*) which centers on the conditions that start actual thinking in a given situation.

Most of these approaches are important in their philosophical and psychological aspects. Although in these developments the situation with regard to our main problem and the crucial points mentioned still seems far from satisfactory, some of them made really new contributions. Some again show the influence of the two classical approaches. In other words, if one penetrates through the new formulations to the nature of the operations which are actually posited *in concreto*, one finds to one's surprise that they are essentially operations of those two traditional approaches. This reminds one of cases that have frequently occurred in the history of logic. In the introduction or in some early chapter a book may seem to start a new approach, altogether different from the customary treatment of logic; in fact, certain formulations may almost appear akin to those of gestalt theory. And yet, when it comes to dealing concretely with a problem, the old operations, old rules, old attitudes appear again.

I have been able to do no more than briefly mention these approaches here. The expert will, I think, see in the text what in them is in line with and what is basically different in nature from the approach in this book.

This book focuses on some elementary, basic issues. The nature of the topics discussed permits us to deal with thought in terms of "relatively closed systems," as though thinking about a problem were a process that occurred independently of larger issues. Only occasionally shall we refer to the place, role, and function of such a process within the personality structure of the subject and within the structure of his social field. For the moment it will suffice if I remark that the same field principles discussed in this book also seem basic to an adequate treatment of processes within such larger regions.

CHAPTER ONE

The Area of the Parallelogram

Among the problems with which I worked was that of finding the area of the parallelogram.

I do not know whether you will enjoy as much as I did some of the experiences of which I am going to tell you here. I think you will, if you will travel with me on this exploratory journey on which problems arose and difficulties had to be faced for which I had to find tools and methods in order to clarify the psychological problems involved.

I

1. I am visiting a classroom. The teacher: "During the last lesson we learned how to find the area of a rectangle. Do you all know it?"

The class: "Yes." One pupil calls out: "The area of a rectangle is equal to the product of the two sides." The teacher approves, then gives a number of problems with rectangles of varying sizes, which all solve readily.

"Now," says the teacher, "we shall go on." He draws a parallelogram on the blackboard: "This is called a parallelogram. A parallelogram

Fig. 1

is a plane quadrilateral the opposite sides of which are equal and parallel."

Here a pupil raises his hand: "Please, teacher, how long are the sides?" "Oh, the sides may be of very different lengths," says the teacher. "In our case one line measures 11 inches, the other 5 inches." "Then the area is 5 × 11 square inches." "No," answers the teacher, "That's wrong; you will now learn how to find the area of a parallelogram." He labels the corners *a, b, c, d*.

"I drop one perpendicular from the upper left corner and another perpendicular from the upper right corner.

"I extend the base line to the right.

"I label the two new points *e* and *f*."

FIG. 2

With the help of this figure he then proceeds to the usual proof of the theorem that the area of a parallelogram is equal to the product of the base by the altitude, establishing the equality of certain lines and angles and the congruence of the pair of triangles. In each case he states the previously learned theorem, postulate, or axiom upon which the equality or congruence is based. Finally he concludes that it has been proved that the area of a parallelogram is equal to the base times the altitude.

"You will find what I have shown you in your textbook on page 62. Do the lesson at home, repeat it carefully so that you will know it well."

The teacher now gives a number of problems all of which require finding the areas of parallelograms of different sizes, sides and angles. This being a "good" class, the problems are all correctly solved. Before the end of the hour the teacher assigns ten more problems of this kind for homework.

2. At the next meeting of the class, one day later, I am there again.

The lesson begins with the teacher calling on a pupil to demonstrate how the area of a parallelogram is found. The pupil does it exactly. One sees that he has learned the problem. The teacher whispers to me: "And he is not the best of my pupils. Without doubt the others know it as well." A written quiz brings good results.

Most people would say, "This is an excellent class; the teaching goal has been reached." But observing the class I feel uneasy, I am troubled. "What have they learned?" I ask myself. "Have they done any thinking at all? Have they grasped the issue? Maybe all that they have done is little more than blind repetition. To be sure, they have solved promptly the various tasks the teacher has assigned, and so they have learned something of a general character, involving some abstraction. Not only were they able to repeat word for word what the teacher said, there was easy transfer as well. But—have they grasped the issue at all? How can I clarify it? What can I *do*?"

I ask the teacher whether he will allow me to put a question to the class. "With pleasure," he answers, clearly proud of his class.

I go to the board and draw this figure.

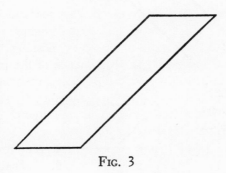

FIG. 3

Some are obviously taken aback.

One pupil raises his hand: "Teacher, we haven't had that yet."

Others are busy. They have copied the figure on paper, they draw the auxiliary lines as they were taught, dropping perpendiculars from the two upper corners and extending the base line (Fig. 4). Then they look bewildered, perplexed.

Some do not look at all unhappy; they write firmly below their drawing: "The area is equal to the base times the altitude"—a correct subsumption, but perhaps an entirely blind one. When asked whether they can show it to be true in this case, they too become perplexed.[1]

With still others it is entirely different. Their faces brighten, they

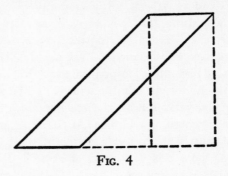

FIG. 4

smile and draw the following lines in the figure, or they turn their papers through 45°, and do it (Figs. 5A & B).

FIG. 5A   FIG. 5B

The teacher, observing that only a minority of the pupils has mastered the problem, says to me with some indignation: "You certainly gave them a queer figure. Naturally they are unable to deal with it."

Now just between us, haven't you too been thinking: "No wonder so many failed when he gave them a figure so unfamiliar!" But is it less familiar than the variations of the original figure which the

[1] A boy from another class, observing these difficulties, whispers to me, "In our class we have learned how to work this overlapping example. It's the teacher's fault. Why didn't he teach them how to do it in the overlapping diagram too?" To my surprise this special and complicated proof is sometimes taught from the start in the textbooks; really to understand it is not only difficult for children but it is also unnecessary for the solution.

teacher previously gave and which they solved? The teacher did give problems in which the figures varied greatly with regard to length of sides, size of angles, and size of areas. These were decided variations, and they did not appear at all difficult for the pupils. Did you notice, perchance, that my parallelogram is simply the teacher's original figure turned around? With regard to all the part-qualities it was not more but less different from the original figure than the teacher's variations.

Here I shall tell briefly of experimental proceedings with children who were taught the area of the rectangle, then the area of the parallelogram with the auxiliary lines and the result: base times altitude, with or without being taught the proof. They were then asked about figures other than the original figure.

3. There are extreme cases of thoughtless reactions, in which a child, if given simply the figure,

FIG. 6

repeats what the teacher has said word for word like a blind slave, mumbles, "One perpendicular from the upper left corner," and draws it; then, "Another from the upper right corner," and draws it, "Extend the base line to the right," thereby getting this figure:

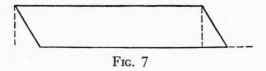

FIG. 7

4. On the other hand, it *does* happen that children even as young as six, who have learned nothing of geometry, after being shown briefly how to find the area of the rectangle, *do* produce the solution for the parallelogram in fine, original processes without being taught what to do. Some of these cases will be described in the third part of this chapter.

And it does happen that, having found or having been shown how to get the area of the parallelogram, children who are asked to find the area of the trapezoid, or of any of the following figures, are not at all helpless, but after some deliberation, sometimes with a little help, produce fine, genuine solutions of the kind that follow.

These are the tasks:

Fig. 8

In all these figures it is possible to solve the problem by changing the figures sensibly (A-responses) or to apply the learned operations, or some of them, blindly and unsuccessfully (B-responses).

A-responses:

Fig. 8A

The subjects change the figures into rectangles by shifting the triangles. They will not give

B-responses:

Fig. 8B

5. But others do give B-responses, or give A- and B-responses indiscriminately. Many pupils refuse to touch problems 1, 2, and 3 at all, with the comment: "How should we know? We haven't learned how to do those figures."

6. I then conducted experiments with children. I put before them

single figures or pairs of A- and B-figures right after showing how
the area of the parallelogram is to be found with the auxiliary lines.

Examples of   A-Figures   B-Figures

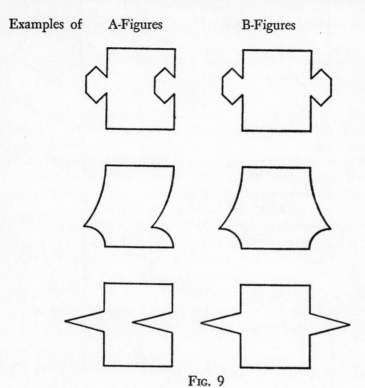

Fig. 9

In these pairs of figures, one member of the pair, the B-figure, can
have no A-solution, whereas the A-solution is possible in the A-figure.
For some children there seems to be no difference between the A-
and B-figures. They are all new. "How should we know!" is their
attitude. They either show no reaction or, if they do, they in no
way differentiate between the A- and B-figures, draw some auxiliary
lines and give blind answers.

But some consistently solve the A-problems and, sometimes after
a brief period, reject the B-problems with: "This one I can't do;
I don't know what the area is"; or even, "I don't know what the
area of these little remainders is." By contrast the area of the remainders is generally not mentioned in the A-cases; or the child

may say: "Of course I do not know the area of the little figures, but that does not matter as long as they are equal."

7. Also in the figures here illustrated, the A-figures, viewed piece-meal, are clearly more changed with reference to the original than

Fig. 10

the B-figures; in fact the changes are the "same" in A as in B, only there are more of them. The simple answer of "familiarity" is obviously of no help in understanding the positive reactions—the straight solution of the A-cases, rejection of the B-cases.

Our observations with the A-B pairs already involved examples of how to proceed with experimental analysis. Although the task here seems easy enough, foolish reactions sometimes occur in the classroom.

8. Another step in the experimental analysis is to give two movable solids instead of one figure. These may be separated or adjacent, and in various positions:

Fig. 11

Again foolish reactions are possible—and sometimes occur.

9. In order to become clear about the theoretical questions involved, it is sometimes helpful to consider extreme cases. Take the following foolish reaction:

A child is taught the proof of the theorem for the area of a parallelogram with the help of a figure drawn on graph paper. The

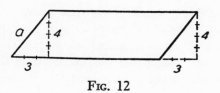

FIG. 12

auxiliary lines are drawn. The side a happens to be 5 inches, the segment c happens to be 3 inches long.

The teacher says: "See! From each upper corner I drop a perpendicular of 4 inches; I extend the base line 3 inches to the right, you may measure it."

After a time another example is given, a parallelogram of different size. Suppose that a child were to proceed in a slavish way, distracted by an observer perhaps, or thinking of a game he was going to play, or wondering where his mother was at that moment; suppose a child were to repeat to himself, "Four inches down, three inches to the right," and were sheepishly to produce this figure:

FIG. 13

Then, asked if the goal, the area, has been reached, he replies: " . . . no," but could go no further for the time being. I myself have not found such a response, but it *may* happen. Similar things do happen in cases structurally less simple, as teachers know.

Clearly this would be an extreme B-reaction: copying what the teacher taught, blind to the context. Everyone sees what is wrong with it. But what is it, theoretically? One might say: "This child did not properly adjust what he had been taught to the new situation." But what does "properly" adjusting mean?

Or one might say: "Clearly this is a case of lack of 'generalization,'" and dismiss the matter as settled. Is it settled? What of foolish generalizations, which are no less generalizations for being foolish? What if a child were to generalize, for example, from the figure above (I have not found such a case): "The perpendiculars have to be one inch longer than the extension of the base line," or "The length of the perpendicular must be an even number," etc., and act accordingly?

To dismiss our problem with the term "generalization" does not help at all. Of course there is generalization here, but we have it in *both* kinds of cases. Often the emphasis on generalization does not answer the question; rather it covers up the problem.

10. What is the real issue in the A-B reactions, in the A-B cases? I had characteristic experiences: there are the intelligent reactions, the subject refusing to apply blindly to the B-problems what he has previously learned, giving the intelligent, genuine solution in the A-cases, altering the procedure as sense requires. And there are the blind reactions in which the subject is unable to deal with A- or B-cases, or applies operations foolishly.[2]

---

[2] The foolish drawings in the examples on pages 17-18 one actually finds only comparatively rarely. Children with a spontaneous, natural attitude do not tend to behave that way. The habit of thoughtless repetition, as developed in certain schools by emphasizing blind drill, does seem favorable to responses of this kind; the same is true of situations in which a blind, piecemeal attitude has been created, e.g., by some distraction, by worry, or by personal difficulties. In schools that use drill the attitude often develops of responding to a new problem by just waiting to be told how to do it; if the pupil is asked to try it by himself, one often finds just passive refusal—"We haven't had that."

That the psychologist felt uneasy in the class (see p. 15) meant that he felt the prevailing drill atmosphere. The behavior described there seems especially connected with the drill attitude, sticking blindly, as it does, to the words of the teacher—generally young children are not much bothered by the spatial positions of figures (cf. W. Stern, "Über verlagerte Raumformen," *Zeitschrift für Angewandte Psychologie*, 1909, Vol. 2, pp. 498-526).

There are grownups who carry into their later life the acquired habit of blind, mechanical activity. It is astonishing to see how educated and otherwise intelligent people sometimes react in similar situations, especially in an "Einstellung" (see Chap. Four, Sec. IV). (See also Chap. Six and Appendices 2, 3, and 4.—M. W.)

If a subject applies the method he has learned to a variation of the original problem, not realizing that it is out of place in the given instance, this is an indication that he has not understood in the first place, or that he has failed to realize what it is that matters in the changed problem. But if he deals appropriately and consistently with the A-cases even when there is more piecemeal dissimilarity with the original, and if at the same time he refuses to apply the learned procedure to more similar B-variations, then it means that he has a real grasp of the problem. Thus A-B variations, systematically investigated, may furnish the basis for an "operational definition" of understanding. And in the course of experimental analysis the various structural factors may be studied by the A-B method.

What is the central difference between the two kinds of reactions to the variations? What, psychologically, is the issue? How does the subject find the A-reaction? What decides, in the mind of the pupil, between the A- and B-procedures?

First: one might say, "The difference is quite clear. The B-reactions do not lead to the correct solutions, while the A-reactions do." But this assertion states the problem; it does not solve it.

Second: "The degree of similarity to the original problem is decisive." No. Similarity does play a role, but what kind of similarity? Viewed in a piecemeal way the B-cases are often more similar to the original than the A-cases.

Third: is the matter explained by "generalization"? No. Of course generalization is involved in all these cases, but a foolish B-reaction, as previously stated, may involve as much generalization as an A-reaction. And so generalization in itself does not help. It would of course help if one were to speak of "properly selected generalization." But what are we to understand by this qualification? That it leads to the solution? This would again be like the first proposal.

Fourth: the situation remains unchanged if one asserts (correctly) that the various A-cases are characterized by grasping the essentials, by grasping what is really relevant. But what is that "grasping"? What are "essentials"? What determines what is and what is not essential? Only the result?

The theoretical proposals 2, 3, and 4 all fail to differentiate satisfactorily between the A- and B-reactions and cases, unless proposal

1 is implied, which does differentiate, but only on the basis of results. None of these proposals in itself brings psychological understanding.

I address myself to the reader: please think this over. Do not be satisfied with superficial solutions. I think you will see the answer if you face these cases directly. You may have it on the tip of your tongue without being able to express it in so many words. I shall not pursue the analysis here, but shall return to it later.

II

11. The psychologist, under the strong and vivid impression of the strange behavior of children in certain schools, makes another and more extreme attack on the problem.

As in the case cited, I have often been puzzled to see how some classes behave while learning. Frequently they follow obediently enough the steps of the proof which the teacher is showing them. These they repeat, learn. One has the impression that "learning" is going on—yes; thinking—perhaps a little; but real understanding— no.

Another procedure was tried for greater clarification.

What I am now going to say is somewhat unpleasant, ugly. But you see, the psychologist must sometimes, for theoretical reasons, use methods which are not in themselves so nice.

FIG. 14

Instead of using the usual, sensible method of deriving the area of the parallelogram, the pupils are told: "In order to get the area of a parallelogram, one has to measure the sides—we will call them a and b; mark the point on the base line which is directly underneath the upper left corner, then measure the distance between the left end on the line and the point, which we call c. In our figure $a=5$ inches, $b=9$ inches, $c=3$ inches.

"Now add a and c! $(a+c \ldots 5+3=8)$

"Subtract c from a! $(a-c \ldots 5-3=2)$

"Multiply the results! $(\ldots 8 \times 2 = 16)$

"From the product extract the square root! You have learned that $(\ldots \sqrt{16}=4)$

"Multiply the result by b, and you have it $\ldots$ $(\ldots 4 \times 9 = 36)$

"The formula for the area is $b\sqrt{(a+c)\ (a-c)}$."

This procedure is ugly and it would never occur to any reasonable teacher or mathematician. It takes the psychologist to introduce such a troublesome, unpleasant, and senseless method. But it does lead to a correct result.

Usually such a procedure seems strange and weird to children—one cannot help seeing that at certain points they draw back. In the end some of them look at the teacher with ill-concealed disdain. Others burst into peals of laughter.

It is a serious matter that in some schools one may *not* be able to observe any essential difference between the reactions of the pupils to this lesson and to a sensible method. When you find that children in a class swallow such a procedure piously, without any reaction, then look into the kind of education they are getting! I should think something must be wrong with it. And if you do make experiments of the kind here reported, I hope your classes laugh out loud, or at least that they are politely dismayed.

In instances of this kind it is sometimes touching to see the close concentration, the strong determination of the pupils to note every single step, the mumbling repetition of the teacher's words, the pride when they can reproduce exactly what they have learned, solve problems precisely in the way they have been taught. Teaching and learning is just that for many. The teacher has taught the "correct" procedure. The pupils have learned it; they can apply it in routine cases; that is all.

Let the reader consider whether he has not often learned things in school that way. Isn't it the way in which perhaps you have learned differential and integral calculus? Even theorems of plane and solid geometry? Of course you had good reason to feel that the teacher was teaching sensible, serious things you had to learn. But did you have the possibility of any other kind of learning, of really grasping? Could you do anything but put up with and submit to the teacher's demonstration, step by step, when you were unable to see why he did just this, then that? Could you help just following obediently as the steps dropped out of the blue?

I think you will agree that you could not. Nor would I be surprised if you were to add that surely it was the right way if the teacher did it that way, that probably there was no other. Or you may object: "One cannot compare this ugly example with the usual teaching in which the teacher sets forth reasonable things with their proofs."

You are perfectly right in this last remark. In our example the proof is lacking, an omission which, by the way, certain classes do not notice. And for a real decision we do need an example which includes a proof. This point will be further considered in ¶17.

12. But let us first get to the end of our story. I asked the class: "Are you sure that this result is really correct?" Most of the pupils were plainly dumfounded by the question, surprised that it should be asked. Their attitude was clearly: "How can you expect us to question the solution you have given us?" The question was strange to them, it touched the very essentials of what school, teaching, learning meant to them. No answer. The class was silent.

I changed my question, asked in a friendly way: "Could any of you show that the answer obtained in this way is really right?"

Little M. raised his hand. Looking quite shrewd, he said: "I know how one can prove it. It's very simple. We found that the area of this parallelogram is 36 square inches. Now I can cut the parallelogram out of tin, place it on one side of an accurate scale, and on the other I can place a rectangle which I know to be 36 square inches—I bet they'll balance."

"Yes, they may, but can you show that this would be the case generally?"

"Why, yes," he answered, "I can repeat it, if you like, with various parallelograms."

What this boy did is characteristic of many cases of thinking. He now has the *blind* procedure *plus* the proof by weight. That is all; he is satisfied. The proceeding, the so-called induction, is in itself a nice thing, often necessary, in some respects fundamental in modern empirical science. Nevertheless, to couple it contentedly with the blind, and therefore ugly procedure is not the solution for a real thinker, not the end. Modern science, while often based on induction, does not like to stop at induction. It goes on to search for a better understanding than induction alone provides. (See, for example, the development of the Mendeleev discovery.[3]) An important instrument in its right place, induction is a start rather than an end in itself. But here it is not even justified as a start, being unnecessarily, arbitrarily blind to the issue.

13. To make the matter clearer, let us consider another example. The teacher demonstrates to the class how to get the area of the parallelogram by means of the usual auxiliary lines, shifting the triangle at the left to the right, showing at the end that the area equals the base times the altitude. In this example I suggested to the teacher that a parallelogram be used, one side of which, a, was 2.5 inches, and the other side, b, 5 inches. The altitude, h, was measured and found to be 1.5.

I then gave other problems, stating in each case the values of the sides a and b; the altitude was measured, and the area of each parallelogram was to be computed:

	a	b	altitude (measured)	area to be computed
1.	2.5	5	1.5	7.5
2.	2.0	10	1.2	12.0
3.	20.0	$1\frac{1}{3}$	16.0	$21\frac{1}{3}$
4.	15.0	$1\frac{7}{8}$	9.0	$16\frac{7}{8}$

[3] Editors' note. Early in the nineteenth century the English chemist, William Prout, noticed that the atomic weights of the chemical elements were approximate multiples of the weight of the hydrogen atom, and he suspected hydrogen to be the *materia prima*. On the basis of this hypothesis, de Chancourtois proclaimed in 1862 that properties of chemical elements were all governed by number. In 1871 Mendeleev published his famous periodic classification of chemical elements, a table in which all elements were arranged in eight vertical and seven horizontal rows. It enabled him to demonstrate that chemical elements changed their properties, especially their valence, in accordance with changes in their atomic weight. Atomic weight appeared to Mendeleev, therefore, to form the fundamental, essential characteristic of the elements. This was borne out by the fact that he was able to predict the discovery of unknown elements, necessary to fill the gaps in his table, through considerations based on the periodicity of properties and the regular increase in atomic weight of the chemical elements.

The pupils worked at the problems, experiencing a certain amount of difficulty with the multiplication.

Suddenly a boy raised his hand. Looking somewhat superciliously at the others who had not yet finished, he burst out: "It's foolish to bother with multiplication and measuring the altitude. I've got a better method for finding the area—it's so simple. The area is $a+b$."

"Have you any idea why the area is equal to $a+b$?" I asked.

"I can prove it," he answered. "I counted it out in all the examples. Why bother with $b \cdot h$? The area equals $a+b$."

I then gave him the fifth problem: $a=2.5$; $b=5$; altitude$=2$. The boy began to figure, became somewhat flustered, then said pleasantly: "Here adding the two does not give the area. I am sorry; it would have been so nice."

"*Would it?*" I asked.

This may serve as an example of a blind discovery, a blind induction. I dare say that no sensible mathematician likes to make such obviously senseless inductions. He will make them *only* if the matter under investigation is so obscure that he has no idea of a possible, sensible inner connection.

I may add that the real purpose of this "mean" experiment which succeeded, as you saw, was not simply to mislead. Visiting the class earlier, I had noticed that there was real danger of their dealing superficially with the method of induction. My purpose was to give these pupils—and their teacher—a striking experience of the hazards of this attitude.

One might say that the boy was wrong in his hypothesis simply because it was not universally true; that it was a generalization based on too few instances. But to do so is to miss the point. The proposed equality, area$=a+b$, is blind to the question of their inner relation, blind to the problem of how this can come about reasonably in even *one* case—for there is no inner relation between the area and "$a+b$."

Though Mendeleev's classification was presented by him as a purely empirical generalization, it clearly pointed to the fundamental unity of matter.

In 1913, on the basis of the atom theories of Rutherford and Bohr, Moseley, a young British scientist, proved that it was the number of hydrogen atoms making up the atom of a given element, *atomic number*, rather than atomic weight that explained the chemical properties of elements—more exactly the number of protons and, therefore, the number of electrons.

Thus an empirical generalization became finally a deductive theory.

14. I shall give a still simpler example. You ask a pupil:

1) 12=3 times what? Answer: 4
2) 56=7 times what? Answer: 8
3) 45=6 times what?

Suppose the pupil were to say in answer to the third problem: "Seven." And if you asked him for the reason, he were to answer: "Isn't it clear? The fourth digit is one higher than the third:

1) 12   3 4
2) 56   7 8
3) 45   6 7

Is the essential point here that the pupil has based his "hypothesis" on too few instances? No. The hypothesis *is* foolish: the lining up of the numbers in this way has nothing to do with the structure of the situation, is blind to its requirements, to the separation by the equality sign, to the meaning of the positions at the left, to the meaning of the multiplication sign at the right. It is blind to all these structural features, which set the requirements for a sensible solution or for a sensible hypothesis.

15. Here follow some additional examples of ugly procedures which lead to the correct answer. What is wrong here is not only that no proof is given but that none of the steps of the procedure has an understandable relation to the task.

How to get the area of a rectangle:

I

1) $a-b$

2) $\dfrac{1}{a}$

3) $\dfrac{1}{b}$

4) subtract 2) from 3)
5) divide 1) by the result obtained in 4)

$$\text{Area} = \frac{a-b}{\dfrac{1}{b} - \dfrac{1}{a}}$$

II

1) For $a+b$ substitute c
2) a^2
3) divide 2) by 1)
4) subtract it from a
5) multiply it by 1)

$$\text{Area} = \left(a - \frac{a^2}{a+b}\right)c$$
$$= \left(a - \frac{a^2}{a+b}\right)(a+b)$$

16. I have chosen artificial examples in order to clarify the issue, but similar things happen without the intruding psychologist.

A child in school learns with accompanying drill the formulas for the perimeter, $2(a+b)$, and for the area, $a \cdot b$, of the rectangle.

After a time tasks are assigned which require computing the areas of rectangles in the course of larger problems. $2(a+b)$ comes to his mind and he uses it—all wrong without knowing it.

Or he tries to recall what the formula for the area was. He may even try to recall the page of the textbook on which the formula appears, and actually succeed in recalling it, but the formula just will not come to mind. He feels at a loss, looks at his neighbor's result, notes that the area was found to be 25—the sides, a and b, happen to be 10 and $2\frac{1}{2}$, respectively. "I see!" he says to himself. "Now I remember how it's done: $10 + 2\frac{1}{2} = 12\frac{1}{2}$, times $2 = 25$, $2(a+b)$," is relieved and busily solves the subsequent problems this way, again getting wrong results without knowing it. (Should it happen by chance that the next task has $a = 12$, $b = 2.4$, and that he looks for corroboration at the result his neighbor got, he will be reassured). It does not even occur to him to consider whether this formula could be at all reasonable here. On the other hand, if the pupil actually faced the problem, he might be able to reconstruct freely even a forgotten formula.

Now, is the decisive thing only that the boy got the wrong result, that his formula does not generally work? In order to bring out the issue sharply, think of a fantastic situation. The business of solving the problem could conceivably be done by a machine that cuts the rectangle into little squares. You put the rectangle into the slot; the machine does its work, the little squares drop out and are counted by you or by an adding device in the apparatus. Let us further suppose that as this machine works, it discards a certain number of the little squares, a number varying with the size of the rectangle; on the other hand, that four little squares are always added.[4] Such a machine can easily be constructed and would then by a general law invariably produce the result, $2(a+b)$.

The thinker urgently feels the need of looking into the machine to discover how this funny result comes about lawfully. If one could

[4] In the formula $2\ (a+b)$ for the area, the area m disappears and the four shaded squares occur twice (see Fig. 15).

only open the machine and look inside! But suppose you could not, or even that there were no machine at all, that the same thing happened without the machine—miraculously, just in the course of cutting and counting . . .

FIG. 15

You would have universality, a factual, constant formula, but the law expressed in the formula would still be ugly, blind to the issue, entirely ununderstandable.

17. Returning to our question, demonstrative *proof* was lacking in these ugly examples, and one might be of the opinion that this alone was the essential point. Let us consider what is necessary in order that a thought process be a good, sensible thought process. The usual answer seems to be:

> that a true solution of the problem is reached,
>
> that it is reached by logically correct operations,
>
> that the result is proved correct, universally correct.

Is that all? Is that an adequate expression of what we are facing in a real, sensible process?

Let us consider a proceeding which embraces all these features, and still is somehow ugly. Suppose I were to teach the area of the rectangle to a child who had heard nothing of geometry. First he is shown that the area of the square is a^2 . . . "*a* times *a*." He learns this and computes the areas of some squares of different sizes. He is then shown a rectangle, and the area of the rectangle is taught in the following way:

FIG. 16

1. First subtract b from a	$a-b$	$7-2=5$
2. Square the remainder	$(a-b)^2$	$5^2=25$
3. Square b and subtract it from the last result	$(a-b)^2-b^2$	$25-4=21$
4. Square a and subtract it from the last result	$(a-b)^2-b^2-a^2$	$21-49=-28$
5. Multiply it by -1 (make it positive)	$a^2+b^2-(a-b)^2$	$+28$
6. Divide it by 2	ab	14

This is the area of the rectangle: $a \cdot b$ — which can be proved geometrically, as the figure indicates. The proof involves the demonstra-

Fig. 17

tion that the two rectangles are congruent, and the subtraction of the overlapping b^2. Although it is somewhat intricate, it derives the general solution by logical necessity. This procedure is a little less ugly than the previous one; still it is ugly.

Some reactions of children: "What grownups will do!" "Why not do it straight? It must be like the square—the number of little *squares in the base row* times the *number of rows*."

18. Let us look back now. Why are these various proceedings "ugly"? What is the decisive point?

1) Is it that the operations are not carried out correctly? No, they are in some examples.

2) Is it that they lack generality? No, the examples that are generally true are nevertheless ugly (cf. ¶11 and ¶15).

3) Is it that they lack demonstrative proof? No, not all the examples do.

If we look at the concrete proceedings in the ugly examples, see how the problem is attacked, how the individual steps in thought are related to the whole line of thinking, then the answer seems to be clear: I want to solve a problem; I face the problem situation; I want to see how I can clarify the issue in order to reach the solution. I try to see how the area is determined, how it is built up in this figure; I want to understand it. Instead, someone comes and tells me to do this or that; viz., something like $\frac{1}{a}$ or $\frac{1}{b}$ or $(a-b)$ or $(a-b)^2$, things which clearly have no inner relation to the issue, which go in another direction, a direction alien to the problem. Why do just this? I am told, "Just do it"; and then another step is added, again ununderstandable in its direction. The steps drop from the blue; their content, their direction, the whole process does not reasonably grow out of the inner requirements of the situation, appears arbitrary, blind to the issue of *how the area is built up* structurally out of the small units in *just this form*. In the end the steps do lead to a correct, or even proved answer. But the very result is seen in a way that gives no insight, no clarification. And this is true for all the examples—proof or no proof.

"Look here," the reader may say indignantly, "are you not demanding too much of human thinking?" I am not; happily there are thought processes which do not proceed so blindly.

19. The positive, productive course of thinking, as indicated in the reactions of children, is of an entirely different character. The question of the area in terms of the sum of the small unit squares is faced *in* the figure, with reference to *its characteristic form*: it is discovered that there are parallel rows which fit, each to the other, which are equal, containing the same number of small squares. Then the number of *squares in one* such row, determined by the length of one side, is multiplied by the number of *rows*, determined by the length of the other side. Here the essential thing is seeing the area structured in accordance with the characteristic form of the figure. None of the steps implied is in a direction blind to the issue, to the inner nature of the problem situation.

And the very same result, area = $a \cdot b$, is psychologically not the same in sensible and in ugly procedures: "$a \cdot b$," as viewed in the sensible process, is not simply a "multiplication of two terms," for one of them *means* the number of *squares in one row*, the other the number of *rows*. The two terms in the multiplication have different structural and functional meaning and unless this is realized the formula, even the meaning of multiplication itself, cannot be understood.

Fɪɢ. 18

20. I shall illustrate the last statement. A boy is shown a rectangle divided into the small square units. He is told that the total amount, the area, is equal to $a \cdot b$. Now, when he is given a number of different rectangles, he figures out the areas correctly by multiplying the sides. I ask him: "Are you sure this is correct?" And he replies, "Certainly, you taught it to me; but if you want me to, I'll count it out." And he starts counting sets of 5 squares, beginning at the base in the following way:

8

3	4	5	1	2	3	4	5
5	1	2	3	4	5	1	2
2	3	4	5	1	2	3	4
4	5	1	2	3	4	5	1
1	2	3	4	5	1	2	3

(**5** labels the left side)

Fɪɢ. 19

When he reaches the end, he turns to me. "See? It's correct."

One can see that something essential is lacking here. This boy has not grasped how the area is built up by the row times the parallel repetitions. He hasn't used the fundamental structural feature that each row has the same number of squares. And so he has failed to get a basis for a sensible structural understanding of the area.

To put the matter differently, if the area is to be found by the kind of counting this boy did, the figure need not be a rectangle at all. Any other figure made up of continuous little squares would do as well. His procedure is blind to the structure of the figure in its inner relation to the multiplication.

Such structural understanding, or lack of it, plays a decisive role in transfer also. Here is a brief example: for the sake of experiment a child is shown how to find the area of a square. He masters it, applies it in various cases, and is then asked about the area of a rectangle. He sees no way of finding it. I ask: "Why don't you do it the same way as you did the square?" Hesitation, and then answer: "I can't do that . . . here the two sides are not equal."

But if the matter is really understood in the case of the square, the area is seen as the number of small squares in the base row times the number of rows, the transition offers no such difficulties. The fact of the equality of the two sides of the square is not disturbing then, being structurally peripheral, having no reasonable connection with the issue.

The transfer could also be blind. One could *without* this understanding simply believe blindly that the area of the rectangle too could be obtained by multiplication of the two sides. If one wishes to call both these cases generalization, one must realize that there is a basic difference between structurally blind, or senseless, and reasonable generalization.

21. Someone objects: "Why do you speak of grasping inner structure, inner requirements, implying that a grasp of the structural features in your example makes the thing reasonable? What of non-Euclidean situations? What if we choose other axioms for our geometry? What is reasonable in one system may be wrong in the other. Only as long as one presupposes the naïve, old-fashioned belief in the unique validity of the Euclidean axioms does what you say seem reasonable."

The objection is blind: it does not touch the issue. Non-Euclidean geometry has structural features of its own, to which again considerations of reasonableness apply within the new, enlarged framework. After having introduced the feature of space curvature, certain assertions of Euclidean geometry no longer fit, since they were made without taking into account the conditions introduced by the curvature and fit only the special case in which the curvature is zero.

To take a short illustration: a figure consisting of four "straight" lines and four right angles on the surface of a sphere *is* different from a plane rectangle also with respect to area; but here again you might get at the new area reasonably, grasping the inner structure, or you might derive it in an ugly way analogous to our ugly cases.

"Why do you speak of reasonableness in this context?" a logician asks. "Reasonableness is nothing but a question of old, formal logical consistency. Any theorem, any law—even your example [pp. 30-31] of the area of the rectangle as equal to $2(a+b)$ in the artificial world you described—is funny or unreasonable *only* in so far as it contradicts other laws, as it is not consistent with the axioms of its own system. That is all."

But this argument simply shifts the issue from theorems to axioms. If we envisaged changed axioms suited to just such structurally blind connections to give formal consistency, the result would be not just an ugly theorem, but the whole axiomatic system would be ugly.

To be sure, there are now trends in mathematics toward systems which would preclude reasonableness in the structural sense. Some believe it necessary to ignore all such reasonableness. A similar tendency appeared in the development of logic, the tendency to reduce logic to a game, governed by a sum of arbitrarily combined, piecemeal rules. As a division of labor such specialization is a meritorious enterprise, particularly with regard to criteria in the problems of rigid, logical validity. But if it is meant really to describe the whole business of logic, it reduces thinking to a poor thing, emptying it of features which play an important role in genuine productive processes. However the relation of the structural problems to formal logic and the theory of knowledge may be viewed, whether the structural problems should or should not be faced in logic, they constitute decisive issues in genuine, sensible productive processes.

The development of modern mathematics has moved in the direction of dispensing with all features of geometrical intuition as completely as possible. This was done with good reason, with an eye to questions of validity in an ideal, axiomatic system in which concrete theorems are obtained only by applying syllogistic and similar formal operations to the axioms. But this extremely well-justified interest should not be confused with the problems of understanding and of genuine productive processes. I have not found a really productive mathematician who did not feel the difference. Some have said: "This is not a logical or a mathematical question. It is a psychological question or, if you prefer, concerns the aesthetic side of the matter." To me it seems that such assertions view logic in too narrow a sense. The steps, the operations, in ugly procedures are not *reached* in a logical way—the direct procedure seems also the more logical. Indeed the difference between arbitrary, blind procedures and those which are not blind lies at the very heart of logic.

22. These have indeed been ugly, senseless examples, and the reader may have wondered why they were introduced. Common sense does in fact show them to be artificial and senseless; common sense feels the difference between these and really sensible proceedings. But it is necessary to focus on the obvious, in order to see the issue clearly and deal with it scientifically. Certain theoretical developments in logic, in the theory of knowledge, in psychology, have become blind to this issue or have tried to substitute criteria of a character that is blind to it.

Furthermore, things that we are inclined to take for granted as "obvious" need scientific clarification and work. I have used terms here that have the appearance of unfamiliarity, that are not too easy. But one must realize that the situation is fraught with problems. And it is not strange that it should be so. Whereas the operations of traditional logic have been richly and highly developed, those dealt with here are still largely unexplored. Gestalt theory is an attempt to develop them.

23. "The one point that suffices for the differentiation of what you call the ugly from the reasonable procedure," the logician interposes, "you have not mentioned. These examples do not look sensible simply because they employ *more* steps, a longer way around. You have forgotten the 'lex parsimoniae.' "

All the preceding solutions, it is true, do have more steps than the corresponding sensible ones. But one should not be deceived by this superficial feature; it is not the main point.

Do such "tricky" procedures always, and necessarily, employ more steps? Are they always more "difficult" than the corresponding sensible proceeding? No. In the area of the rectangle and the parallelogram the sensible proceeding is structurally too simple to allow of any shorter method, but mathematics offers such cases. Consider, e.g., the following problem.

What is the sum of the series

$$S = 1 + a + a^2 + a^3 + a^4 \ldots ? \quad (a < 1)$$

The usual answer is:

1) Write down the equation	1. $S = 1 + a + a^2 + a^3 + a^4. \ldots$
2) Multiply both sides of the equation by a	2. $aS = a + a^2 + a^3 + a^4 + a^5$
3) Subtract the second equation from the first	3. $S - aS = 1$
4) Solve for S	4. $S = \dfrac{1}{1-a}$

That is correct; it is correctly derived, proved, and elegant in its brevity. A way to get real insight into the matter, sensibly to derive the formula is not nearly so easy; it involves difficult steps and many more. While compelled to agree to the correctness of the above proceeding, there are many who feel dissatisfied, tricked. The multiplication by a, together with the subtraction of one series from the other, gives the result; it does not give understanding of how the continuing series approaches this value in its growth.[5] Real understanding proceeds by considering what happens in the growth of the series and derives the law of this growth, leading to the limit.[6] Many do not

[5] I cite an example of a subject's responses in one of my experiments: "Strange thing . . . multiplying by a . . . why this? Does it bring me nearer to the goal? . . . Subtraction—why? And now—in (3)—all that I know of the structure of S has disappeared! Was I not looking for the sum of such a growing series? I do not know more about it than before—only that it equals $\dfrac{1}{1-a}$. But why? How?"

[6] For a solution of a very similar problem which, though requiring considerably more steps, does lead to a more direct understanding, see Appendix 6. Applying to the problem here the structural approach used in the Appendix will enable the reader to see whether he has really understood the solution to this problem.—M.W.

really understand. They are satisfied to have the result.[7]

There are theorems in mathematics for which we have at this time only "external" solutions because the problems are still too complicated for constructive understanding. Extreme are certain cases of the so-called negative, indirect proof in which the principle of the excluded middle is used, showing that the opposite assumption is impossible, leads to contradictions, yet without any possibility of seeing how the positive solution comes about constructively. The famous mathematician, Brouwer, contemptuously called these indirect proofs "thinking with the spine." I am not here concerned as to whether he was right in demanding that results should be dropped which are derived only in such a way. What I want to emphasize is only that there is a striking difference between sensible solving, understanding the subject matter, and solving by external procedure.

III

24. Before reporting on some genuine thought processes of children in finding the area of the parallelogram, we pause to ask: What are the steps in a really sensible thought process solving the problem of the area of the rectangle? We shall enumerate briefly steps which seem to us essential on the basis of experiences with children and adults.

1) The problem is confronted: what *is* the area of the rectangle? I do not know. How can I get at it?

2) I feel there must be an *inner relation* between these two: the size of the area—the form of the rectangle. What is it? How can I get at it?

3) The area may be viewed as the sum of the small squares in the

Fig. 20

---

[7] For the expert, to be sure, the usual procedure contains a sensible feature, based on the discovery that the series remains the same, with the exception of the first member, if you "shift" it, e.g., multiply it by a. Still, the procedure remains external to a real understanding of how the sum comes about.

figure.[8] And the form? This is not *any* figure, not any heap of small squares in any form; I have to understand how the area is built up in this figure! (Fig. 20.)

4) Are the little squares not *organized* in this figure, or *organizable* in a way that leads to a clear structural view of the total? Oh, yes. The figure is throughout equal in length, this has to do with the way the area is built up! The parallel straight rows of small squares fit together vertically in mutual equality, thus closing the figure: I have rows equal in length throughout, which together form the complete figure.

5) I want the total; how *many rows* are there? I realize that the answer is indicated by the altitude, the side *a*. How long is *one row*? Obviously this is given by the length of the base, *b*.

6) So I have to multiply *b* by *a*! (This is not multiplication of two items equal in rank: their characteristic functional difference is basic for the step.)

In this structurization of the rectangle the question of the area becomes clear. The structure obtained is seen comprehensively and transparently. The solution is reached[9] in the realization of the inner structural relation between area and form.

25. I do not mean to assert that these enumerated steps are always separately formulated in actual thinking processes![10] They are mostly in global interplay; yet I think they are needed for any real understanding of the issue.

[8] I here omit processes that start with variation of the size of the rectangle; introducing the small squares simplifies the picture. This procedure was sometimes found by children; sometimes the experimenter gave the rectangle as an arrangement of cube blocks or drew the lines from the beginning; in these cases essential steps had still to be taken by the child.

[9] In step 4), instead of the horizontal rows, the vertical rows could have been chosen. But one should not, in thinking, mix up these two ways. If the child does, the difference between "number of rows" and "length of a row" easily becomes blurred; it is advisable therefore to start with a rectangle the sides of which are markedly different. Step 5) is easily clear if the sides are simple multiples of the side of the measuring square; if not, another step is involved, viz., to decrease the measuring square. In 5) and 6) multiplication comes in. This is by no means simply or necessarily recall of the operation learned in arithmetic. It may be just the opposite: the idea of multiplying or the meaning of multiplication may arise in just such a context.

[10] I would not advise predigesting each of these steps for the child in teaching. But it is sometimes helpful to ask a question in one of the indicated directions.

They involve a number of operations, a number of features, which were not really seen or dealt with in the approaches of traditional logic and associationism.

1) There is *grouping, reorganization, structurization,* operations of dividing into sub-wholes and still seeing these sub-wholes together, with clear reference to the whole figure and in view of the specific problem at issue.

These are operations performed not just in any way; we have here not *any* grouping or organization, even though in fact many different kinds are possible; the steps are conceived and carried out *in accordance with* the whole-qualities of the figure and with the aim of getting at a *clear structure* of the area.

There is involved the realization of how parts (sub-wholes) *fit* together and *complete* the area; the realization of the *inner relatedness* between their fitting together and the whole-features of the figure, such as straightness of the lines, etc.

2) The process starts with the desire to get at the inner relatedness of form and size. This is not a search for just any relation which would connect them, but for the nature of their intrinsic interdependence.

Here some people proceed to introduce changes, observing, studying what a change (e.g., in the width of the figure) does to its form and size; and in this way they get at the kind of inner relatedness involved.

3) Outstanding relations of this kind—sensible with regard to the inner structural nature of the given situation—which we will call ρ-relations, play a large role here:

Equal, straight, parallel rows fitting together:	form of the rectangle involving straightness of lines, not for instance a structure like
Number of rows:	length of one side
Number of squares in a row:	length of the other side
Multiplication:	completing the structure

4) There is the feature of the functional meaning of parts, e.g., the characteristically different meaning of the two terms entering into the multiplication, a feature decisive for the productive solution and for any real understanding of the formula.

5) The entire process is *one consistent line of thinking*. It is not an and-sum of aggregated, piecemeal operations. No step is arbitrary, ununderstood in its function. On the contrary, each step is taken surveying the whole situation. No step appears here that is of the character of $a-b$, $\dfrac{1}{a}$ or $(a-b)^2$ in our ugly examples.

The essential features of the operations mentioned are basically different in character from the operations of traditional logic and associationism, which are blind to the view of the whole, to the structural requirements which actually bring the operations into existence.

I hope the reader realizes the dramatic and consistent character, the beautiful clarity of such a process and its stark difference from processes in which the operations drop in senselessly.

26. By contrast, a description of the process in terms of traditional logic only, or of associationism, looks poor indeed.

Here I want to mention one point with regard to these approaches. In traditional logic the feature of universality is basic: in the concepts, in the judgments, one looks for common qualities in many or all cases (in this instance for the common qualities in many rectangles). Similarly in associationism the question of many cases, of many repetitions showing some constant connection, is fundamental. In line with this, the ugliness of our cases of induction was viewed as due to their lack of general validity. But the issues of sensible structurization, organization, of fitting of items into each other, of completion, etc., are not necessarily connected with thinking of other cases; they may be envisaged, realized in the single concrete case, viewing *it* structurally, sensibly. This does not of course give assurance of universality in factual questions; but it often leads to reasonable understanding and to genuine discovery of essential features, in contrast to performing operations on the basis of blindly generalized features common to many or all cases. And it may imply structurally sensible transposability of items (see ¶[4], leading to sensible generalization and universality. But the steps do not necessarily come into existence by viewing many cases and stating what may be factually common in them.

27. Finding that the usual concepts did not suffice, some theorists arrived at the formulation that using *relations* makes thinking productive. Of course realizing relations does play an important role in thinking, but the assertion in itself is still blind to the main issue, is not the solution. For the difficulties that we encountered with regard to elements recur similarly with relations. To realize *any* relations, even if they are correct, is not decisive; what is decisive is that they must be the relations structurally required in view of the whole, arising, conceived, used as parts in their function in the structure. And this holds equally for all operations of traditional logic and associationism, such as generalization, abstraction, etc., when used in genuine thought processes.

Incidentally, ugly and unsuccessful proceedings involve relations no less than do productive ones.

28. In line with another modern approach one might reflect: "The difference you emphasize between the ugly and the good cases is in fact simple and means only this: in what you call the ugly cases, means are employed, steps, operations, concerning which I do not know in advance that they will help in the end. Whereas in the procedure you call sensible, I do know this on the basis of past experience. I know beforehand, for example, that where an amount is divided into equal parts I can use the learned technique of multiplication. I am using means here which have been associated with their effects by previous drill. Association brings about the recall."

There is nothing to be said against the first part of this formulation, that in the ugly cases means are employed concerning which I do not know in advance whether they will help. But the second part of the formulation is inadequate: first, it ignores the operations of fitting, grouping, etc., and their characteristic features; secondly, knowing some constant connection between means and ends and employing it is not the issue here. "Knowing" is an ambiguous term. To know a blind connection, such as the connection between the switch and the light, is very different from realizing or discovering the inner relatedness between means and ends, their structural fitting in our case (see ([38). This difference *is* of importance in this context precisely with regard to the coming into existence of the sensible, productive processes.

And the formulation with regard to the recall of multiplication learned by drill does not fit our sensible cases. For multiplication and its meaning are sometimes initially conceived through realization of structural needs in just such tasks. And even if the technique of multiplication has been learned before and is recalled now, the essential thing is what is known and what is recalled: some drilled operation blindly applied, or just the operation structurally required, recalled and used for that reason and not on the basis of some peripheral association (such as having done a lot of multiplication just the day before or heard the word "area" connected with the word "multiplication").

29. Multiplication is not simply a matter of being taught operations in terms of associations, connections between numbers. If sensible, it rests on a structural discovery or realization that is necessary even in its application. It is unfortunately true that many children are drilled in multiplication, can react instantaneously but have no idea where to apply it.[11]

30. Now I shall tell what happened when I put the problem of the area of the *parallelogram* to subjects, especially children, after having briefly shown how the area of the rectangle is found, saying nothing

---

[11] I used to ask a child—there were often guests in the house—"How many men and how many women are there at the table? How many are there altogether?" I asked this question often, when the child was six, then seven, then eight years old. In school she was good in arithmetic. If you asked her to multiply, say 6 × 2, she would answer correctly in "instantaneous reaction." But in this case, even when there were four men on one side of the table and four women on the opposite side, or if the men and women were sitting in pairs, she would proceed to count tediously: "One, two, three, four men; one, two, three, four women." Not until she was eight and a half years old did she have the idea, after having counted the men, of saying, "And there are just as many women," or "One, two, three, four pairs." And she is an intelligent child. Only she did not realize the bearing of the grouping on the amount, habituated as she was to counting one by one.

On the other hand, at the age of six, in more difficult but structurally clearer situations, her performances were astounding by comparison. I asked her, as I did many children, to figure out, in imagination, the number of sides and corners in a cube of sugar, then in the pyramid and in the double pyramid. She was able to find the answer structurally, and to apply it generally to the pyramid and double pyramid, even to a pyramid which had 3 × 7 lines, although she was not able to count to, or even say, 21.

further, giving no help, simply waiting for what they would say or do. There were grownups of all types, students who showed by their reactions that they had entirely forgotten this theorem, and children who had never heard of geometry, even children as young as five.

There are different types of reactions.

First type. No reaction at all.

Or someone says, "Whew! Mathematics!" and dismisses the problem with, "I don't like mathematics."

Some subjects simply wait politely for what is to come or ask, "What else?"

Others say, "I don't know; that is something I have not learned." Or, "I learned that in school but I have completely forgotten it," and that is all. Some show indignation: "How do you expect me to be able to do that?" To which I reply, "Why not try it?"

Second type. Others search their memory intensively, some even frantically, to see if they can recall anything that might be of help. They search blindly for some scraps of knowledge that might apply.

Some ask, "Could I ask my older brother? He surely knows." Or: "Could I look for it in a geometry book?" Which is certainly one way of solving problems.

Third type. Some start making speeches. They talk around the problem, telling of analogous situations. Or they classify it in some way, apply general terms, perform some subsumptions, or engage in aimless trials.

Fourth type. But in a number of cases one can observe real thinking at work—in drawings, in remarks, in thinking out loud.

1) "Here is this figure—how can I get at the size of the area? I see no possibility. The area just in this form?"

2) "Something has to be done. I have to change something, change it in a way that would lead me to see the area clearly. Something is wrong." At this stage some children produce Fig. 21. In such cases

Fig. 21

I add: "It would be nice to be able to compare the size of the area of the parallelogram with the area of the rectangle." The child is helpless, then starts anew.

There were other cases in which the child said: "I have to get rid of the trouble. This figure cannot be divided into little squares."

FIG. 22

3) Here one child said suddenly: "Could I have a folding ruler?" I fetched one. The child made a parallelogram of it, then turned it into a rectangle.

FIG. 23

I enjoyed this. I asked: "Are you sure this is correct?" "Sure," he said. It was only after considerable difficulty that I succeeded in making him doubt his method—by using an appropriate drawing such as

FIG. 24

Here he said at once: "The rectangle is much bigger—it doesn't work . . ."

4) A child took a piece of paper and cut out two equal parallelograms. Then, looking happy, he put the two together in this way.

Fig. 25

But he did not know how to proceed further.

This was in itself a fine happening (cf. the ring solution, p. 48). I may remark that in a number of cases I myself gave the child two samples of the figure. The reactions I got were sometimes as follows:

Fig. 26

Some indulged in several trials of this kind, even putting one figure above the other congruently or conversely. Such help seems to be effective only under certain conditions. Which ones?

31. But there were cases in which the thinking went straight ahead. Some children reached the solution with little or no help in a genuine, sensible, direct way. Sometimes, after strained concentration, a face brightened at the critical moment. It is wonderful to observe the beautiful transformation from blindness to seeing the point!

First I shall report what happened with a 5½-year-old child to whom I gave no help at all for the parallelogram. Given the parallelogram problem, after she had been shown briefly how to get at the area of the rectangle, she said, "I certainly don't know how to do *that*." Then after a moment of silence: "This is *no good here*," pointing to the region at the left end; "and *no good here*," pointing to the region at the right.

Fig. 27

"It's troublesome, here and there." Hesitatingly she said: "I could make it right here ... but ..." Suddenly she cried out, "May I have a pair of scissors? What is bad there is just what is needed here. It fits." She took the scissors, cut the figure vertically, and placed the left end at the right.

Another child proceeded in a similar way to cut off the triangle.

FIG. 28A   FIG. 28B

In several cases the procedure ran this way:

FIG. 29

1) "Disturbance"   "Disturbance also"
2) "Too much here"   "Too much here"
3) ——————————   "No! This needs over here at the right
                          just what is too much at the left,"
and she put the left end "in order." Then, looking at the other end, she tried to do the same thing there, but changed suddenly from seeing it as "too much" to seeing it as "gap."

There were other ways. A child to whom I had given the parallelogram, a long one cut out of paper (for the previous examples also, a long parallelogram seemed to be better), remarked in the beginning, "The whole middle part is all right, but the ends—" She continued to look at the form, clearly interested in the ends, suddenly took the paper figure, and, with a smile, made it into a ring, bringing the two ends together. Asked what this meant, she answered, holding the two ends together with her little fingers: "Why, I can cut it now, this way" and indicated a vertical somewhere in the middle, "Then it is all right."

Partially different procedures appear also, but I did not find any similar to that developed in modern mathematics, of diminishing the disturbances by cutting horizontal rows with altitudes smaller than any assignable quantity, infinitesimally small. Even for grownups this procedure often involves difficulties. Cutting in rows of smaller and smaller altitude, proposed to children of about twelve and to grownups, brought funny reactions. After being told the whole story some were still puzzled, thought it "insincere" even when shown that if the rows are shifted properly horizontally, the whole figure becomes more and more "similar" to the rectangle. It involves the transition to the concept of infinitely small and to the procedure of reaching a limit. This method became possible historically only after a long development oriented in a much broader region of geometry.

32. What are the operations, the steps in the procedure?

We saw that in such genuine, positive processes as those just described, there are again factors and operations similar to those mentioned in the discussion of the rectangle: regrouping with regard to the whole, reorganization, fitting; factors of inner relatedness and of inner requirements are discovered, realized, and followed up. The steps were taken, the operations were clearly done in view of the whole figure and of the whole situation. They arose by virtue of their part-function, not by blind recall or blind trial; their content, their direction, their application grew out of the requirements of the problem. Such a process is not just a sum of several steps, not an aggregate of several operations, but the growth of one line of thinking out of the gaps[12] in the situation, out of the structural troubles and the desire to remedy them, to straighten out what is bad, to get at the good inner relatedness. It is not a process that moves from

[12] Initially there is the gap concerning the size of the area. The desire is to fill this gap, to realize in the context of the other characterization what the size is, how this quality of size is structurally determined in the context. Especially when the parallelogram is a long one, the first step is clear: the middle region yields a transparently clear determination of the size—as in the rectangle; the ends appear as trouble regions, clarified in the process then by "making the ends good, too," which is based on the further realization of a second kind of gap: the one end viewed not as disturbance to be cut off but as needing completion.

pieces to an aggregate, from below to above, but from above to
below, from the nature of the structural trouble to the concrete
steps.

As far as we can see there is no blind trial and error in the good
cases. And if it does occur, it is quickly dismissed. I have not in such
processes seen really foolish, blind operations. I have not, for example,
seen a case in which the triangle at the left is cut off and placed on
the other side in this foolish position:

FIG. 30A   FIG. 30B

I did not even find cases in which the trouble regions, having been
recognized, were viewed in terms of the four angles individually
(Fig. 30B).

33. It would be possible, of course, to get the externals of this
procedure, even the solution, by senseless drill. Let us see clearly and
honestly what this implies as a general, theoretical approach.

Taking the extreme case, it would be possible to "teach" the
procedure without even stating the problem first; the teacher draws
the diagram. The pupils repeat "one auxiliary line," perhaps twenty
times, in this way building up a connection with many reinforce-
ments, with much recency. Then they continue similarly with an-

FIG. 31

other auxiliary line, "connecting" it with the figure, and so on, in this way reaching the end, the finished result. This *would* be at least a possible procedure, in line with association theory. I myself have not done such experiments. But I should think that even a positive result thus produced in blind pieces would differ strongly from the good cases with regard to future consequences, such as forgetting or application.

Of course these remarks are excessively simplified as regards the theoretical situation. In order to give an exhaustive picture one would need to go into a discussion of all the auxiliary hypotheses developed in the association approach, which tries to base all sensible processes on an aggregate of mechanical, blind connections. What has been said here may serve merely to give a hint of the fundamental problems involved.

34. It was mentioned above that at times the pupil concentrates first on, say, the left end of the parallelogram, deals with the disturbance by cutting it off, then finds his way by dealing with the right end as a gap to be filled, as required by the felt disturbance there *and* the damage done in leaving a remainder at the left.

Such a sequence does not seem to portray adequately what happens in other cases in which the subject envisages the two directions, the correction of the two ends in one comprehensive view of the figure: what is disturbing, excessive, on the left is seen as just needed at the right.

Both directions are here envisaged and dealt with as fitting together, as requiring each other.

This is still clearer in the ring solution: the two ends are seen as fitting together, as requiring to be brought together to make all trouble disappear. There is no real functional difference between them; they are seen as having the same disturbance, to be got rid of in the same way, by mutually completing each other.

The solution by cutting in the middle and shifting is often similar:

    get proper rectangular ends by cutting somewhere vertically, get rid of the disturbing ends by fitting them together (shift).

If one has vividly experienced such cases, one feels that the great dangers to the development of such fine processes are mainly blind recall, blind application of something learned, a piecemeal painstaking attitude, a failure to view the whole situation on its merits, in its structure and in its structural requirements. It seems to me, although I do not have sufficient quantitative data on this point, that the ability to produce such fine, genuine processes often decreases considerably in school children when they become accustomed to drill.

What the diagrams illustrate is the line of the vectors in the process.

Dynamically the essentials in such thought processes seem to be briefly as follows: facing the problem, vectors arise in connection with and determined by the structural features, the gap, the incompleteness in the situation, tending to concretization of the trouble regions, and to the operations of change. Nothing in the place and direction of the vectors is fortuitous. What is used, either out of the present situation or from recall, enters the process by way of its function, as structurally required, changing the start-situation with its gap and unclearness into the clear, complete end-situation: a good transition from a bad gestalt to a good gestalt.

My description appears highly complex because I have described the various steps implied, separately and successively, and because I had to employ formal terms which are not habitual in the traditional approaches. But does it look so complex, for example, in the case of the ring in which the essence of the procedure is simply that the disturbing oblique sides lose their character of boundary lines by closing the figure, disappearing in the plane? The ring has lost the disturbing features, and is seen as a normal, horizontally and vertically oriented band which, cut vertically, *is* a rectangle. That terms like "function in the whole," "change in function," "change with regard to part-items" are needed for exact formulation, should not detract from the simple understandable character of the process.

35. Here I shall not trouble the reader with a thorough structural analysis of these processes. I shall give only an idea of some of the items formally involved in them.

If in such a proceeding the three auxiliary lines are produced, they come into the picture *not* as "this line drawn vertically from the left upper corner, a second from the right upper corner, and the third prolonging the base to the right," later perhaps acquiring some value, some meaning. But they come into existence from above out of the functional requirements, in their role as parts. And in the process parts of the figure change their functional meaning:

1) The auxiliary line at the left originates

a) as the rectified, properly made *end* of the rectangle at the left;

b) and appears at the same time not as some one vertical but as part of the triangle;

c) as such, it is transferred, shifted to the right, becoming the proper end of the rectangle at the right.

a) and b) already involve a double function[13] of the line, closing

[13] M. Wertheimer, "Untersuchungen zur Lehre von der Gestalt," *Psychologische Forschung*, 1923, Vol. IV, pp. 301-350; see also W. D. Ellis, *op. cit.*, selection 5; or D. C. Beardslee and M. Wertheimer (Eds.), *Readings in percep-*

the triangle and forming the left end of the rectangle. In c) the line
is shifted to the right with the whole triangle, functioning there as
the proper right end of the rectangle.

The second perpendicular is again not just any line dropped from
a corner, but comes into existence as the proper end of the rectangle, being the side of the triangle that was lacking.

And the prolongation of the base line comes into existence not
as just any prolongation of the line but as part of the needed triangle, completing the rectangle base.

The three lines come into existence not as lines but as boundaries;
the figures, not the lines, are the issue—the parallelogram, the rectangle, the triangle; the lines come in only as parts of them.

2) What happens to the original lines of the figure? Some subjects describe it vividly. The figure is viewed first as a parallelogram
with its two horizontals in oblique reference to each other.

FIG. 32

But then the horizontals acquire a vertical reference to each other.
The left end of the base is no longer co-ordinated with the left end
of the upper horizontal but is separated, to be taken away as the
base of the triangle. The part of the base at the right appears unfinished, as lacking its proper end.

tion. Princeton: Van Nostrand, 1958, pp. 115-135. H. Kopfermann, "Psychologische Untersuchungen über die Wirkung zweidimensionaler Darstellungen
körperlicher Gebilde," Psychologische Forschung, 1930, Vol. XII, pp. 293-364.

The two oblique sides become disturbing: "The ends of the figure should not look like that"; a vector arises not to have them as boundary lines; in the shift of the triangle, they jump into identity, are no longer two but one, and this one is no longer a boundary line, is now in fact structurally unessential.

Similarly in the case of the first solution (p. 48) and of the ring solution: the introduced vertical line is conceived, comes into existence with the double function of becoming the proper end of the rectangle at the left and the proper end of the rectangle at the right. (Real understanding of the line involves this splitting into the two functional items.) And the oblique lines fall into identity, disappear structurally.

Changes of a similar character can be studied in perception. Both the structure of the events and the strength of the forces involved are comparable in this region.

Here is a simple example:[14] the two figures shown below are cut

FIG. 33

of wood or cardboard, black on a white ground. Observe as somebody moves them slowly toward each other. Will they meet? Close each other? It is quite a sudden thing when they reach each other—fit—and the jagged sides disappear in one homogeneous, undisturbed rectangle.[15] And what takes place in observers if near the end the quiet, slow movement in the horizontal suddenly changes its direction slightly? Some people actually jump to correct it, to make the parts fit.

Similarly in our parallelogram task: a child pondering on the task gets the idea of cutting off the triangle at the left; cuts it; you take the triangle to shift it to the right; what reaction do you find in children if you leave the triangle in these positions?

[14] Cf. M. Wertheimer, "Zu dem Problem der Unterscheidung von Einzelinhalt und Teil," *Zeitschrift für Psychologie*, 1933, Vol. 129, pp. 353-357. (See Appendix 1.—M.W.)

[15] Compare also the square-sets in Chap. Four, pp. 124-125.

or even in this?

FIG. 34

Some are flabbergasted; some laugh; some passionately interfere and put it in its proper position.

It is also interesting to observe the behavior of children (even of very young children) in the following situations. Four solid figures of this kind are given:[16]

FIG. 35

Children often show a strong trend to bring them together properly, to fit c into a, d into b. If the grownup tries to do it the other way,

[16] Cf. M. Wertheimer, "Zum Problem der Schwelle," *Bericht über den VIII Internationalen Kongress für Psychologie*, Groningen, 1926.

insists on placing *d* with *a*, and *c* with *b*, or puts *c* with *a*, and *d* with *b* but improperly, children are often not only puzzled, or amused, but interfere passionately, fitting the figures into their proper positions.[17]

In all these cases we have structural changes, tendencies toward the better structure, toward fitting, with the disappearance of disturbances.

Such changes are often dramatic in productive processes, much more so than in this modest example of the parallelogram. Indeed, the whole process is often a kind of drama with powerful dramatic forces—with tension and dramatic structural changes in the transition from an incomplete or inadequate structure to a view of the complete, the consistent structure,[18] in the transition from not having understood structurally, from being troubled, to really grasping and realizing the requirements.

36. The most urgent need in the experimental investigation of the problems seems to be not so much to get the quantitative answer, "How many children achieve a solution, how many fail, at what age?" etc., but to get at an understanding of what happens in good and in bad processes.

A physicist studying crystallization may try to find out in how

---

[17] It is easy to blind oneself to the real problems by simple recourse to "familiarity" of the complete figures (Cf. ([38). Familiarity often works in the same direction as a good gestalt but a real decision is found in cases in which the structurally good figure is the less familiar and the structurally less good the more familiar. This way of deciding the issue can be generally applied to structures. Cf. W. Krolik, "Über Erfahrungswirkungen beim Bewegungssehen," *Psychologische Forschung*, 1934, Vol. 20, pp. 47-101; M. B. Hubbell, "Configurational properties considered 'good' by naive subjects," *American Journal of Psychology*, 1940, Vol. 53, pp. 46-69.

[18] Cf. M. Wertheimer, "Zu dem Problem der Unterscheidung von Einzelinhalt und Teil," *Zeitschrift für Psychologie*, 1933, Vol. 129, pp. 353-357. The experimental set described on page 356 of this paper strikingly demonstrates characteristic features of many thought processes. First a simple clear dot-figure is shown; additions appear, quite reasonable ones, with a gap calling for proper completion; but now a new set appears besides, one that strikes the observer as nonsense, as senseless, disturbing. What sudden relief, then, what a change, when with some further additions *all* the parts suddenly form a consistent clear whole, in a new orientation, in strong reorganization and recentering, all fitting the structural requirements. Often one observes signs of strong tension in the subjects, surprise, uncertainty and, in the end, sudden relief. Afterward, when subjects describe the situation they refer to the striking structural changes in most vivid terms. (See Appendix 1.—M.W.)

many cases he finds pure crystals and in how many he does not—
there are crippled crystals some corners of which are jagged, there
are impure crystals, there are Siamese twin crystals improperly grown
together, there are even crystals shaped by artificial polishing into
perfect forms entirely incongruous with their nature. All such cases
are of primary interest to the physicist, not as problems of statistics
but for what they reveal of the inner nature of genuine crystallization.

It is also important to find out what are the conditions under
which pure crystallization may take place, what conditions favor it,
what factors endanger it.

And so in psychology.

IV

37. An easier way out? The role of past experience?

A wise friend, whom I told of the scissors solution (p. 48), exclaimed: "The child is a genius!" But many psychologists would say,
"What of it? Obviously this is nothing but past experience. Why
trouble with complicated and difficult explanations? Isn't it much
easier, and more in line with many other processes in psychology, to
view what these children did simply in terms of recall of past experience? By chance, or by some association mechanisms, the child recalled what she had in the past experienced with scissors. That other
children failed to solve the problem is due to the fact that they did
not recall, or that they had not had sufficient experience with scissors.
They had not learned the connection, the association which would
have helped, or they did not recall it. All that is essential in such
processes is recall on the basis of learned connections. It is memory
and recall that constitute such a process."

There are certainly cases in which such a thing as the use of
scissors comes into play by chance or by external recall. There are
cases, even in good processes, in which such suggestions from memory
are tried and used, or dismissed as of no help. Unquestionably beside
the present experience, whatever it may mean, much previous experience is needed in order to make such processes possible or probable.

But—is it adequate to discuss such things only in theoretical generalities? In our case, for example, the assertion is made that recall
of the scissors and of associations connected with them is decisive.

Suppose a child trying to solve this problem does not think of scissors. There is a lack of this content, and of its associations. Why not take the theoretical bull by the horns?[19] Let us give what is needed and see what happens. If the essential thing is to recall the scissors, we may furnish them directly without troubling memory to recall them. Or we may introduce stimuli eliciting the recall.

I put the scissors on the table at the beginning of the experiment or even have the child cut some paper. Sometimes it helps (e.g., if I bring the scissors after some deliberation by the child, after some remarks showing that the structural requirement is felt).

But there are cases in which it does not help. The child looks at the scissors, then looks again at the figure. Seeing the two he is clearly troubled but nothing happens.

I increase the "help." "Don't you want to take the scissors and cut the figure?" The reaction is sometimes a blank stare; the child obviously does not know what I want.

Sometimes children may obediently start to cut the figure in some way or other:

Fig. 36

Occasionally it happens that a child then puts the two parts together differently, getting another parallelogram. . . .

Fig. 37

When does giving the scissors help? When does it fail to help? We see that furnishing the scissors, and its common use, does not in itself help; it may result in entirely blind and foolish actions. Stating it briefly, it does seem to help if the structural requirement is already felt or if it is elicited by the scissors;[20] it does not easily help if it occurs without realization of what is required structurally, if the subject does not see the scissors in their function, in their role, in their context, with regard to the structural needs of the situation, with regard to what the situation itself requires—then he has them only as an added thing in an and-sum of contents. In fact, in some of the observed positive processes, there were remarks first that showed some realization of the structural need, leading then to recall or trial, which is quite different from blind recall of past experiences.

Moreover, not only does recall not seem to be blind, the real issue is: *what* was learned in this past experience in the positive cases? Some special and foolishly generalized movements with the scissors associated with some results of the cutting? Or the inner relation between the manner of cutting and the results? There is a ρ-relation between operation and effect, a clear fitting of the effect with the operation. This makes possible the sensible application to a new case.

Another similar explanation: the decisive thing is whether the child recalls his experiences with mosaic games which involved putting figures together and separating them into parts.

Procedure: just before giving him the problem, I have the child play a mosaic game with shapes more or less similar to those of the problem, containing within a variety of arrangements one that is even partly identical with the task. This proves somewhat helpful. Nevertheless, in a number of cases it leads to no solution.

I do not know whether the reader realizes the infinite number of theoretically possible ways there are of putting things together. Even with two such triangles as those in the figure, there is a great multiplicity of possibilities, of which only few types regularly occur with children.

There is a wide field here for experimentation. The observed facts do not seem to go in the direction of some, of just any arbitrary factual connections; they soon go in the direction of fitting, closing, getting a good, complete figure.

FIG. 38

Even if a positive procedure could be explained by the working

[20] See N. R. F. Maier, *op. cit.*

together of experienced connections, on the one hand, and of the goal-idea of the rectangle on the other, it seems to be in our case generally not just past experience but the nature and the structural fitting of past experience that has to be taken into account.

Introducing "helps" provides a technical tool for the experimenter to get an understanding of what happens. Sometimes it is more helpful to give other tasks which, in piecemeal details, may be even more complex, unfamiliar, but which have a more transparent, a clearer structure, as for example some of our A-B pairs. It sometimes happens in such cases that the subject sees the light, returns to the original problem and finds the solution. On the other hand, it is possible that he remains blind in spite of "help" which actually gives him just what he needs.[21]

The results of such experiments seem to show that it is essential that the help be seen *in* its functional value, in its place, role, and function within the requirements of the situation.

Now it becomes understandable why one can sometimes give one, two, or even all three auxiliary lines as help without their actually proving helpful. A child who does not see them in their role, in their function, may receive them as added complications, ununderstandable additions. The situation may as a result become more puzzling than before. The lines themselves need not necessarily throw light on the problem.

And was not the lesson the teacher taught at the beginning of this chapter, the extreme of such procedure? He gave *all* the items needed, explicitly; he drilled the pupils, achieving knowledge in routine cases but for the most part no real understanding, no ability to deal with varied situations.

It is not enough to try to substitute for the sensible process a sequence of drilled connections, even if this results in the ability to repeat, to perform what was taught in routine cases. For it would then be necessary to provide additional drill for variations in the situation, for A-B cases. It might be necessary repeatedly to furnish added mechanisms for new types of A-cases. To show that a sensible process can be replaced by a number of associations does not prove anything so long as the applications to variations in A-B cases are

[21] Cf. N. R. F. Maier, *op. cit.*

not taken into account and provided for. Such an enterprise is like trying to simulate the curve of a thrown ball by having it move across the open ends of a row of parallel open pipes with appropriate air pressures. By varying the pressures one could produce other curves corresponding to various angles of throwing and various weights of the ball. Or, again, it is like putting a calculating machine to work to deliver exact solutions of mathematical problems—forgetting or not realizing the piling up of devices that would be needed in the machine in order to make it properly perform some specific A-variations as well. It may be very efficient for solving routine problems, but it cannot adapt itself to new A-variations. Moreover it does not know which operations to apply; this you must tell the machine by setting the problem, by pushing the button for addition, subtraction, etc.

In short, the role of past experience is of high importance, but what matters is *what* one has gained from experience—blind, ununderstood connections, or insight into structural inner relatedness. What matters is how and what one recalls, how one applies what is recalled, whether blindly, in a piecemeal way, or in accordance with the structural requirements of the situation.

In addition to the specific structural experiences which we have in facing a problem—experiences which refer to structural perception, to changes in structural perception, to observing the results of trials, etc.—there are many general features in our world which generally play an enormous role in our dealing with objects, and which do so specifically in the concrete steps required for the solution of this concrete geometrical problem. They are so obvious that most of us do not think of them explicitly. Indeed, the reader may be shocked even to see mentioned, for example,

> that in shifting the triangle from the left to the right no change
>   occurs in the size or the form of the triangle;
> that in doing so no changes occur elsewhere in the figure, no
>   contraction or expansion in other parts;
> that objects like the parallelogram, etc., have their constancy,
>   are not changed in size by drawing lines in them;

that stated equality of some separate lines or angles secures
equality of whole figures in distant places;

that cutting into parts and rearranging them in an actual operation does not change the area;

even that mere thinking operations—stating equalities, etc.—
in no sense change the material;

and so on . . .

Most of the foregoing statements seem trivial and so obvious to
us that they look like hidden axioms, true by necessity. They are
not. If taken in connection with real happenings, they are by no
means "necessary" facts. Worlds are possible in which they do not
hold. Even in our own world modern science had shown them to
be in many respects too simple assumptions; and in some regions
of daily experience they are not true factually.

But leaving aside the question of factual truth, are they of the
character of just any connections, of associations in the exact meaning of the term, such as may connect nonsense syllables? No. They
have the character of simple expectations on the basis of structural
context, negating sheer arbitrary, blind connections. To make the
point concrete, as long as no other factors come into play, it is
structurally simplest, most reasonable, not to expect such changes
as, e.g., a queer contraction of, say, 7 per cent somewhere in the
right part of the parallelogram when it is cut at the left.

If we ask whether these features are learned, are acquired in accordance with the traditional associationist conception of past experience, this seems improbable indeed in the light of experiments
concerning gestalt laws, etc. They center in laws of organization and
reasonable structure; they are an outcome of the structural way of
working of our mind and brain rather than of blind associations.[22]

Thus the mentioned hidden axioms appear by no means as simple
products of sheer association which may connect any items, irrespective of their inner relatedness, of their structural features, of
reasonable requirements.

Still other, entirely different factors of experience play a role in

[22] M. Wertheimer, "Untersuchungen zur Lehre von der Gestalt," II, *Psychologische Forschung*, 1923, Vol. IV, pp. 336 and 349; see also W. D. Ellis, *op. cit.*,
selection 5; and D. C. Beardslee and M. Wertheimer, *op. cit.*, pp. 115-135.

such thought processes, and an important role. The attitudes one has developed in dealing with problem-situations—having had the experience of achievement or only of failure, the attitude of looking for the objective structural requirements of a situation, feeling its needs, not proceeding willfully but as the situation demands, facing the issue freely, going ahead with confidence and courage—all these are characteristics of real behavior, growing or withering in the experience of life.

Thus problems of personality and personality structure, structural features of the interaction between the individual and his field are basically involved. In connection with the latter we have also to realize the structure of the social situation, the social atmosphere one is in, the "philosophy of life" developed in the behavior of the child or person in his surroundings; the attitude toward objects and problem-situations eminently depends upon these factors. So also the social atmosphere in the schoolroom is sometimes of considerable importance for the development of genuine thinking. In the solution of this kind of problem it is more helpful at times to create the right mood than it is to force on the subject certain operations or drill.

Interested in clarifying certain fundamental features, we limited the scope of our discussion. We were able to do so since we were dealing with a relatively closed sub-whole. But if we want really to understand how the performance comes about (or does not), a much broader field must be confronted. The question then is one of the organization of the whole field in which the actual happening is only a part[23]—the personal, the social, the historical field. As to the last, our present generation stands upon the shoulders of previous thinkers in long historic developments. These are large tasks. I regret that I cannot deal with them explicitly here. In all these realms structural issues are involved no less, I think, than in our

[23] Cf. M. Wertheimer, "Über das Denken der Naturvölker, Zahlen und Zahlgebilde," *Zeitschrift für Psychologie*, 1912, Vol. 60, pp. 321-378; reprinted in Wertheimer, *Drei Abhandlungen zur Gestalttheorie* (Erlangen: Philosophische Akademie, 1925); see also W. D. Ellis, *op. cit.*, selection 22; H. Schulte, "Versuch einer Theorie der paranoischen Eigenbeziehung und Wahnbildung," *Psychologische Forschung*, 1924, Vol. 5, pp. 1-23; K. Lewin, A *dynamic theory of personality* (New York: McGraw-Hill, 1935); E. Levy, "Some aspects of the schizophrenic formal disturbance of thought," *Psychiatry*, 1943, Vol. 6, pp. 55-69.

little examples. Some work has been done in these directions; much more is needed.

There are still psychologists who, in a basic misunderstanding, think that gestalt theory tends to underestimate the role of past experience. Gestalt theory tries to differentiate between and-summative aggregates, on the one hand, and gestalten, structures, on the other, both in sub-wholes and in the total field, and to develop appropriate scientific tools for investigating the latter. It opposes the dogmatic application to all cases of what is adequate only for piecemeal aggregates. The question is whether an approach in piecemeal terms, through blind connections, is or is not adequate to interpret actual thought processes and the role of past experience as well. Past experience has to be considered thoroughly, but it is ambiguous in itself; so long as it is taken in piecemeal, blind terms it is not the magic key to solve all problems.

38. Let us return now to the question we had left unanswered in the end of part I, ¶10, the problem of the A-B responses. Our discussions in the previous paragraphs indicate a direct answer.

The teacher has shown the procedure: he has taught the class to draw the three auxiliary lines (p. 14). *If* the pupils have really grasped the issue, then for them the three lines are not just "this line, and that line and the other line" or, as the teacher had said, "a vertical line drawn from the upper left corner, another from the upper right corner, and a prolongation of the horizontal line from the lower right corner." They are not an and-sum of items, blindly connected with the solution. If that were what the pupils had got from the lesson, they would be lost in the critical A-B tasks, they would have no basis on which to deal sensibly with the new problems.

But if they have grasped the problem—and this is what grasping means—then they see the lines *in their structural role and function,* in their meaning within the sensible context. They *see how* these lines, just these in this situation, bring about the solution in the *inner relatedness,* the structural relation ρ of these operations *to* reaching the goal. The operations are viewed "from above," from the vantage point of the inner structure of the whole procedure, as they function within the context and fit its requirements. This then gives a basis for sensible dealing with the A-B problems.

Two things that are related are decisive here: the structural meaning of the parts and the character of their inner relatedness with reaching the goal, actually, transparently. The first has been clarified in many aspects; the issue in the second is a ρ-relation between the operations and reaching the goal.

A first approach may view our problem in terms of what the lesson learned has provided as to structural transfer in changed situations. Suppose we speak of drawing the three lines as the "learned means to the end." In the figure used in teaching, situation s_1, means m_1— drawing the three lines—leads to the goal, g. This is learned:

$$s_1, \ m_1, \ g.$$

What has been provided as a basis, as help for finding the appropriate m_2 in a situation s_2, the appropriate m_3 in s_3, etc.? What has been provided as to structural transfer of the m in changed situations?

Obviously we have to discriminate. m_1, objectively the same, may yet function in different ways: if the three operations have been learned only as an and-sum, without grasping or focusing on the inner, structural relation between just this kind of m in this situation, and successfully reaching the goal, then we have a set of operations that may be repeated, applied correctly to routine variations in some sort of structural transposition, or by blindly following the abstract wording of the teacher according to which the length of the lines is variable. The problem may be solved as long as the variations in s allow applications of just those lines. But if they do not fit the new situation, then there is no basis in what has been learned for dealing with it. In other words, if the meaning of the three operations is centered only on the wording of the teacher (two verticals from the upper corners, prolongation of the horizontal to the right), then the length of the lines and the distance between them are variable and adjustable to a routine form s_2; *but* for situations in which these three general helps are not applicable, which require that *they* be changed, nothing is provided.

Contrariwise, if the procedure is structurally understood, solving is centered in quite a different way and the resulting structural transfer is something fundamentally different. If the center of the procedure is the structural grasp—getting rid of a disturbance in the figure by the compensating shift—then the new situation too may be viewed in terms of looking for the disturbance, for the gap, and for what is required here in order to deal with them. Accordingly, the number, the length, the place of the auxiliary lines are variable, and they may change according to the features of the new situation.[24]

As in the genuine processes (pp. 47-49) the steps came about on the basis of the structural trouble, the structural requirements; here the responses to these changed situations come about sensibly, with the help of what has been understood in the learning situation.

There are characteristic cases in which a subject has not really understood in the learning situation. He has succeeded in routine variations, applying what the teacher had shown; but confronted with new tasks, he is lost. Spontaneously he goes back to the taught lesson, ponders over it, then suddenly cries: "I've got it!" and having understood the s_1, m_1, g structurally, he goes at this new task and he solves it easily. Subjects often describe in the most vivid terms what happened to them in the transition from copying what the teacher had taught to "seeing the light"—how drawing the three lines in the teacher's example suddenly became transparently clear, meaningful, in the realization of the inner structure, the inner requirements of the process. "And then it was easy to deal with the new problems."

In short, this is our formula: in real A-reactions behavior is determined by the requirements of the given situation, in B-reactions by some external details. In A-reactions the subject deals with the new situation on its merits, having understood the lesson situation on its merits.

The problem of transposability is of some importance and, although I think that the reader who has followed through sees the decisive point, I may add that the problem is by no means settled by stating the general formula. A number of problems arise for the scientist: here is a broad field in which experimental investigation seeks clarification, the conditions and laws governing the extent and character of

---

[24] E.g., in some cases (see example p. 47) m_2 easily becomes two lines instead of three. For the case on page 16 a different position is sought which allows the clear interchange of the disturbances. In the case on pp. 17-18 a hint is provided to search for interchangeable parts, out of which the idea of bisecting the slanting line may arise.

variability that result from different learning situations. In order to understand the problem, it is necessary to study it *in contrast* with cases in which the learning gives no material aid for dealing sensibly with changed situations, in which even the greatest genius could find no basis for sensibly transposing the well-known and much used "rote" learning situation.

On the other hand, there is the possibility that the subject grasps the inner structure of the situation, which will then help him when he is dealing with variations of the original problem. Let us consider an entirely crude case of s_1, m_1, g in which no such possibility is given. Suppose, instead of drawing the three lines which bring about the transformation of the parallelogram into a rectangle of equal size, a subject is shown a parallelogram on a screen; furthermore, there are several buttons and the subject learns that by pushing a red button, a blue button, and a green one, the parallelogram disappears and a chocolate drops out—or a rectangle appears on the screen. He may learn that. But if afterward you give him another figure—of the A- or B-type—naturally he will be at a loss. He may try to push the same buttons but with no result. He may try other buttons in blind trial and error, he may even by chance hit on the right ones; but he will again be lost when another figure is presented, for there is no possibility of discovering a sensible inner relation in the s_1, m_1, g. The connections are arbitrary, or hidden, and no basis for sensible variations can result.

Many theorists are blind to the problem, to the difference between such cases and cases which are solved sensibly. They have an easy ready-made way of avoiding the issue; they notice, and notice correctly, that, in the former, help from past experience is precluded, not in the latter; and they conclude—but the conclusion is blind— that the difference in the former responses is explained simply by the working of previous associations, all basically of the same nature as in rote learning. Sensible learning and applying is to them nothing but the work of a pile of previous associations. I hope the reader sees after all our discussions that this would be dismissing the problem far too easily: even if all the factors involved were due to past experience, our problem would remain. The crucial question is not *whether* past experience, but *what* kind of past experience plays a role—blind connections or structural grasp with resulting sensible transposing; also *how* material gains from past experience come in, whether by external recall or on the basis of structural requirements, of material functional fitness. Recourse to past experience does not therefore settle the problem; on the contrary, the same problem repeats itself with reference to past experience.

To study the use of what one has gained in past experience is of profound interest; but for our problem, in a first approach, it is not decisive whether the material used stems from present or from past experience. What is important is its nature, whether a reasonable structure is grasped, and how it is brought in. Even if everything, including grasping itself, were due basically to repetition of past experience—a hope some psychologists entertain, but which I regard as misleading, or at any rate unproved—or if we were to apply the concept of drill learning even to reasonable structures, it would still be important to face and to study the described difference, as it is decisive for the possibility of structurally reasonable processes. In everyday language, to have gained experience means for the most part something quite different from piling up external connections of the character of rote learning in the last example; more sensible gains, more sensible processes are meant.

We can summarize the A-B questions relating to the parallelogram as follows: for the role which a given s_1, m_1, g plays in facing new situations, the decisive point is *what* is learned from the taught example as well as from other past experience. Whether such experience established blind connections or insight into the structural issue is decided by seeing whether or not the subject is capable of dealing sensibly with A-B variations. To this I may add that the role of the particulars in s_1, m_1, g, may be of greater or of less importance; the extreme case is reached when the gain for new tasks is mainly the fine experience of being able to go ahead by looking for the requirements of the *situation at issue* and trying to deal with them straight.

39. If in such processes one looks for the operations of traditional logic, one can find quite a number of them. One can even describe the process in a succession of propositions. But the aggregate of these propositions does not represent what really happened in the process. Much has disappeared. The dynamics, the life is gone.

Traditional logic is not so much concerned with the process of *finding* a solution. It focuses rather on the question of correctness of each step in the proof. Here and there in the history of traditional logic there have been hints of how to proceed to find a solution. Characteristically these attempts have been of the following nature: "Look for any general propositions you know, the content of which refers to some of the items in question; gather these propositions together; look for pairs among them which, containing a common concept (middle term), permit of a syllogism," and so forth. (Cf. the example in Chap. Three, p. 101, which, though foolish, is much in line with such a procedure.)

We shall return to the issue of the proof; we shall then see briefly that the sensible proof itself involves structural factors. But for the moment let us examine some characteristic aspects of the attitude of traditional logic by considering the following remark of a logician: "The whole thing comes down to the use of the principle of commutability, $a+b=b+a$, just as $2+5$ equals $5+2$; both give the result 7." (An empiricist might have formulated it in much the same way.)

Fig. 39

Think it over yourself, reader. Compare this assertion, in the spirit of traditional logic, with a genuine finding process. Maybe you will agree; maybe not. If you see differences, are these unimportant, peripheral? Or do they involve factors that are decisive for just this problem of productive thinking? If you are a logician, accustomed to the ways of traditional logic, very sure in your definitions of what logic is and what thinking is, you may react violently against some of the remarks that follow. Please do not make use of the habitual escapes and dismiss the matter; try to do justice to the points I am going to mention. Do not misunderstand: this is in no sense an attack on the correctness of traditional logic. It is an invitation to realize certain problems and to see the teachings of traditional logic in their proper place.

The principle $a+b=b+a$ is somehow involved in the process of finding the area of the parallelogram, but in a way quite different from its meaning in traditional logic. And just this difference seems essential for making possible the genuine productive process.

1) First let us mention briefly that the a and the b in the figure above are *not* there from the start. This division of the parallelogram has to be reached in the process of solving the problem! And it is quite important that just this triangle a, just this kind of division is found, created, whereas for the formula that is no issue, the a and b are there, ready-made from the beginning.

2) A second point: while $a+b=b+a$, a is supposed to remain unaffected by the change of position, but in actual thinking about the area of the parallelogram the triangle a changes its meaning as it is shifted. The a at the left side is found, created in the desire to get rid of the disturbance. The a at the right side of the equation is the part needed for completing the gap. Only with regard to bare equality of size do we have an equation; the equality of size is important but the transition from left to right is a transition from one thing to quite another thing: $a+b$ is not the same as $b+a$ in regard to form, and quite essentially not the same for the process itself.

Even if we abstract from the actual processes, the formula $a+b=b+a$, taken exactly, is not the equivalent of the equation expressed in the diagram (see diagram below). It would be really adequate

Fig. 40

only if the two parts a and b had nothing to do with each other, were just two pieces, the mutual positions of which were of no importance whatever. But the form is important—or we would have no parallelogram and no rectangle either.

Examination of the parts in the figure clearly shows that there are striking differences between the left and the right of the figure. This holds not only for the whole-features—the parallelogram versus the rectangle—but also for the single parts of the figures. If the reader will study and compare the meaning of the lines, he may be surprised to realize how strikingly different the situation is with regard to them at the left and the right. I shall mention only a few points. The lines 1 and 6 at the left are boundaries; at the right they become identical, are no longer two lines, as they disappear from view in the completion of the rectangle. At the left 1, 5, 6, 2—7 form the figure, with the added, introduced line 3—4, whereas at the right side, 4, 5, 3, 7—2 form the figure and 6—1 is a line that disappears from the picture. The equation ignores the fact that together these lines form the periphery which, after all, is important for the figures the size of which must be determined.

Similarly with the angles: their meaning, their function in the figures is basically different on the two sides; angles which play an essential role at the left disappear at the right, etc.

If one makes the exact analysis of all such factors, one arrives at quite a huge number of structural differences. Viewed from below, piecemeal, such structural differences would look extremely complex. It would be very hard indeed, in all probability impossible, to get the clear process if one were to start with a mere sum of such detailed features. But there is no disturbing complexity if the approach is "from above," from the whole-qualities of the figures and the functional meaning of the lines, etc., in them.

3) Basic in the productive process is the *change* that results when $a+b$ becomes $b+a$. We have not in the figures, as in the equation, simply a relation of mutual equality of two things, but a change with a *direction*,

$$a+b \rightarrow b+a$$

and a *required* change. It is a change from one thing to something quite significantly different. We have not just an equation, we have a *transition*. The problem of validity, though important, is fundamentally blind to this directedness. Here is a basic difference from the approach of traditional logic. Whereas traditional logic is mainly interested in the question of whether or not an a_1 is "equal" (or "equivalent") to a_2, here the issue is the transition from a_1 to a_2, the fact that just this transition is made, etc. And it is a fundamental issue; it involves the step from statics to dynamics.

Do not such transitions involve the alternatives, "logical" or "illogical," sensible or blind and arbitrary procedure? Should these not be a matter of logic?

Such a "transition" often involves "structural reorganization." I may remark here that this term, important in gestalt theory, is often misunderstood, so that its meaning is cheapened. Some years ago a psychologist illustrated its meaning by a series of nonsense syllables to be learned first in one sequence, then in another. No such arbitrary procedure is meant here, but reorganization as sensibly required by the structure of the situation. The vectors for and in this change grow out of the functional requirements of the structure of the situation.

And I may mention that in such genuine cases as this, the transition seems inadequately characterized by stating that it is a transition to a more familiar figure; the transition here is to a form in which the matter becomes structurally clear. The size of the area in terms of unit squares becomes transparently clear in the form of the rectangle.

4) It may be noted that the equation $a+b=b+a$ does play an important role in the process with regard to the question of mere size also. The principle that such operations do not affect size is an outstanding case of structural simplicity in contrast to the possibility that such operations could be accompanied by changes in size (see p. 62). This does not mean that it is true by necessity. Nature is not obliged to show such simple properties. What is comfortably true with regard to the sum—we are dealing here with the *size* of the area, which is an and-summative issue—is not simply true generally, is not true for issues that are not of an and-summative nature.

The order *ba* versus the order *ab*, though irrelevant to the and-summative question of mere size, is very relevant in other aspects of this process. In fact, the order of the succession often does much more to the thing, to the nature of the parts, to the dynamics involved, than in our case. In our example, after all, one again gets a closed figure in the change. Contrast the two ways in which *ab* is changed into *ba* in these simple instances:

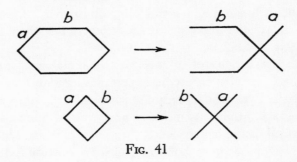

FIG. 41

And to assume the principle of commutability, e.g., in melodies, would be quite blind, quite senseless. The same is true in many other cases. Great problems are involved here, fundamental questions in logic. Some of the problems, such as those illustrated above in the hexagon and the diamond, are partially studied in the modern theory of relational networks, etc.; but deeper problems arise in regard to whole-qualities and whole-dynamics.

Many still view the principle of commutability as a general, basic principle in logic, generally presupposing the summative, atomistic character of facts, of propositions, etc., to such an extent that the doctrine could arise that logic fundamentally deals with "tautologies." In the light of our discussions such a view seems fundamentally blind to real problems in thinking.

The principle of commutability certainly does not hold true generally for the items in a real thought process. If one were to put the items, operations, or steps in a genuine thought process into some mixed-up order and state equality in terms of the principle of commutability, it would be quite a blind statement. The items of such a process are not an and-sum of pieces.

5) For the logician the principle of commutability is one of the statements among the propositions which make up the proof. Now it seems necessary to remark that the proof itself has its structure. If a subject is blind to the structure of the proof, sad things happen. Often a pupil, facing the series of statements in the proof in his textbook, is puzzled, worried, at a loss. He reads the statements,

checks them in the diagram, reads the theorems, starts a procedure of trying to fit the pieces together as in a jigsaw puzzle, to get at the sensible context. If he still does not succeed, he may memorize the statements in the given sequence; reproducing the proof, he may try frantically to recall what the next statement was in the textbook; if he does not succeed, he may produce some other statement which, though correct, is simply senseless in this context. The bright pupil, of course, does what is needed but in many textbook proofs *he* has to do it. He has to change the and-sum of the statements into the sensible structure of the proof. This involves sensible grouping, realization of functional hierarchy, of direction, of the structurally sensible place, role and function of each statement, its meaning in the whole. If a subject fails to see, for instance, that one of the statements, together with certain others, belongs to one sub-whole in the proof (say, the congruence of the triangles), and groups it wrong, he is far from seeing the light. There are cases in which a subject, trying to get some order into the statements about lines only, then about angles, then planes, is rather proud of now having a logical order, but becomes desperate again as he recalls the task. It is of no little importance to realize whether a statement has the function of a premise or of a conclusion, itself serving as a further premise, etc.

Similar considerations hold for *finding* the proof. Sensibly finding the proof does not proceed in the manner described above (p. 70) which is so characteristic of the attitude of traditional logic. It is not just a matter of making correct statements, recalling some learned theorems, etc. The sensible discovery proceeds by realizing the requirements for the proof, by facing what is needed in a structurally sensible order.

But whereas the structure of the proof in our case of the area of the parallelogram is comparatively simple, it is not nearly so easy to find a psychologically adequate, structurally sensible procedure in other teaching matters. Here improvement, productive work, is urgently needed.[25]

[25] For several years I have been dealing with these tasks in lectures on teaching and learning and in research with a number of fellow workers. Dr. George Katona has dealt with some of these questions in his book *Organizing and memorizing* (New York: Columbia University Press, 1940) and in the following papers: "On different forms of learning by reading," *Journal of Educational*

40. We have discussed the factors which are essential in solving the problem, reaching the goal. But what of the goal itself? Often thinking processes are viewed as processes of solving a problem, reaching a set goal; and so far we have done so ourselves. The task of thinking consists, in many theories, of just that. But are not our problems repeated with regard to the goal itself?

Here, in our case of a modest geometric problem, the situation is generally innocent enough. The very joy in solving such a problem is at work, the joy in achievement, in using one's mental powers. To this extent thinking may be a relatively closed affair. Moreover, there are situations in which the task is sensible in a larger context. This is the case when the problem of the area is set in a context in which a farmer wants to determine the area of his field; or when the question arises in a broader context of geometric thinking—as, for instance, when one has grasped the area of the rectangle and is interested in determining the area of other figures, in the general problem of area-determination.

But there are situations in which it is quite foolish just to work on the task of the area of the parallelogram because the task of the area does not structurally fit the situation, because the goal itself is out of place, and the situation calls for other things. If, in such a situation, the task is put or the question arises somehow, some people, blind to what is needed, start to work and stick blindly to the set goal. On the other hand, we often find quite wise reactions, the subject refusing to do the problem, because he is concerned with what really matters in the situation.[26]

I shall give a simple example. A teacher quite innocently uses some occasion for practice problems. In the last lesson he has taught the class how to get the area of a trapezoid by drawing the auxiliary lines; he has taught the formula $\frac{a+b}{2}h$. He refers now to a

---

Psychology, 1942, Vol. 33, pp. 335-355; "The role of the order of presentation in learning," *American Journal of Psychology*, 1942, Vol. 55, pp. 328-353. Dr. Catherine Stern reported on her work in the teaching of arithmetic in a paper read at the 1941 meetings of the Eastern Psychological Association. [This now forms part of her book *Children discover arithmetic* (New York: Harper, 1949.)—M. W.]
[26] Cf. the case in Chap. Four, p. 134 ff.

framed picture hanging on the wall, saying: "I want the area of the frame around the picture"; he labels the lines *a, b, c, d*; gives the dimensions, and adds: "You see, here are four trapezoids. I hope you remember how to find the areas."

FIG. 42

Some children work busily on the task set by the teacher; tediously they determine the areas—some falling into errors, correcting them with strained attention. But some children just look amused, do nothing of the kind, multiply *c* by *d, a* by *b*, subtract *ab* from *cd*, saying, "So what? Why should I get the areas of these trapezoids?"

Thinking is not merely to solve set problems. The goal itself, as a part of the situation, may be structurally sensible or foolish. Just as the operations within a real thinking process function as parts in their place and role with regard to structural requirements, so does the goal itself, as part of the broader context. Often the thinker, in the course of trying to solve a set problem, stops, realizing that the situation requires quite different things, requires changing the very goal. To stick to set goals, to insist on reaching them, is often sheer thoughtlessness.

In life such cases are often of a serious character. Sometimes men, for instance, politicians, after trying hard to reach a certain goal and working at it a long time, suddenly realize that the goal itself, as set, was out of place, unrelated to the real requirements, to more essential goals. This in itself may be a discovery of something that was not at all realized before—namely, that the means for a sought goal would endanger, would kill a much more important goal. Thinking is not merely concerned with means; it concerns the ends themselves in their structural significance.

In our geometric tasks such questions are not so serious: these are tasks in a quiet, pure, peaceful, clear region of life, tasks in which it is possible to proceed in a transparent, crystal-clear way.

This was one of the reasons why educators again and again urged the study of geometry, which allows the development of mental abilities in an atmosphere of clear, transparent consistency, and which may then help toward similarly straight attitudes in thinking about more complex and less concise matters.

This is one of the reasons why in this book we chose these simple geometric examples for discussion; it seemed better first to discuss the basic theoretical issues in structurally simpler materials.[27]

[27] For further material relevant to this chapter, see Appendices 2, 3, 4, and 5.—M.W.

CHAPTER TWO

The Bridge Problem*

In 1911, while engaged in research work at the Psychiatric and Physiological Institute of Vienna, the director of the children's clinic came to me, asking for some help with a special problem. A pediatrician and a psychologist had been engaged in the clinic to find ways of educating a group of deaf-mute children, ranging in age from four to fourteen years. The specialists felt that since the children lacked language, their intellectual abilities were extremely low. Would I not come and try to find out whether they were really so unintelligent?

In dealing with these children I first tried a method which I will report in outline.

1. Sitting at a table with one of the children, I take three blocks

Fig. 43

and build a bridge. Then I tear it down. Most of the children, after such a demonstration, begin to build a bridge. (In one variation I put the three blocks back into the pile at the side. The children then search for the blocks and begin to build.) In some cases in

---

* This chapter was not included in the original edition, although an early table of contents found among Max Wertheimer's papers indicated that he had at one time intended to use it in this place. The manuscript for this chapter did not seem to be in as finished a form as the chapters that comprise the original edition. Some editorial work seemed necessary, but an attempt was made to keep it to a minimum.—M.W.

which this spontaneous reaction does not occur, I take a little doll and make it walk through the door or across the bridge. This often helps.[1]

All this they can do. But what is it they are actually doing? Are they simply repeating what I did, or do they grasp something? It sometimes happens that, when picking blocks out of the pile, the child does not choose just the blocks I had used, but some others. And, after a few trials with poorly chosen blocks, they sometimes succeed only in building a bridge in which the construction falls

FIG. 44

down before it is completed. Then, soon after, they look for the right blocks. Other children solve the problem from the beginning. They transpose. They choose blocks which correspond, and also one

FIG. 45

[1] In these and nearly all the following attempts I used no language and no signs; I made my building and waited for the child.

which bridges the distance between the verticals. If the third block picked up is too short for the distance between the verticals, they either exchange it for a longer one, or bring the verticals nearer to each other. Some—very few—do look at first for exactly the blocks I had used, but most do not try at all to copy either the original distance or the size of the original blocks, adjusting distances and sizes to the building materials they have in hand. (Only one child searched anxiously for the original blocks, placing them at the original distance.)

2. I now put before the child a pile of blocks from which the original blocks of Step 1 have been removed. It works; they build a bridge. In other cases I place on the table only three blocks. All manage them reasonably. No child, when building with group c,

a
(original)   b   c

Fig. 46

used as a vertical the block that had been the vertical in the original set. It was clear that not the original stimuli but the relations were governing their behavior. The two equal and smaller blocks are chosen as verticals, and they are placed at such a distance as makes possible the use of the third block as a top.

3. In other experiments (with some children who were regarded by the doctors as dullest) I work with a crucial situation. In the set of three blocks with which they are to build, there is one block the size of the original verticals, and two blocks identical in size with the original horizontal. Will they stick to the learned and-sum

stimuli and their connections, and put two of the blocks in their
original place?

a   b
(original)

Fig. 47

Some do. They place the short block vertically, the long one horizontally, holding it in this position, and appear anxious to find
another small block. I do nothing. Then they begin to try to put
the third block in a vertical position; it falls down. (Others try this
from the start.) After it falls down, they do it again, but most

Fig. 48

children, after about two trials, suddenly smile, and change the
place and role of the blocks! Many of the children do this at once
after a short pause, without any previous trials. (See Fig. 49.)

For many children, these trials were clearly not simply negative
experiences. One could see that they learned something positive from
the unsuccessful trials: they had attentively observed the essential
point in the collapse of the blocks: the relation between stability and
equality.

FIG. 49

4. In the experiments with others of the children, I use colored blocks, the verticals being equal in size and color, the third being different in both. In the test, one pair is equal in size, and a different pair is equal in color. Nobody is misled. So it is not simply a relation of *any* equality that is decisive, but the inner coherence between a structure that is horizontal (stable) and the property of equality *in size* of the two verticals—a ρ-relation.

red   red   green   red   green   red

a   b

(original)

FIG. 50

5. Is the equality of size of the vertical blocks decisive? Before the test I build a staircase out of big blocks, and this time indicate with gestures that I want them to build the bridge on the steps of the staircase. They do—as you see in Fig. 51; they choose one of the equals for the vertical, the other for the horizontal. This shows that equality is not itself decisive, but rather the inner connection between being horizontal and stable, and that the role

of the part is determined secondarily out of this.

The layman will wonder why I thought it necessary to test in such a way (as in ([s 2, 3, 4, 5). "Is the result not obvious?" he is likely to ask. It is not. First, there are—though rarely—children habituated to act like little slaves, to stick exactly to what they have learned, to stick exactly to the painfully learned and-sums of pieces and their connections, and who do not succeed in such variations. Similarly there are children, although again rarely—I found none in this group—who in the course of unhappy trials repeat and repeat

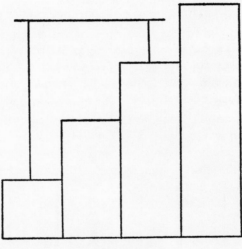

FIG. 51

without achieving the idea of changing the situation in the sensible, required way.[2]

Second, the state of affairs of our science of psychology is such that crucial experiments of this kind are needed—and very much so. To reach a real scientific clarification of the issues involved, science needs such crucial questions. (Despite the fact that common sense knows. Sometimes the obvious contains just the funda-

[2] In the few cases of this kind which I have seen, a change in the surroundings that gives the child more freedom, a change toward friendliness and optimism, helped quickly. See Chapter Seven.

mental, fascinating problems for the scientist—and sometimes common sense errs.)[3]

6. Still, it is possible that some theorists may think this way: "After all, relations or no relations, at bottom the whole thing is nothing but a sum of connections." Could we find a crucial experiment to test this assertion? Is it possible to decide by experiment whether we have here nothing other than an arbitrary learned connection?

It is possible. What is needed is to introduce arbitrariness into the connection. How can we do this? We might construct a magic set of blocks, blocks which make a stable bridge if the *colors* are equal in a vertical pair, which fall down if the colors are not the same, regardless of the relative size of the verticals.

Or in accordance with a different kind of experimentation we need not bother to construct such a magic world. Instead, the teacher simply says after one construction: "That's right," and gives the child a piece of chocolate; and after another construction he says: "That's wrong," and, God forbid, punishes the child before waiting to see whether the structure falls down.

Will the learning effect here be equivalent to the situation we have dealt with before in this chapter, which is, fortunately, to some degree reasonable, natural?

But we will leave this question for now and proceed with simple experimentation.

7. As in (1), I start building a bridge, but for the subsequent test I place the two verticals a little further away from each other. The child looks at the third block, then pushes one of the verticals nearer to the other,[4] into a more appropriate position. I move it

[3] I may remark in the interest of some who may wish to repeat such experiments with children that you must be to some degree cautious in the matter of selecting blocks. If you use blocks which will also, because of friction, permit a bad construction to stand, this will hinder your investigation. (It is necessary, for example, to use polished blocks in order to reduce friction.) Compare the chimpanzees who did not need to pile up the boxes in a stable way in order to reach the bananas, because they were quick enough to jump from the top just before the construction tumbled down. (W. Köhler, *The mentality of apes*, New York: Harcourt Brace, 1925).

[4] This decrease in the distance between the verticals did not take place if the third block was in view and if it was no shorter than this new distance. We see in this situation that the functional requirement, that the block must be longer than the distance between the verticals, worked clearly. And observ-

back to its first position. Sometimes there develops a nice pushing back and forth of the block between the child and myself. After a while (and for some children, without this game of pushing back and forth) the child turns back to the pile, where he searches clearly for a longer, "proper" third block. Failing to find one—there being no block of the required size in the pile on the table—he takes two small ones, and builds the construction in Figure 52. We see

Fig. 52

then that the relation between the distance and the length of the third block is decisive. (One child did take the original third block, which was not long enough for the distance between the verticals, and held it between them. It fell down, but the child did it again and again.)

8. When this problem is solved, I tear it down, take the verticals, and place them still farther apart, so that the preceding solution is no longer possible. The child builds the structure in Figure 53.[5]

Fig. 53

If by chance this holds up, I increase the distance. The child does it again; this time it breaks up. The child repeats the performance with the same result.

I watch the child observing the constructions and reconstructions as they fall down again and again. The child places the middle block

ing these children one could see that the behavior was directed by the understanding that the two short ones do not "close," do not give stability, etc. Not the repetition of original concrete items, but the requirements of the structure of the situation shaped the behavior.

[5] Again, in the selection of blocks for such experiments, care should be taken that constructions of this kind do not hold up.

carefully on top of the two horizontals, while continuing to hold it. But before the structure is about to fall, at the moment that there is a danger of tilting the horizontal blocks and throwing them completely off balance, he suddenly lifts the middle block again, and builds, with some difficulty but consistently, the construction of Figure 54, putting additional small blocks at the extreme for balance!

FIG. 54

Several do so without many trials, the behavior within the trials just before the solution showing clearly how the child becomes interested in the direction of falling down of the blocks.[6]

This may be an example of a real, if modest, discovery or invention. In this situation it is clear that, for the child, it is something newly found.[7] He is himself surprised. Other children could not do it. And a considerable number of grown-ups with whom I repeated this experiment did not solve it, among them some very intelligent and highly educated, sophisticated people. Some of these later told me that they spent a sleepless night without reaching the result.

Sometimes other inventions occurred, as, for example, doubling the vertical pillars, introducing a third vertical pillar in the middle, etc.

I may remark that one child, after the first construction broke

[6] Discovering the direction in which the blocks fall down is not just a turning of attention to one stimulus. There is involved the important procedure of discovering the decisive region within the structure. Compare experiments with grown-ups and children, in which they try to copy a magic trick: how difficult it is for them, under certain structural conditions, to get at what really matters! Not having understood, they try, in such a situation, to copy the operations in succession so exactly and so slavishly that they miss the essential point.

[7] I took pains, while questioning the teacher before the experiment, to make sure that these children had not previously had experiences of this kind.

down, took, with a shrewd expression on his face, a single pillar, tried to balance the horizontal, tried to place the two blocks on the horizontal, and watched with strained interest what was going

FIG. 55

to happen. When this construction stood, he returned to the long bridge and solved the problem.

I want to add that the building of the structure is in itself not a simple job. One must take pains to put it up in such a way that it will not fall down before it is finished. It is, in reality, a precarious enterprise, because one cannot place the horizontal and both end blocks simultaneously, with only two hands. But in spite of these difficulties, the building was done, in the positive cases, clearly and consistently. When negative performance occurs, whether in children or in grown-ups, it need not simply be a sign of lower intelligence. Quite different factors may play a role: difficulties in the handling of the blocks, awkwardness, clumsiness. In some grownups there is the additional factor of dislike for being tested, of disdain for such problems, of being subjects in experiments, of being before an audience, etc.

Many psychologists, hearing of these experiments, said: "This would make a nice intelligence test; should it not be standardized?" (There is nothing against this, providing it would not stop us from thinking, from looking for what is happening, for the real factors involved, for what the performance really means psychologically.) Very often in intelligence tests the psychologist does not know what he is measuring. And so whether a certain test item is solved or not does not actually say very much, when it remains ambiguous what the positive performance is, when we cannot say whether it

is a blind repeating of a learned and-sum of actions (choosing this
block and putting it in this place), or whether it has more to do
with a real grasping of what is to be done.

If the reader should now ask: "You said earlier that some solved
the problem and others not. How many did it? How many failed?
What are their ages?" he would miss the point at issue. We are interested here in finding out how the children reached the solution,
what factors were involved in this productive performance. Not
being satisfied with answers just in generalities, such as past experience, the functioning of learned connections, the drive to reach
a goal, etc., we had to employ these variations. We will now try to
formulate the way these proceedings look.

9. In the solution of the last problem (which for many children
clearly involved the enjoying of a new experience, a new achievement), the decisive step was the placing of additional blocks at
the extreme left and right of the horizontal blocks. How did this
operation arise? How did the children hit upon just this step?

Through blind trial and error? Certainly not, because they did
not, as such a view would imply, make a number of foolish trials
before hitting on this solution. They certainly did not proceed to
the solution via a number of arbitrary operations.

Through chance? Extremely improbable.

Through the use of past experience, the recall of similar operations performed with success? It is very probable that some past
experience played a role, but is the matter really cleared up by
referring to past experience in such general terms? Let us *introduce*,
here and now, what would be needed. I showed Figure 55 to the
children, not only as a finished product, but while I was building
it; I also let the child build it and achieve the effect of balancing
himself. It did not help in the solution of the long bridge problem,
not even if I added the remark: "Now certainly you will be able
to build the long bridge." Conceivably some children might be
helped by such a procedure; it was not so with these children. What
conditions would be necessary to turn this procedure into a help?
Why did it fail to help in these cases? (As I mentioned, there were
some children who spontaneously interrupted their work on the

long bridge, tried to build just this structure, and when they achieved it, returned to the first problem and solved it.[8]

What then *is* decisive here? How can we find out?

If one observes the behavior of the children—what they do, where they look, what they seem interested in, how they come to their real achievements—the process seems to be the following:

1) The child puts the middle block on top; the building falls down. (Negative experience; no success; some children are desperate; some children repeat the operation several times.)

2) This is for the child not simply a negative experience. He is clearly interested in trying to locate the trouble, to find out how the negative effect of falling down comes about, how and why it happened.

3) The falling of the middle block is now no longer the center of the problem. There are things happening at the left and right too! And *what* happens here is related to the trouble, or is important in relation to it. (All this amounts to more than getting all the details in a piecemeal analysis of the events; it aims at the region important in the interrelatedness of the events.)

4) The stability of the building is touched upon right here. How? The observed direction of fall of the pillars is seen to be due to the instability produced by the overloading of one side. (This is, of course, not formulated by the child in such abstract terms, but he feels the need to compensate symmetrically for the overloading in order to achieve stability. The situation cries for some help.)

How is the help given? In a blind way? By means of recall? As I mentioned a little while ago, one child interrupted his work on the bridge, and set up the structure in Figure 55; after realizing, beaming, that the small block on the left could compensate for the added weight of the block on the right, he returned to the long bridge and solved the problem.[9] Another child, without doing this,

[8] *Cf.* N. R. F. Maier, "Reasoning in humans: the solution of a problem and its appearance in consciousness," *Journal of Comparative Psychology*, 1931, Vol. 12, pp. 181-194.

[9] We now also see that an operation, given as a help, is effective only in the light of the functional need, in its function within the whole structure. For the children mentioned above, who were shown Figure 55 as a "help," this operation performed by me seemed something entirely strange. They did not see the interrelatedness of this step with the long bridge problem, and were

clearly focused on these critical happenings within the long bridge, touched the endangered ends with his fingers, clearly experiencing what had happened, and then solved the problem.

The gravitational conditions have to be included in the structural picture. But it does not help to think of the matter in such terms as "gravitational experiences must be taken into account." The gravitational side of the matter enters here structurally as part of the picture involving stability, symmetry—not simply geometrical symmetry, spatial symmetry, but *gravitational* symmetry—in its reasonable place in the whole structure.

There are in this structure a number of ρ-relations which are connected with whole-qualities. We could now build, as in (7), a substitute and-summative copy in which, instead of ρ-relations and meaningful whole-qualities, we introduce blind connections. We could, for example, make a magical set-up in which one-sided loading produces the effect of stability, while symmetrical loading produces just the opposite effect, pulling the structure down.

We may add at this point that the situation is, for the children, less simple than here stated. They have to get at the ρ in spite of technical difficulties: sometimes a building topples even though it is symmetrically balanced, frequently because of clumsy, unskillful handling of the blocks and of placing them with inappropriate force.

In any case, it is my impression as a result of such experiments that children can be able to find out, by actual reasonable working at a problem, just what is needed—without special previous experience. They find the needed experiences for themselves, in a reasonable way.

The experiencing of such processes may appear to the child to be just a game, or the solution of a puzzle. But observing their behavior afterward, one gets the impression that what they achieved was a deepening of insight, or understanding some reasonable features of our physical world. The "curiosity" often to be observed in such cases seems not just the curiosity for something new, for getting a

---

not able to use it just because it did not have this functional meaning for them. Here is a problem for future experimentation: perhaps if one gives this help just at the right moment, at the moment the child has already entered the region of the difficulty—perhaps then it would help.

trick down pat, etc., but a working toward a deeper understanding of our world.

Introducing rewards, such as chocolate or money, sometimes does seem to increase the drive to be successful. But in many cases it seems actually to work against a real solution. The desire to get the chocolate, if strongly in mind, provides in itself no material direction for the vectors needed. These must stem from the structure of the situation, from what the requirements cry for. It looks as if reward works positively only if forgotten in the demands of the work, or, in other words, if a transformation takes place from "what I want: the chocolate" to "what the situation requires."

Looking at the problem as a whole again, we see that we have here not simply an aggregation of some items, or of some relations, but a process that is governed by whole-qualities embracing a hierarchy of logically higher and lower items. Also, one sees that each of the items (or relations, or connections) is not an arbitrary addition to the place which it occupies, but that it completes in a reasonable way the structure of the whole, being the "proper" one, the adequate one, the reasonable one, in its place, role, and function within the structure.

If we study the reactions of the children or the grown-up subjects in the different variations, the processes involved seem to go not from below to above, from the "logically" lower terms to the higher ones, but the other way around. Determining the behavior, in the reasonable reactions, are, in the first place, the whole-qualities (of being stable, closed, symmetrical), and what they demand in the choosing of blocks, positions, distances. Logically the whole-qualities imply or demand the relation of relations; through these, the relations; through these, the items.

Certainly the child does not have this abstract logical structure in mind. It may also be too complicated to get into one view by adults (especially for those educated to read such statements with their attention centered on the piecemeal details). Logic, to be sure, tears things apart in such a way, formulating the items, relations, etc., separately—everything for itself. But this should not be done in order to have them all in addition to one another (as some logicians think), but in order to have them in their place, role, and function within the structure. For many logicians there exists the danger that when they have made their analysis they see only the additive characteristics, instead of seeing the picture from above to below, and realizing the ρ-nature of the events.

Fortunately the working of perception (and action) is not so piecemeal that the matter is psychologically as complicated as it looks in the logical picture.[10] If perception were fundamentally a getting of the and-sum of stimuli, with perhaps additional mechanisms, it would be very complicated indeed.

10. Let us try to express the logical structure of the proceedings, the structural features which hold true for the psychological picture.[11]

The two verticals, V_1 and V_2, are homotypic—they have the same logical place, role, and function in the whole. Between them there is the relation of being equal in size (s) on the one hand, and their horizontal distance (d) on the other. The third block, the horizontal (H), has homotypic logical relations to V_1 and V_2, the left end of H coinciding with the top of V_1, the right end coinciding with the top of V_2. But H has, further, a relation to the relation d (length of H longer than d), and a relation to s, the equality of s in V_1 and V_2 making possible the horizontal position of H. And just these last two relations of relations, if this term may be allowed, have an outstanding relation to the whole-qualities of the construction—its stability, the fact that being closed gives stability, together with the relation that, with d, a hole is formed in the construction.[12]

11. A number of different operations enters into the process of building the bridge: selections of blocks, putting them into a certain position, etc. In order to test various types of theoretical ap-

---

[10] Cf. M. Wertheimer, "Untersuchungen zur Lehre von der Gestalt," *Psychologische Forschung*, 1923, Vol. IV, pp. 301-350. See also W. D. Ellis, *op. cit.*, section 5; and D. C. Beardslee and M. Wertheimer, *op. cit.*, pp. 115-135.

[11] I hope the reader will not be repelled by the complicated logical picture which is drawn here. Certainly the reactions and the behavior of children, as of grown-ups, are not at all based on such abstract logical notions. These are just logical tools used in order to formulate the logical structure of the proceedings. Their merit is to express, in a model, the structural features which seem to be true of the psychological picture—a picture which proceeds in a way which is very different from logical abstraction.

[12] Some details have been omitted here, such as the position of H on V_1 and V_2, which is symmetrical, the gravitational character of the situation, etc. These are in the picture; because they do not change the essentials, they are not considered here, in order to prevent the situation from becoming too complicated.

proach, to test the essentials with the help of variations, the following
method was also used: to formulate the operations, as objectively
and as exhaustively as possible, and to project them into the terms
of a certain theory. For example, what would be a set-up "equivalent"
to the one we have discussed, if we assume that what is going on
in the child in the bridge situation is nothing other than arbitrary
connections or associations, blind to the inner relations, to the
structure as a whole, to the relation ρ?

The following operations are involved in the building of the
bridge:

1) Taking one block (either the same one the teacher used, or
simply any block), and

    1b) Placing it vertically on the table.

2) Taking another block equal to the first (in size, color, form?)
and

    2b) Standing it up, again vertically, like the first,

    2c) In a place beside the first, at a certain distance from the
first (either copying the distance the teacher used, or taking
a similar distance),

    2d) (Or at a distance a little shorter than the length of the
third block);

3) Taking a third block (again copying the teacher, or simply
selecting any one that is the appropriate length),

    3b) Choosing one a little longer than the horizontal distance
between the first two, and

    3c) Putting the third one horizontally on top of the others,
perhaps symmetrically.

In short, take a block "a," place it vertically (v), and perhaps
at the left side (l); take a second one, again an "a" (equal to the
first one), place it vertically (v) again, and perhaps at the right
side (r), and at a certain distance (d) from the first "a." Now
take "b" (the third block), put it horizontally (h), on top (t);
symmetry! (s).

We might suppose that the essential thing is to have learned this
in the sense of having the correct connections, associations between
the items; a correct solution or a correct process here would mean
that the operations are done, determined by these "connections."

If we envisage the proceedings in this way, as some psychological theories do, then it is possible to "copy" them, for example, in the following simple way. There is no bridge, there are no blocks, etc., but there are cardboard squares with letters on them, and some boxes, each with a small slit in the top and with a sign on the front. The teacher shows, or has the child learn, the following operations:

1) Take a card with the letter a on it, and put it in the box with the signs v and l.

2) Take a card with the letter a on it, and put it in the box with the signs v, r, d.

(Variation: instead of taking a square with the letter a, in step 1, take a square with any letter at all. Then in step 2, take another square with the same letter as the square in step 1.)

(Another variation: there are three letters on the cards—corresponding to length, color, and form. One must then teach that one of these three letters must be the same in 1 and 2 above. Which one? Are there any other restrictions?)

3) Take a card with the letter b, or with the letters b, ld (meaning longer distance), and put it in the box with the signs h, t, s.

Now, with regard to the operations to be learned, to the connections allegedly the essential of the proceedings, this is fairly equivalent to the first bridge problem. (With some additions it could be made logically exactly equivalent.)

It is also possible to use, instead of boxes, a procedure similar to the original without in any way omitting the point that in this copy we have an and-sum of operations, or arbitrary connections. One could also introduce some "relations," building up a constellation involving an and-sum of relations. Spatial relations could also be used directly.

Such a "copied" set-up gives the possibility of studying the proceedings of learning and performing, in order to find out if perhaps copies of this kind do not miss the very essentials of the first kind of proceeding.[13]

[13] A psychologist—and he is by no means the only psychologist who has used this approach—tried to study the psychology of the formation of general concepts, and of operations with regard to logical concepts, in a way very much like this. He came to me afterward and said: "Now, do you see at last that I

It is certainly possible to learn what is taught in such a copied set-up. The psychologist can study the differences in difficulty of learning, remembering, and transfer. It looks as if the copy will take longer to learn, will be forgotten much sooner, while the errors will, when compared with the original, be by necessity of a fortuitous and senseless character. The possibilities for the kind of transfer described in the original situation are drastically curtailed, and by necessity almost invariably blind.[14]

---

am not blind to philosophy, that I am not a man engaging in blind experimentation? I think you'll have to admit that I am a philosopher too, and that, with these procedures, I am investigating the essence of logic and of logical principles."

[14] See Appendix 5 for a problem related to the one in this chapter. (Also see G. Katona, *Organizing and memorizing*, New York: Columbia University Press, 1940.)—M.W.

CHAPTER THREE

The Problem of the Vertical Angles

HERE is an elementary question in geometry. Two straight lines intersect and form two angles, *a* and *b*. Can you prove that they are equal?

FIG. 56

Very likely you have learned this theorem in school. Perhaps you have forgotten it; all the better. Try to do it before reading what I report in this chapter. You may enjoy what follows more.

Putting this question to bright children and to grownups, one often gets reactions such as the following: "What are you asking? Isn't it obvious? Naturally the angles are equal; can't anyone see that?" And if one insists, one may get the answer: "It is clear; two straight lines first come together, then diverge in the same direction."

One of the main difficulties in dealing with the problem is that the pupil does not see—cannot see—the sense of the question. It appears artificial, senseless. Often the demand for a proof cannot be understood in such a situation; many do not know or are not able to realize the value of a proof here, the need for which came into existence in the development of theoretical mathematics.

Some say: "Of course you can prove it if you want to. Cut the paper vertically, turn the half page around putting one angle over the other. Hold them against the light. You will see that they

Fig. 57

coincide." If I say: "I agree, they will, but can you demonstrate here, on the figure, that the two are equal?" then for the most part subjects do not know what to do. Some fall into deep thought, which may contain little that is positive.

I shall tell first of what happens in schools.

I

The teacher demonstrates the theorem. He draws the lines, labels the angles, and proceeds as follows:

$$a + b = 180°$$
$$b + c = 180°$$

$$a = 180° - b$$
$$c = 180° - b$$

$$a = c \quad \text{Q.E.D.}$$

Fig. 58

One can describe the process in terms of traditional logic or of association theory. The teacher shows a number of successive operations, makes additions, writes equations, transforms them, finally derives the result. He may start with axioms or some general propositions, and apply them to the case in question. The pupils learn the proof and are then able to repeat it.

Certainly the proof can be described in terms of a number of operations and, for the problem of validity, these have to be considered. But is such an aggregation of several operations what really matters?

Some days later the teacher calls a pupil to the blackboard and asks him to demonstrate the equality of the angles. If the pupil now repeats word for word what the teacher has taught him, one is at a loss to know, "Does he repeat what he has heard blindly, like a slave, or has he grasped, has he understood?"

It sometimes happens that the pupil does not recall exactly, writes

$$a+b=180°$$
$$c+d=180°$$

then boldly: therefore $a=c$. Others become lost, look desperate, or get a stupid, sheepish expression. Still others may do

$$a+b=180°$$
$$b+c=180°$$

$$a=180°-b$$
$$b=180°-c$$

and then become equally helpless.[1]

But you also find such performances as:

$$a+d=180°$$
$$c+d=180°$$

$$a=c$$

Some pupils laugh at this: "Look! He has made two mistakes!" But the really superior pupil says, or appears to say to himself: "Why should I bother with the terms? It doesn't matter which way I work it." The teacher asks whether he cannot write the proof exactly as it was given and he writes with assurance

$$b+c=180°$$
$$c+d=180°$$

$$b=d$$

This is certainly fresh, but obviously quite different from the changes made by the first pupil.

We see that the "number of errors" is not decisive. One error makes the response a B-case, a senseless procedure; two "errors" may or may not lead to success, the operations may or may not be sensible. Two "errors" may simply show sensible understanding.

[1] Cf. Chap. One, p. 15 ff. Such foolish performances do not seem to be characteristic of children's behavior in general; they seem to become possible mainly on the basis of teaching by drill, etc.

What is decisive? We shall return to this point later.

There are pupils who are seriously disturbed if the teacher so much as uses a diagram with other than the habitual labels. This is no proof of the assertion that "mind is ruled by habits throughout."[2] It is proof that these particular individuals stick blindly to "what they were taught." Others may be a little surprised at the change, but what they are trying to do is a different thing from slavish, senseless repetition.

Here are examples for testing A- and B-solutions.

Fig. 59

1. We have a straight line; two other lines form a known angle, e.g., 90°. If one bravely applies here the steps of the learned demonstration, one shows that one has understood nothing.
This is a B-task.

Fig. 60

2. There is a right angle. The two dotted lines, too, form a right angle. Some refuse to make an attempt, "But, teacher, we haven't learned this." But some proceed consistently, in spite of the much changed situation.
This is an A-task.

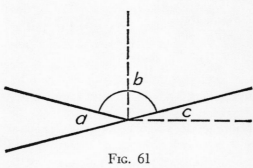

Fig. 61

3. The angle *a* is drawn and one of its lines is prolonged, giving the *b*-angle. *b* is bisected by the dotted vertical line. The fourth line is added, forming a right angle with the bisecting line. The task is to demonstrate the equality of angles *a* and *c*. The reader may discover for himself whether this is an A- or B-case.

[2] E. L. Thorndike, *The psychology of algebra*, p. 458 (New York: Macmillan, 1920). See Chapter Six on Thorndike.—M. W.

II

Now I shall tell of experiences I had when I gave the initial task of proving the equality of the two angles, $a=c$, without showing how to do it. The task is hard. Most subjects do not succeed. I hope the reader will see why: the structural operations required are not easy to envisage (cf. p. 103 ff). I shall illustrate by three examples:

1. I shall tell first of a subject (adult) who proceeded much in accordance with some classical remarks in traditional logic. He said: "Let's see, what general propositions have I at my disposal?" After a while he became busy writing down true propositions:

Fig. 62

$$a + b = 180°$$
$$a + d = 180°$$
$$b + c = 180°$$
$$c + d = 180°$$
$$a + b + c + d = 360°$$
$$(a + b) - (c + d) = 0$$

Then he searched for more such propositions. After a time he started making permutations, combining pairs of equations, adding them, subtracting them, seeing whether something would turn up. He finally arrived at the equation $b=d$, but did not think of stopping and proceeded until he reached $a=c$.

The procedure was similar to the answer a composer gave to a curious visitor who wished to know how he got the ideas for his melodies, how he found them. The composer, bored by the visitor, said: "Oh, that's simple; I take a number of notes and make permutations."

2. Here is a fine example of a process going ahead sensibly. The subject, fortunately, was thinking out loud (sometimes mumbling). I am sorry that I could not make a sound picture to show the illuminating changes of expression in voice and face in the course of his work.

Looking at the drawing he said slowly: "Now these are not two separate angles whose position is arbitrary with reference to each other." Asked what he meant, he drew:

FIG. 62A   FIG. 62B

"They are not like those angles. They are corresponding parts in the figure. The straight lines go clear through. This straightness of the lines must have something to do with the equality of the angles! . . . Straightness in terms of angles means—180° . . ." Then he drew:

FIG. 63

and he said: "*What a is as part of its 180°, b is as part of its 180°!* The remainder in both cases is the angle above; identical in both!" He labeled it *c*, and wrote the two equations:

FIG. 64

$$a + c = 180°$$
$$b + c = 180°$$

He continued: "What a is in $a + c$, b is in $b + c$," and wrote:

$$a = 180° - c$$
$$b = 180° - c$$

"Therefore," he concluded, "$a = b$."

3. In another procedure which was somewhat similar at the beginning, the last steps were different. The subject saw the requirement to understand a and, similarly, b as part of 180°. But he did not at first see the requirement with regard to the remainder. He proceeded as follows: "I have to use a as part of 180°; I have to use b as part of 180°. He drew:

FIG. 65A

Then he hesitated, saying: "There is another possibility of pairing."
Beaming, he changed the figure into:

FIG. 65B

III

A sensible process such as was described in our last two examples
involves operations of grouping, of grasping structure, equality, symmetry, of "playing the same role," of having the same function in
the group, of realizing relations, more particularly the ρ-relation
in which is realized the inner relatedness with the given structure of
the needed grouping.

Probably the reader has already seen what is essential in the A-
and B-cases and reactions. What matters in the A- and B-reactions
(see Figs. 59-61, p. 100) is not repetition of items, copying a learned
aggregation of steps; what matters is the structural issue. To establish the equality of a and c, the one angle, a, is viewed as part of
180°, as part of the angle $a+b$; c is also viewed as part of the—
equal—angle $c + b$. With the remainder identical, the angles a and c
must be equal. The structural issue in the two equations is:

$$a + b \qquad\qquad = 180°$$
$$\updownarrow \text{identical} \qquad \updownarrow \text{known as}$$
$$\text{remainder} \qquad \text{equal.}$$
$$c + b \qquad\qquad = 180°$$

FIG. 66

Thus what matters is how the two equations are structurally related
to each other; a sensible procedure looks for these structural requirements. The B-reactions violate them, are blind to them. The A-reac-

tions are determined by them but deal freely with the items; it is immaterial whether the steps in the demonstration are "correctly repeated."

Putting it generally, the structure is:

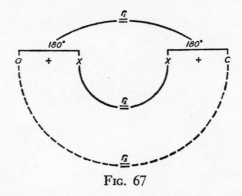

FIG. 67

It is not the items that are decisive but the kind of grouping in connection with the relations: r_1, the equality of the sub-wholes,

r_2, the identity of the remainder,

leading to r_3, the equality of the two angles.

This is not any aggregation of relations or operations: they are interlocked with the task, are sensible parts of a closed whole.

Some theorists recognize that the view of the whole is required but still miss the issue. They formulate certain B-reactions, for example, as follows: "The subject was wrong because he did not take all the items or relations into account." All items? All relations? It is just characteristic of sensible processes *not* to take all items into

FIG. 68

account. If this figure is given with the task of proving $a = b$, the fifth line is sensibly neglected. In short, "whole" does not mean "all," but refers to the structure of the items as they must be related in view of the task; it refers to the "good gestalt."

The reader may get clarification if he applies the structural scheme (p. 104) to the A- and B-reactions. In some of the B-cases—the senseless cases or the desperate cases—one main relation is lacking; in others, there are two main relations, as in Fig. 69. But the pro-

FIG. 69

cedures are blind because of the structural place of the items they interrelate. This leads to the conclusion that not the relations alone are decisive, but the relations with regard to their places within the good structure.

In the figure on page 104, relation 1 is a relation not between items but between two groups or sub-wholes, which are seen as symmetrical. Their equality (relation 1) plays the decisive role in the process, whatever the item may be, whether 180°, 90°, etc. Relation 2 is a relation between "homotype" items in the two sub-wholes. Relation 1 with relation 2 reasonably implies relation 3 which was sought: $r_1\ r_2 \supset r_3$. (The logician must not be mistaken about the formula $r_1\ r_2$ leading to r_3. It is not a case of a transitive relation. The formula is meaningless if the relations are not meant in their structural places.)

The task of finding the proof for the theorem, $a = c$, without help, seems very much more difficult than, e.g., the problem of the area of the parallelogram. Why?

In addition to the point mentioned earlier, that the reason for asking for the proof at all is often ununderstandable, the main reason seems to be that the situation calls for seeing the figure in *two* organizations, ab/bc—symmetrical, to be sure, but overlapping, while still tending to the pairing of the two critical angles a and c.

To view the angle a "as playing the same role in ab as c does in bc" demands considerable clearmindedness.[3] There are subjects who help

[3] Often after just sensing the structural requirements, the procedure becomes easier by transition to algebra.

themselves by drawing two figures:

FIG. 70

And in teaching this also seems to help understanding sometimes.

IV

The decisive thing in the A- and B-reactions was the structural relation of the pair of equations. But this is not sufficient. Often in genuine cases the very idea of the first equation, of grouping the given angle with the third angle, clearly comes into existence because it is seen that this can be done symmetrically for both the angles in question. It is not an operation in and for itself, but justified as part of the plan. One feels that the two operations (later equations) will interlock and in this way bring the solution. In such cases there is not simply a succession of two acts, but when the first comes into existence, it does so already *as* one of a pair. It is written down as a separate item but it is not separately conceived.

Thinking does not, as many believe, necessarily proceed merely by passing successively from one item to another, by formulating successive propositions; it does sometimes, but in the very act of thinking, in genuine processes, often it does not. Here the procedure goes from viewed whole-qualities to the items viewed as parts of the whole.

$$a + b = 180° \longrightarrow a = 180° - b$$

$$\text{corresponding role}$$

$$c + b = 180° \longrightarrow c = 180° - b$$

$$a = c$$

introduced   drops out

FIG. 71

The line of thinking, the direction, is in this case not *one* succession of items; there is a symmetrical two-directedness, each critical angle being dealt with as a part in its whole, formed by the introduction of the third angle, which subsequently can drop out again through the symmetry of the operations.

A comparison: some performances require both hands symmetrically, jointly, to co-operate with each other, to supplement each other's movements. In some cases it would be senseless to proceed with a sheer succession of separate items: you give two playing cards to a child, and ask him whether he can make them stand. The child may take one card and incline it about 30° from the vertical, an action that is sensible only in relation to the idea of the completed structure. To do this with one card, without viewing what will be done with the other, is senseless. There are subjects so educated that they are hampered in their thinking by the habit of proceeding only successively, step by step. But one should not suppose that one always has to do one thing after the other with the idea, "I'll take care of the other things later." Try first to see what you are doing in its context, deal with it as part of the context.

The successive habit—and so the widespread theory that thinking is by nature so[4]—is due to its adequacy in summative situations in which the performance of one operation is merely additively connected with others. It is due further to the fact that we cannot say two sentences at the same time, that we cannot write down two propositions simultaneously, that in reports we have to proceed with one thing after the other. That is one of the reasons why diagrams are often useful.

Further, the sheer successive habit is often caused by the demand for exactness, correctness in every step, which is of course seriously needed but which is not enough. And still further it is due to the fact that correct expression, or logical, formal expression, seemed to be possible only in and-sums of items: to repeat, in connection with the axiomatic assumption that thinking is, must be, verbal by nature, that logic is a matter of language, both of which assumptions are blind generalizations. Viewing the whole seemed unsuited to exact formulation.

---

[4] Cf. Kant's formulation that human thinking is by necessity *discursive* only.

CHAPTER FOUR

The Famous Story of Young Gauss

I

FIRST a question to the reader:

A staircase is being built along the wall in the hall of a new house. It has 19 steps. The side away from the wall is to be faced

FIG. 72

with square carved panels of the size of the ends of the steps. The carpenter tells his apprentice to fetch them from the shop. The apprentice asks, "How many panels shall I bring?" "Find out for yourself," rejoins the carpenter. The apprentice starts counting: $1 + 2 = 3; +3 = 6; +4 = 10; + 5 = \ldots$

The carpenter laughs. "Why don't you think? Must you count them out, one by one?"

Dear reader, if you were the apprentice, what would you do?

If you do not succeed in finding a better way, I will ask: "What if the staircase were not along the wall and required the square wooden panels on both sides? Would it help if I suggested thinking of the patterns of the two sides cut out of paper?"

The foregoing are some of the various experimental questions by which I studied features in the range of problems involved in the Gauss task.

Now I shall tell the story of young Gauss, the famous mathematician. It runs about as follows: he was a boy of six, attending grammar school in a little town. The teacher gave a test in arithmetic and said to the class: "Which of you will be first to get the sum of $1 + 2 + 3 + 4 + 5 + 6 + 7 + 8 + 9 + 10$?" Very soon, while the others were still busy figuring, young Gauss raised his hand. "Ligget se," he said, which means "Here it is."

"How the devil did you get it so quickly?" exclaimed the surprised teacher. Young Gauss answered—of course we do not know exactly what he did answer, but on the basis of experience in experiments I think it may have been about like this: "Had I done it by adding 1 and 2, then 3 to the sum, then 4 to the new result, and so on, it would have taken very long; and, trying to do it quickly, I would very likely have made mistakes. But you see, 1 and 10 make eleven, 2 and 9 are again—must be—11! And so on! There are 5 such pairs; 5 times 11 makes 55." The boy had discovered the gist of an important theorem.[1] In diagram:

not

but

FIG. 73

[1] $S_n = (n+1)\dfrac{n}{2}$

As the teacher had put the problem to the class, I put it to many subjects, including children of various ages, to see whether a good solution would be found, and what helps, what conditions, might bring it about. In order to study the steps and the features involved, I employed systematic variations some of which I shall describe later. Sometimes I gave very long series. I said directly: "Solve the problem without using the cumbersome additions," or I simply waited for reactions.

Here are the best types of genuine processes that I found.

1. At first no way was seen of dealing with the problem. Then: "If a sequence of numbers is to be added, it is certainly correct to add them as they come—but tiresome." Suddenly: "This is not just any sequence; the numbers increase consistently, one by one—this fact may . . . it must have something to do with the sum. But how the two hang together—the form of the sequence and its sum—what the inner relation is between them—is dark, unclear; I feel it somehow but I cannot clarify it."

After a while: "The series has direction in its increase. A sum has no direction. Now: the *increase* from left to right involves a corresponding *decrease* from right to left! This *has* to do with the sum.
—————————→ more and more; ←————————— less and less; in the same amount. If I go from left to right, from the first number to the second, there is an increase of one; if I go from right to left, from the last number at the right to the next preceding, there is a decrease of one. Hence the sum of the first and the last numbers must be the same as the sum of the next inner pair. And this must be true throughout!

"There remains only the question: how many pairs are there? Obviously the number of pairs is one-half of all the numbers; hence of the last number."

Essentially there is involved the regrouping, the reorganization of the series in the light of the problem. This is no blind regrouping; it comes about reasonably as the subject seeks to grasp the inner relation between the sum of the series and its structure. In the process the various items clearly gain a new meaning; they appear functionally determined in a new way. Nine is no longer viewed as 8 plus 1, it has become 10 minus 1, and so on.

If one gets the general formula $S_n = (n+1)\frac{n}{2}$ in some such way, then one understands its terms in the light of this structure: $(n+1)$ represents the value of a pair, $\frac{n}{2}$ the number of pairs. But many know only the formula, in a completely blind way. To them all forms $(n+1)\frac{n}{2}$, or $\frac{n+1}{2}n$, or $\frac{n(n+1)}{2}$, or $\frac{n^2+n}{2}$ are simply equivalent.[2]

The two n's seem to them to stand for the same item. They do not realize that, in the first formula, n in the expression $n+1$ is one member of a pair, while n in $\frac{n}{2}$ stands for the number of terms in the series, determining the number of pairs. Of course the four formulas give the same end-result and are in a way equivalent, but not psychologically.[3] In reality they are logically different too if one views them with regard to their form and function, and not solely in terms of external equivalence. Of course it is a logical matter only if one does not exclude from logic the functional meaning of terms, the genetic question, the question of the approach to the formula—finding or understanding the formula sensibly.

The formula applies equally when the series ends with an uneven number, e.g., 1 2 3 4 5 6 7. Here the grouping described

sometimes produces hesitation: what is to be done with the number in the middle which cannot be paired? A further step is required in this kind of procedure. Looking at the single number there comes a sudden discovery: "This must be half a pair, $\frac{n+1}{2}$!" And after some deliberation it is found that this does not change the formula:

---

[2] Even, e.g., $\frac{(n+\frac{1}{2})^2}{2} - \frac{1}{8}$. Or compare a blind generalization of the formula $\frac{n^2+n}{2}$ into $\frac{n^\bullet+n}{x}$.

[3] The difference shows itself objectively in responses to varied tasks. See p. 115, footnote 7.

there are 3 pairs and there is the remainder in the middle, now understood as half a pair.[4]

There are other ways of proceeding productively and sensibly. The following procedure by an 11-year-old boy is in line with what I have just described. After I had simply put the question to him: "What is $1+2+3+4+5+6+7+8+9$?" he asked, not too well pleased, "Should I count them?" "No," I answered. Suddenly smiling, he said, "There at the end is 9. Eight with the 1 in the beginning is also 9, and so must be the other pairs . . . ," then he stated the result.

2. Another way found by a 12-year-old boy started out differently. The task was: $1+2+3+4+5+6+7$.

Told not to do it by counting step by step, he said slowly: "The numbers ascend consistently . . ." And then, suddenly happy, "Oh, I have an idea! I simply take this number in the center and multiply it by the number of terms in the series—which is of course equal to the end number." It was clearly a discovery for him. Asked to show what he meant, he took the middle number, 4, and multiplied it by 7. Given a series ending with 8, he took the middle value between 4 and 5, viz., 4½.

In terms of a general formula, this means

$$c \cdot n \text{ (central value times } n \text{), or } \frac{n+1}{2} \cdot n$$

The formula is structurally different from the first in which $n+1$ was the sum of each pair, and $\frac{n}{2}$ the number of pairs.

I wanted to become clearer as to what he meant and how he had reached his solution. He was not able to give any clear-cut mathematical formulations, but what he said was: "The numbers ascend consistently. This means that for the sum the central value is significant. The numbers increase to the right of it; and they decrease in the same way to the left of it. So what is added on the right is just what is lacking on the left." In diagram:

$$[4] \ (n+1) \cdot \frac{n-1}{2} + \frac{n+1}{2} = (n+1)\frac{n-1}{2} + (n+1)\frac{1}{2} = (n+1)\frac{n}{2}$$

pair	number of whole pairs	half-pair

Fig. 74

3. The following was a structurally different procedure: realizing the consistently ascending character of the series, the subject viewed finding the sum as: "Very troublesome because of the jagged edge."

Fig. 75

"But"—and here the subject's face lit up—"I can easily make this trouble disappear. If I combine this staircase with another, inverted one, they will have to fit and give a clear figure without any trouble. The sum is clearly base times height, $n \cdot (n+1)$; half of it."[5]

Fig. 76

[5] Cf. Chap. One, p. 47 ff. The structural trouble is realized and made to disappear: the two trouble features fit together and vanish in the structurally clear whole.

This provides a sensible foundation for the well-known procedure in which the teacher says, "To get the sum of such a series, write it out, then just write it below in the opposite order and add each vertical pair. They are equal."

$$1+\ 2+\ 3+\ 4\ldots\ldots\ldots+58+59+60$$
$$60+59+58+57\ldots\ldots\ldots+\ 3+\ 2+\ 1$$
$$\overline{61+61+61+61\ldots\ldots\ldots+61+61+61}$$

I found a number of persons who gave this procedure as the solution. They said they had learned it that way in school. Asked why they wrote the series twice, and in this inverted fashion, all were puzzled, did not know what to answer. When I insisted, "What I want is the sum of the series, why find twice the sum first?" for the most part I got the answer, "Well, it leads to the solution in the end." They were unable to say how the idea of doubling might have originated. I confess that I myself was for a long time at a loss to see how one could reasonably have come to the idea of doubling. It had looked to me like a trick, as it does to many, like a chance discovery.[6]

When I showed these results to a mathematician, he said, "Why do you bother about what you call 'functional differences,' 'differences in the meaning of terms'? What matters is the formula, which is identical in all cases."

This attitude is certainly justified if nothing matters but the correctness and validity of the final result. But the moment one tries to get at the psychological process in productive thinking, one *has* to investigate, to view the terms in their functional meanings. These bring about the solution in the sensible, productive processes; they constitute the basic difference between finding the formula in a sensible way and finding it by blind learning or by chance trial and error.

[6] Cf. a similar procedure: getting the area of a triangle by doubling it into a parallelogram or, specifically, doubling a right triangle into a rectangle when the area is asked for.

Fɪɢ. 77

The structural operations in the various procedures which have been described are in some respects different.[7] But there are also characteristic identities: first the problem is seen, realized. It calls for grasping the concrete structure of the series in the light of the problem. The aim of discovering the inner relation between structure and task leads to regrouping, to structural reunderstanding. The steps and operations do not in the least appear to be a fortuitous, arbitrary sequence; rather they come into existence as parts of the whole process in one line of thinking. They are performed in view of the whole situation, of the functional need for them, not by blind accident nor as the thoughtless repetition of an old rule-of-thumb connection.

Although the whole process sometimes takes no more than a minute—as in the case of the two boys mentioned—the idea often comes in a colloidal manner, first in terms of directions, of main lines of groupings, etc. Often it takes some time before the situation becomes really lucid, fully clear. This is especially the case in finding the formula. Having once got the idea, the subjects are able to envisage some of the structural qualities of the equation to be formulated long before they are able to write the formula in concrete terms.

[7] The organization, the grouping, etc., in the three examples correspond to the following formulas:

$$1. \quad S = \underset{\substack{\text{value of} \\ \text{one pair}}}{(n+1)} \quad \bullet \quad \underset{\text{number of pairs}}{\frac{n}{2}}$$

$$2. \quad S = c \left[= \frac{n+1}{2} \right] \quad \bullet \quad \underset{\substack{\text{center value}}}{} \quad \underset{\text{number of terms}}{n}$$

$$3. \quad 2S = \underset{\substack{\text{one pair} \\ \text{(or height)}}}{(n+1)} \quad \bullet \quad \underset{\substack{\text{number of pairs} \\ \text{(or base)}}}{n}$$

These differences in reaching the solution also have objective consequences: they even seem easier than the odd series in 1 because of the complication with the half-pair; if procedure 1 has been found or shown in an even series and, as a test, an odd series is presented, difficulties often appear—hesitation, longer reaction time. The opposite seems to be the case in procedure 2: an uneven series seems easier because there is a middle term present, whereas in an even series there is not; if procedure 2 has been found or shown in an uneven series and, as a test, an even series is given, hesitation often occurs. In 3 there is no such difference with regard to even and uneven series; and a long series is often more easily dealt with than in 2, because the center need not be found.

That such a period of thought often appears hazy is, I think, due largely to the fact that exact terms for structural qualities, for whole-qualities, are frequently lacking, have not been developed. Of course the matter is really finished only after all the items involved have crystallized. But conceiving of symmetrical compensation is often the essential part in the process. In this phase it often happens that one is clear about rejecting proposed formulas which do not fit the envisaged structural qualities long before one is able to write down the positive formula. This is similar to the state of affairs in which a creative musician has in mind the idea of a melody in its whole-character; he tries to concretize it on the piano, produces something which he definitely discards as not proper, etc., until he does find the tones for what is in his mind.

II

I shall give some examples of the tasks I used in the experimental study of the Gauss problem. As in the problem of the parallelogram, subjects of various ages, especially children, were shown the Gauss method (p. 109) in one example, $1+2+3+4+5+6$, generally without the formula, sometimes with it. Then one or more tasks of the types appearing below were given to see what the subjects would do spontaneously, what help they needed, what kind of help really helped, etc.

The reader may guess the nature of the reactions: what fine productive processes (A-reactions) sometimes occurred (especially with problems d and e), how subjects sometimes even deepened, broadened the formula—and what blind, stupid B-reactions sometimes occurred.

Let the reader try for himself; let him see what happens to him in solving these problems—in one way or another they are all A-tasks:

What is the sum of:

$a.$ $\quad 1+2+3+4 \ldots\ldots\ldots\ldots +58+59$

$b.$ $\quad 17+18+19+20+21+22+23$

$c.$ $\quad 1+2+3+4 \quad\quad +16+17+18+19$

$bc.$ $\quad 96+97+98 \quad\quad +102+103+104$

$d.$ $\quad 1+5+9+13+17+21$

$cd.$ $\quad 9+11+13+15+17+19+21$

What is the product of:

e. $1 \cdot 2 \cdot 4 \cdot 8 \cdot 16 \cdot 32$
ec. $5 \cdot 10 \cdot 20 \cdot 40 \cdot 80 \cdot 160$
f. $\frac{1}{8} \cdot \frac{1}{4} \cdot \frac{1}{2} \cdot 1 \cdot 2 \cdot 4 \cdot 8$

I have said that these are all in some way A-tasks. I hope you see that.

In a) the original series is prolonged. If the formula has been taught, it is simply a special case of the formula.

b) does not start with 1. How did you deal with it? Did you see any direct way? Of course I made it easier for you by choosing a round number, an outstanding number. Did you think of an inclusive formula?

Series c) has a gap. Did it disturb you?

In series d) the difference between the terms is changed. What did you do?

Series e) and f) ask for the product. Were you surprised? Did you find a way? Could you write the formula?

I did not of course teach formulas to young children, nor did I ask for them; I often chose simpler numbers than in series b) and bc), or simpler cases than series e), f), but not necessarily shorter series, often much longer ones. One must be careful about the relation of successive tasks to each other. The nicest thing is to jump from the original to one of the last problems, to d) or e).

Often one has interesting experiences with such tasks: sometimes one gets surprisingly fine reactions, which are also evident in the remarks of the subject; sometimes one encounters utter helplessness, surprisingly stupid or blind responses even in intelligent subjects, especially if they have been blinded by habitual attitudes or by drill (cf. Chap. One, p. 17. The nature of both the sensible and senseless reactions illuminates the psychological issues.

For problems of type e), f), requiring the transition from addition to multiplication, I may cite the following incident: I had shown the Gauss method, in the example $1+2+3+4+5+6+7+8$, to a boy of eleven years. Then I gave him the series $1 \cdot 2 \cdot 3 \cdot 10 \cdot 15 \cdot 30$. "No," he said, "here it is impossible to use that nice method . . . ," but after a while he added spontaneously: "Oh, if I were to multiply these numbers it would work . . . !" and he showed the grouping $30 \cdot 30 \cdot 30$, making the discovery of the application to products by himself.

In the addition form this last series was a B-case; the multiplication form was an A-case. It became possible in experiments to use systematically pairs of A- and B-forms of such series as the following:

$$5+10+20+40+80+160 \qquad \text{(B-case)}$$
$$5 \cdot 10 \cdot 20 \cdot 40 \cdot 80 \cdot 160 \qquad \text{(A-case)}$$
$$1+2+4+8+16+32 \qquad \text{(B-case)}$$
$$1 \cdot 2 \cdot 4 \cdot 8 \cdot 16 \cdot 32 \qquad \text{(A-case)}$$

On the other hand, in some series the problem in addition form was an A-case:

$$5+10+15+20+25+30 \qquad \text{(A-case)}$$
$$5 \cdot 10 \cdot 15 \cdot 20 \cdot 25 \cdot 30 \qquad \text{(B-case)}$$

Or:

$$1+2+3+4+5+6 \qquad \text{Original case}$$
$$1 \cdot 2 \cdot 3 \cdot 4 \cdot 5 \cdot 6 \qquad \text{(B-case)}$$
$$1 \cdot 2 \cdot 3 \cdot 4 \cdot 6 \cdot 12 \qquad \text{(A-case)}$$
$$1+2+3+4+6+12 \qquad \text{(B-case)}$$

Which cases one rejects, to which ones one applies the method, what difficulties one has, etc.—these things are characteristic for understanding.

There are similar examples of B-tasks more liable to induce blind reactions. If, for example, we give, instead of series

$$a) \quad 1+2+3+7+8+9,$$
$$\text{the series} \quad b) \quad 1+2+3+4+7+8+9$$
$$\text{or} \quad c) \quad 1+2+3+4+6+7,$$

subjects sometimes show blindness to the requirement of the symmetrical position of the gap. Some subjects, on the other hand, apply the method correctly and unhesitatingly (A-reactions) in tasks of type a, while in tasks of type b and c they hesitate, even though in piecemeal terms these types are certainly *more* similar than type a to the original series $1+2+3+4+5+6$. They discriminate strongly between the types, looking for the required symmetry and, for the most part, they develop an appropriate, more complex procedure, e.g., restoring symmetry in b by eliminating the 4, adding the missing 5 in c, or changing the 4 to 5, etc.

Other examples of A-B pairs for distinguishing the issues in type
d) are the following:

$$1+2+3+4+\ 5+\ 6$$
A $\quad 3+5+7+9+11+13 \quad$ A $\quad 1+3+5+7+9+11$
B $\quad 1+2+3+4+11+13 \quad$ B $\quad 1+2+3+7+9+11$

Although it does take a considerable degree of blindness, the B-case,
especially when it is longer, provides occasion for blind application of
the Gauss method if the subject acts really thoughtlessly. On the other
hand, B is often intelligently rejected, or dealt with by the cumbersome method, while A is dealt with sensibly.

One can in such ways realize, study and test the structural features
involved in the Gauss task, those which are "essential," the features of
the structural inner relatedness between operations and form, in contrast to other factors which are structurally peripheral. In the various
types of tasks the issues were:

in b), independence of the structural factors from the place of beginning;
in c), the necessary symmetry of the series, tested by means of the
   gap and its position;
in d), independence of the structural features from the amount of
   the constant difference;
in e), independence of the structural inner relatedness from the nature of the particular operations, shown by the transfer to the
   structurally similar cases of multiplication.

It is most interesting to study which forms of tasks are better for
discovering the method with or without help; and it is most illuminating for the theoretical problems to find, for example, that
shorter series are by no means always more favorable for discovery,
nor even that $1+2+3+4+5+6$ is necessarily more favorable than,
e.g., $1+3+5+7+9+11$.

One primitive factor should not be forgotten: a disordered series,
with its numbers mixed up, offers particular difficulties, whether in
application or in discovery. The proper order makes for one comprehensive view, shows the needed consistency of the series. On the other
hand, there are changes of order which do not seem so unfavorable.
What seems important is not the amount of piecemeal deviation from

the original; it is rather the kind of order which may help or hinder a clear view of the whole. In

$$1+10+2+9+3+8+4+7+5+6$$

it sometimes happens that a subject stops, exclaims, "It goes right on consistently—these go up, these go down," showing

FIG. 78

or making the pairs,

1 10   2 9   3 8   4 7   5 6

FIG. 79

The latter procedure borders on the well-known "short cut" procedures used by many bookkeepers in long additions. They look for pairs or triplets, making easy round numbers rather than follow the order of succession. These procedures; of course, lack the fine relation to the "principle" of the series.

III

Confronted with the problem of the sum of a series (cf. §1), and given no help, many fail to find the Gauss solution. Why? What makes the task so difficult for many? What does it mean when one says, "It took the genius of young Gauss to do it"? Or why was it that the young boys in the examples mentioned, did it, and did it consistently and easily? What is at the bottom of these achievements psychologically?

The Gauss tasks involve structural difficulties. To overcome them, really to see one's way in spite of them, requires something. On the basis of my experiences, I would say that the essential features in genuine solving are:

> not to be bound, blinded by habits;

> not merely to repeat slavishly what one has been taught;

not to proceed in a mechanized state of mind,
in a piecemeal attitude,
with piecemeal attention,
by piecemeal operations;
but to look at the situation freely, open-mindedly, viewing the whole,
trying to discover, to realize how the problem and the situation
are related,

trying to penetrate, to realize and to trace out the inner relation
between form and task; in the finest cases getting at the roots
of the situation, illuminating and making transparent essential
structural features of regular series, in spite of the difficulties.

The Gauss situation *is* structurally complex; the main difficulty
seems as follows: envisaging the inner relation between form and
task (sum) is difficult (1) because the compensating differences are
hidden

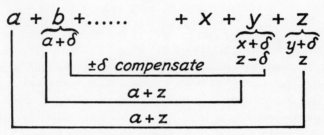

Fig. 80

and (2) because of the psychologically strong form of the ⟶
progressive series which has to be broken down into the required
symmetrical halves ⟶ and ⟵.

What if we simplify the structure of the situation, not just by
giving fewer numbers, but by employing tasks in which the basic
structural features are not so hidden?

Some forms of tasks similar to the previous examples clearly made
matters easier, for example:

$$99.8 + 99.9 + 100 + 100.1 + 100.2 = ?$$
$$273\tfrac{3}{5} + 273\tfrac{4}{5} + 274 + 274\tfrac{1}{5} + 274\tfrac{2}{5} = ?$$
or $$\frac{271 + 272 + 273 + 274 + 275}{5} = ?$$

But let us proceed in a radical way. Let us use tasks in which the compensating differences are not hidden structurally. The achievement becomes natural if, for example, we ask what is the sum of $-3-2-1+1+2+3$.[8]

Of course there are some who still stick to the attitude of drill, who still proceed blindly, piecemeal. But most subjects, looking at the whole line, laugh when they are given such a series, or are puzzled by the important-looking appearance of so obvious a problem; this happens often with virtually all subjects. In such cases it sometimes happens that one gets the response *without* even putting the question, *without* asking for the sum. If the series is long, it is often plain that the thing is done not by actually forming all the individual pairs, but by a view of the characteristically structured whole, based on the consistent progression of the series. If an item is added which clearly does not fit as, e.g.,

$$9-5-4-3-2-1+1+2+3+4+5$$
or $$-5-4-3-2-1+1+9+2+3+4+5$$

it often stands out, segregates itself.

Our case comes down to such tasks as $m+a-a$; or $m+a-a+b-b+c-c$. Operation 1) calls for adding a to m; operation 2) for subtracting a; but operation 2) stands in intrinsic relation to operation 1), being its opposite. Operation 2) appears in this context as demanding the undoing of what would be done by operation 1); and vice versa. That is their structural meaning. Both are viewed and function not as an and-sum of two operations but in their inner relation which makes it unnecessary, indeed senseless, to perform either.

Natural, sensible grasping is at work in the realization of this relation, in the reluctance to perform things which undo each other. The trained psychologist may think of behavior tendencies even in rats. It seems very difficult, often even impossible, to teach a rat maze runs parts of which undo each other. (See Fig. 81.)

We must not forget, on the other hand, that there are situations, forms of performance, in which a kind of doing and undoing becomes sensible —in rhythmical play, in rhythmical dance as in $-1+1$, $-1+1$, etc., or in $-1+1$, $-2+2$, $-1+1$, $-2+2$, etc. The symmetry of the opposite movements plays an important positive role.

[8] Cf. also example *f*, p. 117. Did the reader see it more readily than *e*, *ec*, or even *d* and *cd*?

Fig. 81

In 1931 in the Frankfort Institute I gave Miss Siemssen the task of studying psychological differences between sensible and senseless work. As compared with putting books in order, putting them sensibly on library shelves, we used externally similar Sisyphus tasks: rows of books were to be put on the shelves, then taken out again and replaced in their former places, put on the shelves again, and so on. . . . In both cases the activity was observed for about half an hour. The subjects performed the senseless task politely enough, although reluctantly, and obviously with some difficulty in sticking to it; as time went on, resistance increased and revolutionary tendencies came to the fore. But sometimes, when the performance continued, a striking result emerged: with some subjects the character of the task changed into something nicer—it became a kind of rhythmical dance, the books were taken out and returned in measured dance movements; continuing then was no longer so hard, the task had changed into jolly play. Even this did not last long, however.

To return to the issue: the role of sensible order, the features of sensible grouping in the situation, become technically clear if we give children tasks of the following types, and compare their attitudes and responses:

1. $m+a-a+b-b+c-c$
2. $m+a+b-c-a+c-b$
3. $m+a+b+c-a-b-c$

or 4. $m+a+b+c-c-b-a$ etc., with or without the m item.[9]

[9] Also concrete cases as, for example:
$$96+77-\ 77+134-134$$
or $96+77-134-\ 77+134$
or $48+79-124-\ 79+124$
or $48+79-\ 79+124-124$. The last in blind procedure:
$$48+79=127$$
$$127-\ 79=\ 48$$
$$48+124 \text{ etc.}$$

In the first we get easy, quick responses for the most part: "Of course it is m," with occasional remarks such as, "Should I always undo what I do?" The sensible pairing is done

$$m|+a-a|+b-b|+c-c$$

never

$$m+a|-a+b|-b+c|-c^{10}$$

Similarly, but more decisively, when the series is

$$m-a+a-b+b-c+c \ldots .$$
one gets $m|-a+a|-b+b|-c+c \ldots .$
not $m-a|+a-b|+b-c|+c \ldots .$

Most subjects do not bother to make the addition of $m+a$ or the subtraction $m-a$. Or, if they do, they are soon annoyed with themselves, exclaiming, "How stupid, how blind!"

In the second task we find more piecemeal, blind procedures. Often there is hesitation, uneasiness; remarks such as, "This needs to be put in order," "It is out of order," and the children rewrite the series in sensible pairs.

The third type of task again seems easier than the second, giving a quick view of the corresponding halves; the series is still more easily grasped if the given digits are not arbitrary, but a surveyable principle is used as in $m-1-2-3+3+2+1$, and in other similar examples.

A simple experimental technique for the study of these sensible tendencies of grouping is what we may call the "square set." The task is to add 4 numbers, of which the addition of two gives an outstanding number or mutual compensation.

[10] It is illuminating for the theoretical views of the transfer problem, to consider A-B cases in elementary forms:

		taught:		e.g.,
1)	Original shown,	taught:	$a+b-a$	$35+14-35$
2)	A—form		$c+d-c$	$87+69-87$
3)	B—form		$a+b-c$	$35+14-87$
4)	A'—form		$a+b-b$	$35+14-14$

In 1) the procedure of grouping the first term with the last is "shown, taught." In 2) all the numbers are changed as compared with the original example. In 3) much less is changed; viewed piecemeal, in terms of sum and stimuli, it is much more similar to the taught original. But if any understanding has taken place, the transfer is made by children to tasks 2) and 4), but not to task 3).

1) $+a-a$ ⌐‾‾¬   2) $+a-b$ ⌈ ⌈
     $-b+b$ ⌐‾‾¬ $-a+b$

e.g., 1) $+56-56$ ⌐‾‾¬   2) $+56-27$ ⌈ ⌈
       $-27+27$ ⌐‾‾¬ $-56+27$

Set 1) is usually sensibly conceived and dealt with in horizontal pairs, set 2) in vertical pairs. Similarly, with tasks in which two or more numbers make an outstanding number rather than compensate each other:

1) $+98+2$ ⌐‾‾¬   2) $+98+75$ ⌈ ⌈
    $+75+25$ ⌐‾‾¬ $+2+25$

If we designate the four terms in all such sets by $\begin{smallmatrix} a & b \\ c & d \end{smallmatrix}$ the preferred grouping in sets of type 1) is ab/cd; in sets of type 2) ac/bd. The psychologist sees that these are cases belonging to the results of investigations about the role of organization in perception, which uncovered the so-called "gestalt tendencies" in grouping.[11]

In those experimental investigations, dealing mostly with point sets or simple figures, it was an illuminating moment when a strong tendency was found to perceive consistent whole-qualities, "reasonable groupings" with features belonging to the inner structural nature of the situation—the so-called factor of the "good gestalt."

Those investigations showed that the tendency of perception to be "reasonable" is correlated with sensible, lawful mathematical

[11] Cf. M. Wertheimer, "Untersuchungen zur Lehre von der Gestalt," *Psychologische Forschung*, 1923, Vol. 4, pp. 322-323; see also W. D. Ellis, *op. cit.*, p. 82, or D. C. Beardslee & M. Wertheimer, *op. cit.*, p. 128. For example,

FIG. 82   FIG. 83

Fig. 82 is seen as ad/bc, not as ab/cd. Again, Fig. 83 is seen as $bcfgkl$ . . . $/adehi$ . . . , not as $acegi$ . . . $/bdfhk$ . . . ; it is nearly impossible to realize the latter view of the whole figure in perception.

features of the situations—although with restrictions, because of the importance of whole-qualities rather than of "class-laws" in perception (cf. p. 249 ff.).

The issues with which we are concerned here are by no means peculiar to arithmetic or to arithmetical training. A figural example not unlike the arithmetical square sets is the following optical constellation; especially in solid figures, e.g., black figures on white. Set 1 is usually seen vertically paired, set 2 horizontally.[12]

FIG. 84   FIG. 85

Or take these situations:

FIG. 86

If confronted with such patterns—say in blocks—there seems to be even in little children a strong tendency in the sensible direction. They often get at it spontaneously, "improving," "correcting" the situation. No language is needed—they just put the objects together reasonably, fit them together. Often it is not even necessary to assign a task for a sensible response to appear: it grows out of the inner dynamics of the situation. Again we see the role of "disturbance," "gap," "fitting," "being just needed," "being required," as parts in a

[12] Cf. experiments on movement with the special method of square sets. E.g., P. v. Schiller, "Stroboskopische Alternativversuche," *Psychologische Forschung*, 1933, Vol. 17, pp. 179-214.

consistent whole. These features seem also to be of basic importance for the reasonable teaching of arithmetic.

A simple illustration for our problem is this figure, which reveals[13] a tendency to take away the square, or the remainder, where it is "too much," and to put it in the place where it is lacking.

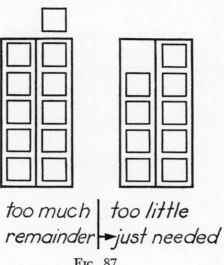

too much | *too little*
remainder ►*just needed*

FIG. 87

Similar considerations seem to be of basic importance in teaching geometry. For example, even to grasp sensibly, what an *angle* is, it seems important to view it as part in the outstanding whole of 360°. If angles of 182° and 180°, 355°, 360°, 363°, are dealt with indifferently as just *any* angles, as of the same rank, one is blind to their structural place, to their functional meaning. Here I will mention experiments with children who were asked to turn the large hand of the clock by several angles in succession.[14] The tasks were similar

[13] In many years of study with children, Dr. Catherine Stern has developed tools and methods for the teaching of arithmetic in which genuine discovery in tasks of a structural nature plays an essential role. The results in learning—and in happiness—seem extraordinarily good as compared with the usual teaching by drill which focuses on forming associative bonds, etc. [These methods and studies have been published in Dr. Stern's *Children discover arithmetic* (New York: Harper, 1949.)—M. W.]

[14] See M. Wertheimer, "Über das Denken der Naturvölker, Zahlen und Zahlgebilde," *Zeitschrift für Psychologie*, 1912, Vol. 60, pp. 321-378; reprinted in Wertheimer's *Drei Abhandlungen zur Gestalttheorie* (Erlangen: Philosophische Akademie, 1925); see also W. D. Ellis, *op. cit.*, selection 22.

to the Gauss problem. For example: what is the end position of the hand if it is turned clockwise, first through 7°, then through 90°, then 180°, then 90° again? Or first through 8°, then 7°, then 83°, 6°, 84°, 5°, 85°, 4°, 86°? In experiments with children who did not know about angles, I said, "It is 12 o'clock; suppose I turn the hand several times, clockwise. Where will the hand be in the end if I turn it first 7 minutes, then 25, 5, 24, 6?"

Here is an experience which occurred in dealing with the following type of task with grownups. I asked for the sum of the vectors, the forces working on a body, in instances like the following: "There is one vector (*a*) working vertically upward (0°), size K; another (*b*) at an angle of 90° to it, size L; a third (*c*) at 180°, size K; a fourth (*d*) at 270°, size L. What is the result of these forces on the body?"

FIG. 88

Now, especially if one makes the diagram and looks at it, the result is clear—zero; the opposites compensate each other, the opposite equals are paired.

But it happened that one person, seeing the complete picture, insisted upon doing it in what he called "the exact way." Making the constructions (Fig. 89), he said, "Vectors *a* and *b* in the parallelogram of forces give the resultant r_1. Combination of the first resultant and vector *c* in a parallelogram of forces gives the second resultant (Fig. 90). This with *d* gives resultant 3, which is zero; and r_3 combined with *a*, gives +*a* as the result." He was clearly puzzled, said hesitatingly, "But this is nonsense! And yet, working it out, it comes out that way . . . where is the mistake?" He did more than 14 minutes of strenuous thinking without becoming clearer, and dropped the matter. Coming back to the problem after a time, he suddenly said rather sadly: "I've got it. I had already used the first vector," and in an apologetic tone he added, "I was dumb. It was clear to me that I had to go all around. With the resultant 3, I felt that I had gone only ¾ of the way, only as far as 270°. . . . I thought I had to complete it. Didn't think that I had used vector a already. How stupid I was. Of course, a and c make zero, so do b and d. So the resultant is zero."

FIG. 89   FIG. 90

Certainly his procedure was correct up to the last step. Construction of every resultant is often needed; it is the general method. But we should not forget that often, in productive situations, the sensible view of the whole plays a decisive role: the realization of symmetry and balance in the whole, and of deviations from it, in sensible grouping. He was obviously misled by the closing tendency which obtruded.

To be sure, this was an extreme case. If the diagram is shown or drawn, almost all responses are sensible—always assuming that the meaning of "vectors" is clear.

IV

I have mentioned before that giving the task in the form of

$$\frac{271+272+273+274+275}{5}=?$$

seemed helpful. Some see their way at once. "This is 273, of course," they say and do not even start the cumbersome additions. Some do not see it, ask whether they really should do all the additions. If the task is given as a test after the Gauss method has been taught, the subject may even then start blindly with "$271+275=546$."

In this form the point is that the denominator requires the numerator to be divided into five equal parts and so helps toward viewing the expression above as being these five parts. When experiments showed that the concrete difficulties of many subjects with such tasks were similar to those of the Gauss problem, structural simplification seemed to be the next step.

When I asked children,

$$\frac{274+274+274+274+274}{5}=? \text{ or } \frac{272+272+272}{3}=? \text{ or } \frac{273+273}{2}=?$$

I got clear-cut results with some bright subjects. Most of them laughed, enjoyed the joke, while others were puzzled that such an easy problem should be given, or were bored; but they had no difficulty with the answer. They realized spontaneously and easily that what the denominator demands is already done in the numerator. Division by five was understood in its structural meaning, as demanding structurization of the amount of the numerator into five equal parts, which is already done. Or, the numerator, viewed as multiplication, showed the compensation of multiplication and division.

To add or really to multiply in order to divide later corresponds here to the doing and undoing we had before; it means working elaborately on something that is already done, trying to reach a solution that is given. Of course, something is to be done, viz., to realize that the solution is already there, to see that one of the numbers is not merely something to be added to the others but *is* the solution. This is an achievement: in the context of the task, intelligent change of the functional meaning of an item into the solution. But that is quite easy; there is no strong "embedding" to be overcome.[15] Although there was sometimes a little hesitation because the subjects had not expected such an easy task, a smile soon appeared with such remarks as, "It is obvious. At first it appeared to

[15] One has characteristic experiences in experiments with tasks in which the solution is factually contained in the text of the problem, but functionally strongly embedded, i.e., given in a definitely different functional place and role within the context of the question. Subjects are often blind even to the exact word-for-word formulation of the solution in the text, and characteristic processes occur when, after a time, they discover it. This again furnishes experimental proof of the importance of realizing the structural place, role, function of an item in its whole. (Cf. N. R. F. Maier's experiments on embedding technical tasks, "Reasoning in humans. I. On direction." *Journal of Comparative Psychology*, 1930, Vol. 10, pp. 115-143.)

be a difficult task but it isn't," and the solution was given.

Thinking of certain school attitudes I had so often experienced, I continued to ask such questions. Quite a surprise was in store for me—I had not imagined how extreme the situation often was. A number of children who were especially good in arithmetic in their school were entirely blind, started at once with tedious figuring or begged to be excused from the cumbersome task—they did not look at the situation as a whole at all. To be sure, when I helped them to see, they were clearly ashamed, exclaiming, "How dumb I was! How stupid!"

These experiences reminded me of a number of more serious experiences in schools, which had worried me. I now looked more thoroughly into customary methods, the ways of teaching arithmetic, the textbooks, the specific psychology books on which their methods were based. One reason for the difficulty became clearer and clearer: the emphasis on mechanical drill, on "instantaneous response," on developing blind, piecemeal habits. Repetition is useful, but continuous use of mechanical repetition also has harmful effects. It is dangerous because it easily induces habits of sheer mechanized action, blindness, tendencies to perform slavishly instead of thinking, instead of facing a problem freely.

An investigation of the blinding effects of mechanical repetition in sequences of assigned tasks was begun in the Berlin Institute in 1924. Duncker and Zener obtained striking results.[16] In recent years, a student of mine, A. Luchins,[17] has made a comprehensive investigation in schools of this effect, and has further developed experimental methods for dealing with it. It is surprising how easy it is, through some kind of mechanization, to blind even bright, highly educated subjects with the beloved method of repetition. Luchins also employed methods of recovery from blindness thus induced, which usually make it easy to regain sensible reactions but which showed no considerable positive effect with many of the children in certain schools. Of course there are a number of possible explanations to be considered both for the blinding effect and for the failure to recover; Luchins and Asch[18] made experiments concerning

[16] See N. R. F. Maier, *op. cit.*

[17] A. Luchins, "Mechanization in problem solving: the effect of Einstellung," *Psychological Monographs*, 1942, Vol. 54, no. 6.

[18] S. E. Asch, "Some effects of speed on the development of a mechanical attitude in problem solving," paper read at the 1940 meetings of the Eastern Psychological Association.

such theoretical issues. This much seems clear: important factors are the habits developed by drill, the attitude toward problems, certain school atmospheres as to learning, doing, and thinking.[19]

I will now report three reactions to these findings.

I once told a famous psychologist of these results. I said that they might have been due to bad schooling, a consequence of the emphasis on thoughtless association and drill, which impairs attitudes toward thinking. "Oh, no," he said, "not at all. The negative result is not at all surprising if you ask such gestalt questions; the children are not taught to solve such problems. They learn arithmetic in school. If you were to teach them such gestalt tasks, they would learn them. It is only a matter of what they are taught."

These remarks illuminate the theoretical situation. This psychologist is himself a fine thinker. His remarks become understandable if one realizes that, theoretically, thinking is for him, as for many others, fundamentally nothing but the working of mechanical associative bonds, habits, acquired by repetition. What else *could* it be?!

A mathematician whom I told of these experiences remarked: "You are wrong. To see the way to such a short cut is not important; the method of counting out, thoroughly, is a correct method, the general method. You can use the short cut only in specific cases."

Now this is a serious question. In my answer I first referred to several things of which I have spoken in previous chapters. Then I asked him whether he regarded the Gauss discovery too as merely an unimportant short cut. But, thirdly, I said: "I regard it as just the opposite, not a matter of a short cut merely, of a special case. The basic attitude toward a problem, toward an operation, is at stake. For many school children division *means* the drilled technique as, e.g., in $\frac{816}{3}$: '3 into 8 is 2; carry the 2; 21 by 3 is 7; 6 by 3 is 2 . . . 272.' This *is* to them division. But though mechanical mastery is of value, especially in freeing the mind for more important tasks in a problem situation, it should not blind the subject. It makes a difference whether the technique of division is viewed, known, applied

[19] As to the consequences of structurally blind teaching, compare Chap. One, section II; compare also the results of Dr. Katona in *Organizing and memorizing* (New York: Columbia University Press, 1939). (See also Chap. Six and Appendix 4 in this book.—M. W.)

as a mere technique or whether a subject is blind to the very meaning of division: the subdivision of an amount into equal parts in all the concreteness of the given structure. And so with multiplication.

"If, in such cases, one is unable to realize the structural meaning of division, one is blinded to the fundamentals. I mean it seriously: teaching arithmetic should not mainly stress drill but should let the child discover the structural features and requirements of given situations, and let him learn to deal with them sensibly. This of course requires a very different procedure from the drill of most schools." I then told him of some developments, especially of Dr. Catherine Stern's[20] structural methods, which of course he enjoyed.

The reaction of another well-known psychologist was different. After I had told him briefly of my experiments in schools, he said: "Of course, I see. It reminds me of an experience I had some months ago which may be typical. My son, who is a bright boy, came and said to me, 'You see, daddy: I am very good in arithmetic at school. I can do addition, subtraction, multiplication, division, anything you like, very quickly and without mistakes. The trouble is, often I don't know *which* of them to use. . . .' "

It is not the teachers who are at fault. Many are somehow deeply dissatisfied with the emphasis on mechanical associations, on blind drill. Many rely on them because they seem to them to be in line with scientific psychology—by which they mean the psychology of learning rote syllable series, and of conditioning. Many rely on them because they see no other, more sensible, concrete, scientific way of teaching. To develop better methods is really the task of a more adequate psychology of thinking and learning.

V

Probably the reader now has a clear idea of the psychological structure of the Gauss problem. One interesting point has not received enough consideration in the variations reported. It is just the point that made the Gauss discovery so beautiful: its inner connection with the principle of the series. In the course of experiments I showed a series of numbers without giving a task. Here is one:

$$-63, -26, -7, 0, +1, +2, +9, +28, +65$$

[20] Cf. p. 127, footnote 13.

Perhaps the reader, looking at the series, has already done something with it. He may, as some do, have noted the similarity of certain numbers (-63, $+65$; -26, $+28$; -7, $+9$), stated that the sum of each pair is two; 3×2 is 6; and the sum of $0+1+2$ is 3; so that the sum of the series is 9. This procedure is somehow Gaussian and yet not quite.

There is another type of reaction. I report a typical protocol: "To the right the series increases progressively; similarly it decreases on the left. These numbers correspond somehow, the -63 and 65, -26 and 28, -7 and 9. What about the middle region?

$$-63 \quad -26 \quad -7 \quad 0 \quad +1 \quad +2 \quad +9 \quad +28 \quad +65$$

FIG. 91

. . . Oh, the series is out of place!! The real center is where the $+1$ is! This 1 should be zero. . . . And if we subtract 1 throughout we get $x_n = n^3$."[21]

Now, such a procedure was also followed in a case in which the sum was asked for from the start. Interested in grasping the series, however, the subject at first disregarded or temporarily forgot this task. After the subject in this way had reached "It is $x_n = n^3$" he was reminded that the task was to find the sum. "The sum?" he said. "The sum of such a series is naturally zero. . . . Oh, forgive me, here is this silly shift. The whole series is shifted by $+1$. Every number gets an additional $+1$. So $+1$ times the number of terms . . . how many are there? It makes 9." He said it not too pleasantly.

Here someone remarked: "What queer behavior! You were asked for the sum; why did you bother with these things at all?" And he showed the short procedure mentioned above, adding: "No principle was asked for. Why not do the task the direct way?"

To which the first subject, somewhat absent-mindedly, seemingly preoccupied, somewhat annoyed, answered: "Oh, yes, yes,—you are right—but please don't disturb me. Don't you see what opens up

[21]

-64	-27	-8	-1	0	$+1$	$+8$	$+27$	$+64$
$(-4)^3$	$(-3)^3$	$(-2)^3$	$(-1)^3$		1^3	2^3	3^3	4^3

here? . . ." He was submerged in thought. There started for him a
long process, a chain of discoveries.

To focus on a set question, to solve it in the shortest way, is not
always the most intelligent attitude. There is such a thing as trying
to get at the root of a situation. Days afterward this same subject
remarked: "That silly shift—I just had to see through it." It is a
fine thing to uncover the "real" structure,[22] to see through a misleading appearance, to get at the core of a situation, to realize what
one is facing.

After a while the subject said: "Here it was $x_n = n^3$ . . . the sum is
zero whether the series is symmetrically continued or cut off at any
particular point. This would not be the case in $x_n = n^2$. There is
equality of the two halves but they do not compensate: $(-2)^2 = +4$,
the same as $(+2)^2$. In general, when the exponent is an uneven
number, the sum must be zero." After a while he proceeded: "The
same will be true of continuous curves, e.g., of the sine curve, properly
cut; of the area or of the sum of the vertical lines between the sine
curve and the axis:

FIG. 92

"And so with the area in . The area becomes a rectangle.

FIG. 93

Even if the curve is shifted!

FIG. 94

[22] In order to make reasonably sure whether such a structural view, here
$x_n = n^3$ (shifted), is the true view in an actual case, one looks ahead to see whether
or not further values, left and right, would be in accordance with the envisaged
principle. One also examines what happens to the values in variations of the series.
But all this is not the issue in this case in which the subject was intent upon
certain whole-qualities of consistent series, as his further procedure showed.

This is a question of symmetry and equilibrium within the whole figure.

"What of other curves? Of course it is true also for $y = x$ (see Fig.

FIG. 95A   FIG. 95B

95A) or $y = ax$ (see Fig. 95B). It holds, however the angle may change, with any straight line symmetrically cut. In $y = ax + b$ the line is only shifted. And the area is the height of the center times

the base in figures such as the following:

FIG. 96

"It holds with corresponding series $x_n = x_{n-1} + k$. The sum of the terms is the value of the center times the number of digits, c times n."

FIG. 97

In this way he arrived at the Gauss theorem, not from a series starting with 1, but from the view of the structural whole-quality of the balance in the distribution as seen from above.

I shall presently return to his thought process. In the meantime it will be realized that this is not just a question of stating the individual differences between successive terms, of stating the equality of such differences, etc., or of dealing with class laws of series— laws which somehow hold for all the points or items. It is fundamentally a question of balance within the whole, of realizing equilibrium with regard to whole-features. And this balance is a dynamic thing, sensitive to deviations or disturbances in any of the parts.

If one makes a diagram of the points of such a Gauss series, one sees that the line is straight, or that there is a deviation from straightness, a disturbance, long before one can state or know the measure of the differences, and whether they are equal, etc. For example,

$$1+2+3+4+6+7+8$$

FIG. 98

or

$$1+2+3+4+6+8+10$$

FIG. 99

There is sensitivity to such disturbances which stand out against the clear whole-quality of straightness. Such series, for example the first of the two series above (without the 5), can be formulated as a lawful series in a consistent general formula, $x_n = f\ (x_{n-1})$, no less lawful than the straight series, only more complicated in its terms. But the series $x_n = x_{n-1} + k$ is outstanding in its structural simplicity, in the structural clearness of its whole-quality. Nobody would spontaneously view the series

$$1+2+3+4+5+6+7+8,$$

especially in its diagram, as a deviation from the more complex formula, with the 5 intruding as a disturbance, even though in the usual mathematical terms a law is a law, each like every other.[23]

Similarly with the sine curve, or with dots in a sine curve. Long before one states or knows the measure of the distances between the single points, long before one has a "class law" for them, one sees—viewing the whole—that the path of the curve is regular.

FIG. 100

One sees that there is rhythmical repetition in regular sub-wholes,

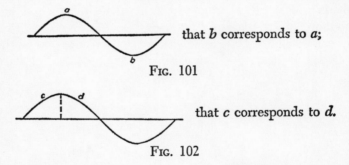

that *b* corresponds to *a*;

FIG. 101

that *c* corresponds to *d.*

FIG. 102

One grasps symmetrical features in the sub-wholes from above. What first matter here, psychologically, are the outstanding features of the whole,[24] and of the sub-wholes. From these as centers, deviations often become conspicuous, are conceived *as* deviations.

Many will say, "Quite so; but these are only inexact, global, psychological views, not to be compared with exact mathematical

[23] Of course the facts have to decide. One may be mistaken in making the structurally simpler assumption. What is decisive is the structural behavior of the terms in the series. Cf. p. 135, footnote 22.

[24] This holds not only for rhythmical forms and symmetrical features; it holds also for the direction of a main vector in changes, trends, etc.

It holds for thinking processes and for action if, in spite of complications, in spite of small deviations, one does not lose the clear whole-direction.

formulations in terms of $y=f(x)$, etc." The objection is blind. Is the mathematical way, the exact way, necessarily the way from below? From the elements? Must it, to be exact, derive whole-qualities such as symmetry merely secondarily? Should there not also be mathematical ways from above, no less exact? Mathematical ways that start from whole-qualities and go secondarily from these to the elements?

Psychologically, the situation with regard to viewing whole-qualities is frequently not essentially changed if, instead of a sine curve exact in all its details, one looks at a crinkled sine curve, or a curve drawn

FIG. 103

in dots in which there is some distribution of errors, even a chance distribution.[25] Here the view from above gets the whole-qualities, the form; the details, the smallest parts, the elements are no longer

FIG. 104

governed directly and simply by the law. Mathematics has exact ways of dealing with such cases, formulating whole-qualities that are valid in spite of variations in the parts.

This is often the situation in modern physics. In such cases we know about whole-qualities, the whole-behavior of systems of which

[25] At the International Congress of Psychology in Groningen, 1926, I reported on investigations in this regard in the context of a paper dealing with gestalt problems on perceptual thresholds ("Zum Problem der Schwelle," *Bericht über den VIII Internationalen Kongress für Psychologie*, Groningen: P. Noordhoff, 1926). And some years ago Woodworth mentioned an illuminating example: a prehistoric ringwall was discovered from an airplane in a field which had been cultivated for many decades. Nobody had noticed it before. Nobody had been able to see it without the broad survey of the whole field which the pilot had.

the behavior of the smallest parts is not known exactly, or is known to follow a chance distribution. In trying to arrive at a mathematical formulation, must we then start with a law for the smallest parts? There are ways of starting with a formulation of whole-qualities that allow for varying behavior in the smallest parts.

Should it not be possible, moreover, to develop methods for dealing with questions of dynamics in this way? To conceive of tendencies toward certain transformations not on the basis of the and-sum of elementary piecemeal forces but as functions of whole-qualities and their disturbance?

Whatever future developments may be, it is certainly not true that the way from above is merely a "global," "inexact" way; what is true is only that the techniques of the other way are mathematically more developed.

Let us now return to the process reported on p. 134 ff. Although similar in its view of the Gauss problem to the procedure of some of the other subjects (cf. §II), there is still quite a difference. This subject took the problem in a broader, deeper way. To him it offered not merely the nice possibility of reorganization in the particular task; no, he was focussing on what opened up in the inner relation between form and sum.

In his next step he compared his formula $c \cdot n$ with the Gauss formula $(n+1)\dfrac{n}{2}$ and remarked that it became $c \cdot n$ with the slight change into $\dfrac{n+1}{2} \cdot n$. Then he said, "$c \cdot n$ seems to be the more general, more fundamental formula in which it does not matter what the amount of the equal differences is, what the end term or the first term is. On the other hand, I have two variables here, c and n, whereas for the Gauss formula one variable suffices, n! So the Gauss formula is the more elegant, requiring only one variable." Suddenly he laughed and said: "No, it is only an external limitation that makes it appear so. This '1' in $(n+1)$ is in fact the first number in the series just as n is the last number. Similarly $\dfrac{n}{2}$ looks only superficially so simple. It is in fact $\dfrac{z-a+1}{2}$, z being the last, a the first number in the series.

It turns into $\frac{z}{2}$ only because $a=1$. That the series should start with just the value 1 is of no importance. It is a special case. Furthermore, that particular kind of formula is a special case because it is limited to a difference of 1 between the terms. The important thing is the basic relationship: some series, some curves, some distributions show this clear inner relation between their whole-qualities, their principle of construction, and their sum. I want to find out more about this. What are the requirements generally? At bottom it seems to be a question of balance in the whole, of compensation at some level among the various parts." Thinking then of the matter of compensation, he recognized that the same principle must hold for products. Although he immersed himself in these problems, I shall not follow his later steps here. They led him to the question of whether an inner relation between a growing series and its sum is possible only by way of compensation, and eventually to the facts of finite limits of infinite series.

In such processes of thinking the solution of an actual task, "Problem solved, task finished," is not the end. The way of solution, its fundamental features, the problem with its solution function as parts of a large expanding realm. Here the function of thinking is not just solving an actual problem, but discovering, envisaging, going into deeper questions. Often in great discoveries the most important thing is that a certain question is found. Envisaging, putting the productive question is often more important, often a greater achievement than solution of a set question, just as here in our example the main thing seemed to be to envisage, to crystallize a basic structural problem—a much broader, much deeper process than the processes reported before.

Just as a task, a problem situation in productive thinking, is not something closed within itself, but tends toward its solution, its structural completion, so even a task with its solution is often not a thing by itself. It again may function as a part that points beyond itself, striving to envisage, to clarify a broader field. Often such a process takes a long time; it is a drama with setbacks and struggles. There are fine cases in which the process proceeds irresistibly, through months, through years,[26] never losing sight of the deeper issue, never getting lost in petty details, in detours, bypaths.

This is one important difference between pedantic thinking and thinking in broad lines, a difference that in life as well is terribly important. Many theorists do not rightly see this difference or its importance, they confuse it with questions of exactness, of piecemeal one-sided exactness which is blind to the great features at issue. But exactness is not inconsistent with great features; it is a needed co-operator.

[26] This is true not only of individuals but of groups, so that great problems are handed on from generation to generation, the individual acting not primarily as an individual but as a member of the human group.

CHAPTER FIVE

Plus Three, Minus Three[*]

In a physics laboratory stands a mirror-galvanometer. A small mirror is suspended with a minimum of friction so that, given a push, it oscillates with a regular motion. A light ray falling on the mirror is reflected from it, throwing a light spot on a milk glass scale, along which it moves back and forth with the oscillation of the mirror.

Some boys visit the laboratory with me and see the moving light. It goes from −3 through 0 to +3, back and forth.

We return the next day. The right end of the scale is now screened from view by a partition. The oscillating light spot moves to the left to −5, back to 0, disappears behind the screen, returns, and so on. I ask: "What do you think is the terminal on the right side?"

1. One boy says eagerly, "Plus three; I remember the end point at the right was plus three yesterday." This remark may be just the result of a piecemeal recall of the value connected by yesterday's experience with the right end; the boy does not seem at all to be think-

---

[*] This chapter was not included in the original edition, although an early table of contents found among Max Wertheimer's papers indicated that he had at one time intended to use it in this place. The manuscript for this chapter did not seem to be in as finished a form as the chapters that comprise the original edition. Some editorial work seemed necessary, but an attempt was made to keep it to a minimum.—M. W.

ing of the inner connection between the values. Later remarks showed that this was just plain repetition; we may call such recall thoughtless.

2. A second boy says: "It should be plus five." Perhaps this answer rests on an entirely different assumption; later remarks suggested that he thought of an inverse equality between the end numbers, without going any further.

3. A third boy says: "The oscillation is stable. The spot should move to the right just as far as it does to the left; therefore it is plus 5."

I say: "Sorry, it is plus 3;" moving the partition and showing that the right end of the swing is at $+3$. He is clearly shocked.

A clear, productive process follows. After a while the boy smiles and says, "Isn't the scale out of place?" Asking permission, he shifts it to the left, so that the terminals of the swing are now -4 and $+4$, saying, "The zero was out of place." He changed

	-5	0	$+3$
into	-4 ←	0 ←	$+4$ ←

4. Still another boy neither asked nor waited, but looked behind the partition, glanced at the moving light ray, exclaimed, "The scale is out of place," and corrected its position. His behavior was clearly based on the realization of the proper position of the zero with reference to the axis of symmetry of the moving ray.[1]

oscillating mirror

How does the thinking proceed in the sensible cases (3 and 4)? Remarks indicate: there is on the left side of the scale the value a, and on the right side the unknown x; there is the stability of the

[1] Numerical guesses on the part of the subject are ambiguous if unaccompanied by characteristic behavior or additional remarks. What about a case in which the response is plus 1? With some subjects, this may be based on the required equilibrium and the idea of shifting the scale, which is recognized as out of place. But the answer is not clear by itself. The subject may well have been blind to the issue of equilibrium, basing his answer just on keeping the same distance (6) between the terminals as on the previous day.

oscillatory motion; this is reasonably, sensibly related to the symmetry of the event; this requires an inverse equality of the end values, *a* and *x*. The stability requires, as a ρ-relation, the symmetry; given *a*, then $x = -a$.

The operation goes from above to below, from envisaging interrelatedness and whole-qualities to specific items. What may the stability reasonably require for the position of the two end values with reference to each other? This leads to the reasonable demand for their symmetry, and from it follows the derivation of the value *x*, by finding a value symmetrical to the given value *a*. The process is focussed on outstanding whole-qualities and on the reasonable ρ-relation between them—between the stability of the motion and its symmetry—which does not hold between stability and non-symmetry.

If the observations of the first day have provided understanding, this means that the terms -3, 0, $+3$ have been grasped in their place, role, and function in the structure, with -3 and $+3$ being homotypes, and zero the middle of the symmetrical distribution. In the -5, 0, $+3$ situation, the required symmetry of the values is in contradiction with the location of the zero, which is therefore out of place, and is responsible for the structural trouble. In the solution of the -5, 0, $+3$ problem, it is not the specific values themselves, but their place, role, and function in the whole that are determining for the thinker. The values change their meaning as parts in the structural interrelatedness on the one hand, and externals such as the structurally arbitrary place of the scale on the other.

appearance:	-5	$(-1)\ 0$	3
scale shifted:	$+1$	$+1\ \ +1$	$+1$
structural value:	-4	$0\ (+1)$	$+4$

There is for all the values a common external shift of $+1$; -5 is now -4 for internal structural reasons; zero becomes plus 1 because of the external shift, etc.

Restating the procedure from above to below more explicitly, we can give a formal expression of the structural view of the original -3, 0, $+3$ situation:

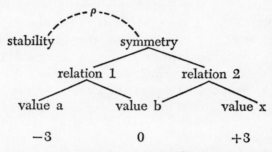

This is not any aggregate of numbers; this is not even a blind aggregate of relations. It is a structure governed by an outstanding whole-quality, symmetry (which is in turn in an outstanding inner relation with the stability of the whole—a ρ-relation). The symmetry implies the inverse equality (not just equality, but with a particular direction included) of relations 1 and 2. Value a is homotypic to x; there is the reasonable requirement that the homotypes a and x be equal, or, better, that they compensate each other; the term between them, value b, is the center. Understanding the structure, the individual values and the distance between them have a certain permissible variability; but given some of these items, the others follow structurally, are required.[2]

If -5 and 0 are given, and $+5$ is expected as the third term—or if all three are given—the expectation, or the understanding of the new set, is not necessarily then due to superficial transfer, to carrying over the notion that "the distances will be equal here as in the original," but may well be due to being structurally required; this requiredness may have been grasped in the original case. There are of course two possibilities for a structural understanding of the

[2] Compare the process described in the chapter on Galileo, especially how Galileo's envisaging of, and focussing on, structural symmetry in dynamics played a significant, important role in his thought process, and in the foundations of modern physics.

situation. The response on Tuesday may have been based not on carrying over some arbitrary features from the experience of Monday, on the assumption simply that "today it will be as it was yesterday," but on considerations of reasonable structural interrelatedness, grasped in the experience on Monday and determining the response in Tuesday's problem. Or it may not develop until the Tuesday problem is confronted.

Here are the explicit steps in a process dealing with the -5, 0, $+3$ situation:

Step 1. What do these numbers really mean? Taken by themselves I do not understand them.

Step 2. The oscillations appear to be stable and in equilibrium. This would require symmetry in the values of the numbers.

Step 3. The end points are 8 units apart; the symmetrical distances from the middle, therefore, are 8 divided by 2, and the values of the end points are thus, structurally -4 and $+4$.

Step 4. But they are given as -5 and $+3$. How can this be understood? Very simply. (At this stage, there occurs a radical separation of structural characteristics from external factors.) The position of the scale partly determines the numerical value of the end points; but the position of the scale, basically entirely external, has nothing to do with the relation of the end points of the light ray's excursion to one another, and is arbitrary with reference to the inner structure of the event. In order, then, to understand the numbers, we must segregate whatever the arbitrary position of the scale may contribute. The scale is out of place by one unit, the correction of -5 by $+1$ gives the structurally proper -4, and the correction of $+3$ by $+1$ the proper $+4$.

Step 5. From the beginning, the place of the zero was puzzling. The structural understanding of the numerical values of the end points brings with it the clarification of the "0" in -5, 0, $+3$. It appears to be in no way a structurally outstanding place in the oscillation. It is not the presumed location of the light spot if the oscillating motion were to come to rest. The "0" is merely an incidental transitional point, of which the structural value is not 0 but $+1$. The -1 point, which was not at all outstanding in the -5, 0, $+3$ situation becomes focussed as the proper center.

In this proceeding, assumptions[3] are implied about the simple reasonableness of the structure, such as that there are no hidden factors making for one-sidedness, or asymmetry, in the oscillation. One of the boys had looked behind the partition to see whether the scale was properly placed with reference to the mirror; another boy, whom I did not mention before, wanted the apparatus stopped so he could see where the light spot would be on the scale, whether at 0 or at −1! If the "0" in −5, 0, +3 had turned out to be the outstanding place, this would have been puzzling indeed, leading to the search for an added hidden cause which would make the asymmetry understandable. Still another proceeding would be to study— if this would be possible with the available apparatus—the velocity of the moving light, to determine at what point the positive acceleration turns into negative, and to see whether this point of maximum velocity is at 0 or at −1.

I have described these events explicitly so that in this elementary case one may see that the questions of whole-qualities and requirements are in no way vague, but can be dealt with exactly. For even though there are still many who are of the opinion that there is no exact way for dealing with the study of thinking from above to below, the thinking process in the example described here can be expressed in operations with symbols quite as exactly as in the procedure from below to above.

[3] I did not give the axioms involved in these structural events explicitly here, but it is not difficult to formulate them. Besides the inner structural questions, there is involved here, as previously stated, a process of separating structural items from features external to the structure, much as in transposing melodies. I might add at this point that transposition cannot always be performed in a completely arbitrary way. In melodies, the general pitch or level of the whole is greatly, but not entirely, external to the structural features of the melody; if shifted too far, the level may become inappropriate to the structure; the structural features of a melody in the bass are different from those of high-pitched melodies. Likewise, if one excessively enlarges or reduces the size of a work of art, one may see that it is inappropriate, that there is something like a "proper size" (as emphasized by the philosopher Georg Simmel). Similar conditions hold in physics or engineering. Compare the question of the stability of the 100-times enlarged elephant, or of the 100-times enlarged frame building. This is one of the reasons why it is a mistake to think that in structures (or gestalten, or "holistic organizations") *only* the organization in terms of the arrangement plays a role, and that the concrete nature of the part-members—or the overall "level"—is always variable or arbitrary. It *is*, in certain cases, but only when the structural requirements do not penetrate to these characteristics.

Some people may object to speaking of whole-qualities. They think that such a thing as symmetry is nothing but a relation of relations. It is not, as can be seen by comparing the two following sets:

I	−3	+3	
II	−3	+3	+9

Between −3 and +3 there is real symmetry only so long as they constitute a whole; if the whole were as in set II, −3 and +9 would be the structurally symmetrical points, with +3 no longer the symmetrical homotype of −3, but the center—the zero—of the structure.

The structural values are   −6   0   +6

shifting the scale +3   +3   +3   +3 yields the

appearance   "−3"   "+3"   "+9"

The relation between the relations −3 to 0 and 0 to +3 is no longer a relation of symmetry; it is only one of many relations. To call a relation of relations a "symmetry" involves the question of the whole; the relation R_1 may be "inverse equality," or "mirror image" of the two relations r_1 and r_2, but it is not symmetry.

To return to the −3, 0, +3 situation, the two relations, r_1 and r_2, are not simply a repetition of the same relation. Their direction is of importance; they operate essentially in opposite directions. Compare 1) ⟶ ⟶ 2) ⟵ ⟶ 3) ⟶ ⟵ ; the first is structurally a basically different case from the other two, which give symmetry, which provide equilibrium, a sort of "closedness," a reasonableness in the balance of the whole. The role of such whole-qualities becomes especially clear in a systematic study of variations. To mention only one point here, more change, in piecemeal terms, often means less change in structural terms, and vice versa. For example, changing the size of both vectors in set 2) from $\longleftarrow\!\!\!\!\longrightarrow$ to $\longleftarrow\!\!-\!\!\longrightarrow$, as against a change in only one of them: $\longleftarrow\!\!-\!\!\longrightarrow$. Or, adding to vectors as in set 2, two further vectors from $\longleftarrow\!\!-\!\!\longrightarrow$ to $\longleftarrow\!\!-\!\!\longleftarrow\!\!-\!\!\longrightarrow\!\!-\!\!\longrightarrow$ as against adding only to one of them, $\longleftarrow\!\!-\!\!-\!\!\longrightarrow\!\!-\!\!\longrightarrow$ These are very elementary examples in the broad issue of variability in terms of whole-qualities, basic for the difference between structurally sensible versus structurally blind or piecemeal comparison, abstraction, generalization, etc.

CHAPTER SIX

The Square of a Binomial;
Learning Arithmetic*

THE A-B method has been exemplified in various preceding examples—the area of the parallelogram, the bridge, plus three-minus three, the vertical angles. The principle of the method is concerned with a central gestalt question, the problem of the basic difference between an aggregation, a mosaic, a concatenation on the one hand, and the conditions of a consistent whole, a good gestalt, on the other. I had introduced and used it in very different fields, such as the recognition of melodies, of figures, and in the study of motor performance. It is applicable in nearly all fields of psychology.

One day I happened to come upon a book by a well-known psychologist.[1] While looking into it, I saw a section (Appendix III, pp. 458-464) dealing with the effect of changed data on the fundamental processes of reasoning. Looking at the experimental set-up and the results described in this section (before having read the other portions of the book), I felt, "Oh, this is fortunate. Here the A-B method is already used."

Then I started to read the first paragraph of the section more carefully. The theoretical formulations seemed strange, especially

* This chapter was not included in the original edition, although an early table of contents found among Max Wertheimer's papers indicated that he had at one time intended to use it in this place. The manuscript for this chapter did not seem to be in as finished a form as the chapters that comprise the original edition. Some editorial work seemed necessary, but an attempt was made to keep it to a minimum.—M. W.

[1] E. L. Thorndike, _et al., The psychology of algebra_ (New York: Macmillan, 1923).

with regard to the A-B method. "So much the better," I felt; "if a psychologist starting with such a fundamentally different approach arrived at the same method."

In my further reading, some things happened which may shed some light on the theoretical situation. Let us read the first formulations. The section starts with the following paragraph:

The older psychology, perpetuated in current educational doctrines and practices, regarded reasoning as a force largely independent of associative habits, which worked back to correct or oppose them. Our present psychology finds that the mind is ruled by habit throughout, the correction or opposition being of certain more simple, thoughtless and coarse habits, by others which are more elaborate, selective and abstract. It defines reasoning as the organization and cooperation of habits rather than as a special activity above their level; and expects to find 'reasoning' and habit or association working together in almost every act of thought.

In reading this, I encountered some difficulties. For example, the terms "thoughtless habits" somehow had the appearance of begging the question. Also, I felt unclear about such terms as "selective," "organization," "cooperation." Are these terms meant, I asked myself, in the same sense in which they are applied to senseless materials, such as the rote learning of syllables? Or to refer to learning in which the teacher calls some stimulus-response connections wrong, others right? I found myself bluntly asking the question: "Now, does the author mean that thinking *is* associative habits, or *not?*" It seemed so, and then again it seemed not. Some formulations in the text did not seem to imply a basic identification of thinking with such associative facts and practices, as for example (p. 462), ". . . one's associative habits do not retire while reason attacks." Or (p. 461), ". . . there is a substantial interference with thought (produced by an experimental change in the contents of a problem)." Then there were formulations such as the following (p. 251) about "abstraction, generalization, and reasoning:" "these higher powers in reality are the cooperation of many connections or bonds selected and given proper weight for some purpose." These words again threw me back into the same difficulty: is this a begging of the question?

Then, on the first page of the preface, I met the following statement: this book "treats learning as the formation of . . . connections or bonds or elementary habits; and finds that thought and reasoning —the so-called higher powers—are not forces opposing these habits but are these habits organized to work together and selectively."

"Good," I thought; "that *is* association theory, and the terms 'selective,' 'organization,' 'cooperation' are certainly intended here as they are usually applied to rote materials, to the learning of nonsense syllables. But how is it possible to come to such formulations in connection with, of all things, the A-B method," I thought, "which in my experience seems to show the fundamental ineptness of a mere associationist, summative theory of thinking?"

In their experiments, the authors compare the reactions of students to pairs of algebraic tasks. One of the pair is an habitual task; the other is similar, but changed into a somewhat unfamiliar problem. ". . . The concrete situation in the one case is that with which our ordinary associative habits have been made, whereas in the other case the concrete particulars are somewhat altered." (pp. 458-459.) For example (p. 459):

Habitual	*Changed*
1. What is the square of $x+y$? (Learned reaction: $x^2+2xy+y^2$)	1. What is the square of b_1+b_2?
4. What are the factors of x^2-y^2? (Learned reaction: $(x+y)(x-y)$)	4. What are the factors of $\dfrac{1}{x^2}-\dfrac{1}{y^2}$?

The experimental results showed that the percent of errors is considerably greater when the task is of the changed sort than when it is of the habitual sort. And so the authors seem to prove the associationist thesis, that thinking is a matter of habits. It seems established: if the original, familiar task is changed into one less familiar, we get poorer results.

I must confess that the large differences obtained in this case gave me a sad feeling. (The change in case 4 requires more—the recognition that $\dfrac{1}{x^2}$ equals $\left(\dfrac{1}{x}\right)^2$). What kind of class was that? What kind of education had they received, that such slight changes, which in fact did not at all touch the character of the problem, should

cause so much trouble? Of course, the introduction of unfamiliar
subscripts and of fractions, and not simply the substitution of strange
terms, such as b for x, c for y, may have been responsible for mistakes.

Looking at the procedure, it suddenly became clear: this is *not*
the A-B method. It is one-sided; it is, in fact, blind to the problem
of thinking. It does not study thinking, it does not test understanding, but defines "more complex" in strictly peripheral ways; it is a
study of half the A-B method, of the counter-influences that come
from adherence to blind habits, of mechanical learning. It *is* a proof
that some processes can be thoughtlessly determined by rote procedures. It does not at all touch the problem of real thinking—with
the possible exception of very routine generalization.

If I want to test, to study *not* the role of slavish, blind, rote
memory and its influence, if I want to get at all to the problems of
thinking, then I cannot confine myself to such changes, but must
introduce pairs of changes of the following kind. I shall take the
first example for illustration. For the sake of simplicity, let us turn
the problem around, asking for the factors of the expression.

Original: $a^2+2ab+b^2= \ldots$ The learned answer is $(a+b)^2$

B example: $a^2+2ab-b^2 = ?$

A example: $a^2-2ab+b^2 = ?$

Externally viewed, in terms of familiarity, in each of the two variations one plus sign is changed into a minus sign. But if the subject
writes $(a-b)^2$ in answer to the B example, this shows that he did
not really think, or perhaps that he had not grasped the problem
at all. Anyone who is blind to the fundamental difference between
these two changes just has not grasped the issue. The minus sign
in the two cases means, structurally, basically different things. The
minus with the ab, in the A example, means "$-ab$ and $-ab$"; this
implies structurally that one of the items, say b, is negative, and the
other positive. There is nothing wrong with this; $-b$ times $-b$ gives
$+b^2$; hence we have the basis for the simple binomial form $(a-b)^2$.
But what about the B case, where we have the $-b^2$? This means
that one of the two members must be positive and one negative
if one is to arrive at a negative product; in the square of the binomial, b would have to be at the same time positive and negative,
which is of course nonsense.

The minus sign in the "$-b^2$" can mean another thing—if the minus holds for the entire expression and not just for the b^2, as in $-(a+b)^2$ or $-(a-b)^2$. But here the symmetry of a and b is required; the a has to share the fate of the b in a squared binomial; this clearly is not true in our B example.

One may object that the algebraic technique has precisely the merit of releasing the mind from such real structural understanding; instead, it permits mechanical rules for proceeding. This is certainly true. But in productive processes, such things as "feeling the requirements for symmetry with regard to the fate of a and b" do play a decisive role in leading to a new understanding, or in dismissing some blind proposal. And even here, in cases like the one just discussed, a "feeling" of the structural difference between the two minus signs (those of $-ab$ and $-b^2$) seems basic for sensible proceeding.

There is here also the possibility of theoretically very interesting changes (method of the "elegant B"):

A B change: $a^2 - 2ab - b^2$

An A change: $-a^2 - 2ab - b^2$

The A case, viewed piecemeal, undergoes the *same*, and *still further*, changes from the original. This clearly shows that it is blind to deal with "any" changes, or "the amount of change." The "same" change, viewed piecemeal, can mean fundamentally different changes with regard to the structure and reasonableness of the answer. And this is the meaning of the A-B method: the "same" amount of change, or a *smaller* amount of change, may produce a B case, and a piecemeally larger change may, for the thinking subject, produce an A case. Decisive is the structural meaning of the changes. The reactions of thinking subjects are, on the whole, not really endangered if the B cases are, item by item, very similar to the original, while the A cases involve changes of nearly all items.

The A case can be extremely different. If, for example, one has really grasped the original situation, and is alive to what is at issue, one may be puzzled, and not do anything with the B case $a^2 + 2ab - b^2$, though it involves the change of only one sign; but one may go ahead quite assuredly with such a task as $-m^2 - 2mn - n^2$ or, sometimes, even with $-m^2 - 6mn - 9n^2$, in which almost all items are changed, but the structure is not.

So far we have been concerned with two changed tasks which were compared with one another. But it is also possible to see A and B reactions using *one* changed task. For example, the original is learned, and then the following problem is set: $-a^2-2ab-b^2$. The B reaction is $(a-b)^2$ and the A reaction $-(a+b)^2$. Now, a subject, thinking out loud, may say, "Oh, I have learned that $a^2+2ab+b^2=(a+b)^2$. This I remember well." He continues, "What did this imply?" Answering his own question, he goes on: "In the example I learned, the answer contains two terms, a and b, which are connected by a plus sign, which is also the sign of each term in the expression. Here, the sign of each term is negative; therefore . . . $(a-b)^2$." This approach clearly involves abstraction—more so than if new symbols such as m and n are introduced. It involves the facing of rules, but in a structurally blind way.

The A reaction involves recognizing the same structure as before, realizing that the signs are negative in the whole expression; hence the result is $-(a+b)^2$, with a separation of the inner structure and the fate of the whole.

The impact of the negative signs is still further increased if a problem such as this one is given: $-(-a^2-2ab-b^2)$. I have seen a bright boy, looking at this example, smile after some hesitation and then write down, despite all the changes: $(a+b)^2$. Does this perhaps mean that he simply gave the learned response in spite of the changes? I doubt it. He may have done it by combining the first minus sign with all the others, changing all of them into plus signs. While working with the problem, he made spontaneous remarks like: "This looks terribly negative. . . . All terms in the parentheses are minus; this makes it $-(a+b)^2$. But the minus sign of the entire expression is itself negated by the first minus sign." That is, it became $--(a+b)^2$, which of course is $(a+b)^2$.

Some other examples: what are the factors of the following?

1) $a^2+2ab+4b^2$
2) $a^2+4ab+4b^2$
3) $4a^2+2ab+4b^2$
4) $4a^2+4ab+4b^2$
5) $4a^2+8ab+4b^2$

One can proceed in a different way than by changing the signs;

one can also introduce changes in the terms. A most brute B case would be $a^2+2bc+b^2$, or $a^2+2bc+c^2$. But returning to the examples above, example 1) is a B case, because of violation of the structure: "$2ab$" demands "b" as a term, while "$4b^2$" demands "$2b$" as a term. Example 2) is an A case; in accordance with the structure, both the second and third parts demand "$2b$" as a term. The reasonable procedure involves grasping the different meanings of the coefficient "4" in the two terms. In "$4ab$" it is 2 plus 2, while in "$4b^2$" it is 2^2. Examples 3) and 4) are similar to 1), with inconsistent demands made on the terms, a violation of the structure. Example 5) is an A case, the "4" in "$4a^2$" and in "$4b^2$" being 2^2, the "8" in "$8ab$" being 4 plus 4 (really 2 times 2 plus 2 times 2); or, one can view it as a transposition, by separating the inner structure as follows: $4(a^2+2ab+b^2)$.

A subject who has grasped the structure and its requirements, sometimes after a short time of looking at the problem, often sees at a glance that 1), 3), and 4) do *not* fit, with regard to the interrelatedness between the number in the ab term and the numbers in a^2, in b^2, or both; he sees in one comprehensive view, on the other hand, that 5) and 2) do fit. Problem 5) seems somewhat easier than problem 2); in 5), the original symmetry is there, while in 2) the equality of the two 4s—which is not a structural equality—is disturbing.

To return to the basic issue. We saw that what is decisive is not the amount of change nor the piecemeal similarity of the new task to the originally learned task. The reasonableness of the operations has an inner connection with the structure, not with the sum of the items, the sum of the bonds, etc.

But even with this we have not stated the real point. The essential feature is not performing an operation in accordance with the identity or the similarity of a present structure to some previous "structure." The structure at hand must itself be a good gestalt, a consistent whole, and must be questioned, viewed, in this way. In the original example we have an equation containing two expressions, one on each side of the equality sign. It is not the basic identity or similarity of the left side of the new task with the left side of the old task (or the right side of the new and old tasks) which is, reasonably, decisive for the answer. What is decisive is the interrelatedness of the answer to the present task. The answer must fit in as part of the relation l (left) $= r$ (right). The equal sign requires that r and l should, in essentials, be identical (with the one difference, required by the task, that r is to be a simpler expression). And this requirement, that the two fit, that they must stand in the relation "equal," is decisive. What the teacher taught is not, for a thinking subject, that the specific procedure she gave is correct, that one just has to perform and transfer. Understanding involves grasping the inner relation, the relation ρ, seeing how r is derived in a sensible way out of l, or the other way around, how l is derived from r; and what the items in the formula mean structurally.

A logician might object at this point, "Why do you speak here of this mysterious ρ-relation? The reasonableness, the correctness of the answers is based simply on axioms and theorems. The correct operations here are in accordance with the axioms of algebra and arithmetic; and if not, they are wrong. The derivations are subject to the norms of logical validity. (And the axioms are only some axioms that happen to have been chosen for the system.)"

I refer the reader to the later section of this chapter on the educational machine (p. 165f). If we think in terms not of abstract mathematics but of real equivalence of the l and r, nature could be more complicated, so that these axioms would not apply. Still, the ρ-relation, with its fitting-in, would distinguish those cases which are simply reasonable from those which are not. Of course we would, in such a case, have to drop the simple consistency, and look for deeper-lying ones. And we could even imagine that nature might make *any* reasonable axioms impossible; but fortunately, the sensible, reasonable approach fits. This analysis also provides an answer to the question of the *a priori*. There is nothing here which would compel nature in cases of "true equivalence" to proceed in accordance with those axioms. Not a blind and absolute necessity, as is envisaged in the *a priori* approach, is at stake here, but the hope and modest assumption that using reason has sense in the world we live in.

For that matter, the recourse to axioms, to very general propositions, as underlying reality, is somehow unrealistic, as old philosophers, like Locke, already demonstrated clearly; it does not provide the answer to our question. Grasping what is called here "fitting the requirements of a concrete case" is, for children—and grown-ups—very much more natural than the conception of, or the ability to face, axioms in their abstract generality.

An associationist might ask here: If a man uses thinking in such examples, if he reacts "sensibly," is this "thinking" not again a matter of habits? Let us take one simple example. If a pupil, in solving an equation involving an x, brings the x terms to one side of the equation, he is certainly employing a habit, and a very useful one. He is doing what he was taught, what he had practiced.

Of course, it *can* be something acquired by drill, by blind habit. But it is, aside from all this, also a reasonable procedure. Since the goal is to find the unknown, x, it is reasonable to have the terms containing x—and only these—on one side of the equation. There is a ρ-relation involved here. Of course, it is practical to make this operation habitual. In dealing with such situations "automatically," our mind is free to deal with "higher" problems involved in the task. Nevertheless, there still remains the difference between blindly using a habit, and performing sensible operations. For example, here is an equation: $100a^2 - 20ax + x^2 = a^2 + 20ax + 100x^2$. Find x. Now a subject, bravely following what he has learned, brings the x terms to one side, and writes $99a^2 = 99x^2 + 40ax$; and thus $x^2 + \dfrac{40}{99}ax = a^2$. Not knowing how to deal with such an equation, he comes to a halt, and is helpless. But a subject who does not follow habits blindly, but recognizes the structure, does not think of starting by bringing all the x terms together on one side, but writes down $(10a - x)^2 = (a + 10x)^2$, and proceeds easily to the solution. In the first case, the x terms were viewed in a way blind to the structure; this was not so in the second case.

Again an objection could be raised here: "The first procedure is not foolish at all, for there is a general formula showing how to find x with the equation he formed. It is simply his lack of knowledge of the general formulas for solving quadratic equations that causes trouble here. And it is certainly better to know this general formula."

Now it seems to me that this objection is blind. First, we see that a reasonable solution is possible *without* a knowledge of the "general" formula. Secondly, with the "general" formula, similar questions arise all over again—blind dealings as against reasonable dealings, procedures which realize the structural requirements.

In Thorndike's *Psychology of Arithmetic*[2] we find the general attitude already presented in this chapter, expressed even more strongly. "Reasoning is not a radically different sort of force operating against habit, but the organization and cooperation of many habits, thinking facts together. Reasoning is not the negation of ordinary bonds, but the action of many of them, especially of bonds with subtle elements of the situation. Some outside power does not enter to select and criticize; the pupil's own total repertory of bonds relevant to the problem is what selects and rejects." (pp. 193-194). And "successful responses to novel data, associations by similarity and purposive behavior are in only apparent opposition to the fundamental laws of associative learning. Really they are beautiful examples of it." (p. 191).

Reading page 192 of this book I was very much struck by the description of how children can become confused in doing arithmetical tasks. The discussion is about children who are given examples of the following kind, after they have mastered adding and subtracting with one- and two-place numbers, and multiplication with one-place numbers:

Multiply	Multiply	Multiply
32	43	34
23	22	26

Thorndike writes that "they will add the numbers, or subtract the lower from the upper number, or multiply 3×2 and 2×3, etc., getting 66, 86, and 624 . . ." Of course, we all know children who would go about the problems in this way. But are they not pitiable products of senseless drill? And don't we know children who would refuse to do such blind and senseless things, but would instead say, "I can't do it"?

Very often, if a child does perform these senseless operations, he

---

[2] E. L. Thorndike, *The psychology of arithmetic* (New York: Macmillan, 1922).

will look insecurely at the teacher, trying to guess from her expression what is right, his attitude being, "the teacher should tell me." This is all too usual, when teachers simply issue orders, declaring that this is the right answer, that the wrong answer.

But if the teacher does not, like a *deus ex machina*, say, "This is right, that is wrong," what about the law of effect? Do psychologists realize that the law of effect cannot help, simply because it does not really apply? Success can help, but if the child does not know whether he has achieved real success or not, how should the principle of the law of effect help at all?

But is it true, as Thorndike and others seem to maintain, that the "child of sufficient genius" (p. 192), finding the right procedure, would do it simply "by the operation of bonds," by blind habit and association? Here is a report I obtained from one child, who was not outstanding. "This is certainly very complicated. First I will try a less complicated problem. May I? Say, for instance, 14×3. Now, if I have 4×3, this is equal to, this means, 4, 4, 4. It doesn't really matter here whether I have 6, or 16, or 216, or another number. ... If I have $3 \times 4 = 12$, this means

twelve, which on the right means $10 + 2$, is the right answer because I have the same amount, only put together differently." (Understanding the "correct answer" means to realize the ρ, the requirement that the amount on one side must equal the amount on the other side.) "Now, 14×3 means the same thing as 10×3 plus 4×3, and now I have to find out what that is." And after solving this, he proceeded happily to the more complex question, mastering it.

I wouldn't necessarily call such a child a genius. The child was just led in his operations not by blind habits, or by the strength of associations, but by realizing the demand of "being equal," by changing an item without changing its arithmetical amount.

Happily enough, children do, very often, show a very normal tendency to proceed reasonably with such questions, a tendency to master such things on their own, and not by blind trying. (To be sure, there are schools in which these fine tendencies are considerably shaken in the first school years. Sometimes it seems to me as if children were, just before entering school, wiser in this regard than after they have become objects of drill.)

More generally, I did not find children who made the senseless mistakes of the first kind described by Thorndike, except in certain schools, as the product of blind drill, or when tired or careless. Secondly, it seems that there are two types of children who refuse to do the problem at all: one type which felt that one should not attempt things one has not been taught, the second type not being able to solve the problem in spite of trying to, who at the same time strongly refused to adapt to the proposed foolish procedures. Third, I did find children who (apparently without being geniuses) quietly solved the problem.

When confronted for the first time with such questions as 24×3, one child proceeded like this: "I can't do this all at once; but, you see, this is 4×3 and 20×3."

$$
24 \times 3 \quad = \quad
\begin{array}{rcl}
4 \times 3 & = & 12 \\
+ & & + \\
20 \times 3 & = & 60 \\
\hline
& & 72
\end{array}
$$

And he proceeded similarly when he was first confronted with a three-place number as one of the multipliers. Or, if confronted with complicated tasks, like 27×34, sometimes a child will proceed this way:

$$
\begin{array}{ccc}
20 \times 30 & + & 20 \times 4 \\
7 \times 30 & + & 7 \times 4
\end{array}
$$

One faces a different task when one tries to get the child to use the short cut, which demands, "you must not do it in the old way; you must write down the product (say, of 27×3) directly." Children often refuse to do this; they do not understand what it is all about. When this happens, I ask them, "Could you do it in such a way that you write down only the result?" Some then understand that this is not a question of getting at the right result, but of inventing a trick technique, a mental gymnastic. And this implies the task of discovering a procedure that contains a number of features, such as cutting into parts, one of which can be written down, and one of which must be kept in mind temporarily, as a different mode of grouping. A realization is required that some numbers can be written down because they will not be further influenced by others, and that some must not be written down yet because they may still be changed.

Concretely, this would mean: in the problem 24×3, I can safely write down the 2 of the twelve I get when multiplying 4×3, but I cannot write down the 1 of the twelve, because this other part, the product of 20×3, may influence it. Therefore I must hold it in mind, and add it to the latter value, and write it down only when it is complete. I have not found a child who could do this without help. The reason is not, I think, because the task is too difficult, but because the mental gymnastics involved are too strange. (Ability in such mental gymnastics is not difficult to develop in many children, but individual differences seem to me to be very great. And the task is not one of productive thinking, but of acquiring skill in such gymnastics.) "What is required" here is *not* required by the problem itself, but by a certain artificial technique, which has practical advantages. Basically, the requirements are directed at a technical goal, not an arithmetical one.

One might think that it is not good to let children use the first procedure, which they will not use afterwards; many feel that one should not teach the child what he will have to unlearn later. I disagree. I should think that the good teacher will start with the first procedure, despite the fact that the child will not use this particular technique. To learn the short-cut method without understanding how it comes about may arm the child with routine skills, but it omits the development of thinking (and if the trick of the procedure is forgotten, the pupil is lost; not so with the other method).

I think that giving 32×23 as the first task is psychologically in error. It not only confuses the pupil by demanding at once the two-sided discovery, but also, the equality of the numbers (in the multiplier and the multiplicand) and their lack of equality as to place-value is disturbing (2×3 is 6 on the one hand, and 60 on the other). The so-called gestalt law of similarity, which says that one tends to group equals, works in a direction opposite to what is to be done. One can observe in such cases how the equality of the numbers is an outspoken distraction, and a cause of increased difficulty.

In case the first task, 24×3, appears too difficult, there is still the possibility of helping with 42×3 or 12×3, cases which require no carrying, and involve no overlapping in the tens place. In any case, the best procedure seems to me to be *not to teach* the pupil the short-cut method *without* real understanding on his part, but to let him do the task, to let him find the necessary steps, but in a reasonable way, by proceeding from structurally easy tasks to structurally more difficult ones—which does not mean that the tasks given also need to be easy in other respects.

The process of thinking in such cases of course makes use of learned things. But the procedure is governed not by applying blindly what has been learned, as in the foolish cases on p. 192 of Thorndike's book.[3]

The ideal seems to me to be to have individual teaching, fitting the procedure to the individual. And it looks as though this might produce an astounding saving of time. Of course, there are, even in arithmetic, things which must be learned by memorization, but these are very few and usually can also be learned sensibly; the fact that there are such things, should not color, or endanger, or destroy the other more important things, to which these others should simply be an aid. Of course the practical impossibility of teaching all things individually, which also involves the impossibility of finding enough good teachers, demands a kind of compromise. But must this compromise be just in the direction of mechanizing minds, destroying abilities?

Let us return now to the basic difference between the two ways of teaching arithmetic. There is a further way in which one can dif-

[3] It is an experimental question to compare, in exact investigation, what happens when one is taught a method blindly through drill, as against what happens if one acquires it through a reasonable proceeding. For certain purposes, to be sure, when one needs not a man but a robot, the first procedure may have the advantage of speed. This issue seems parallel to the historic case of teaching medicine as rote technique, as against trying to educate physicians on the basis of physiology. (See also G. Katona, *Organizing and memorizing* (New York: Columbia University Press, 1940)—M.W.)

ferentiate them. Suppose the children were not taught the objective meanings of numbers, but were instead taught the same associations, *without* giving them experience with the real items, without the realization of "fitting," of structures, with regard to these real items. In some schools, based on associationism and drill, the teaching often comes near to such a state. Would this give the same results, the same possibilities? We could set it up in such a way that it would give exactly the same opportunities for building up all the associations, but would exclude the possibility of real thinking.

We can "simplify" the situation, in a manner very similar to that used in many customary experiments in learning. We will construct an "educational machine," which has a slot on top, into which you can put little boxes; there is another slot at the bottom, out of which other little boxes drop when you put something in at the top. The little boxes have letters marked on them. Now you start teaching subjects that when they put a little box marked *o p o* into the slot machine, another little box marked *t* drops out at the bottom. If you insert a box marked *t p o*, out comes another marked *th*. If you put in a box marked *th p o*, you will get one marked *f*.

Suppose the subject learns this thoroughly, so that in each case, before putting the box in the slot machine, he can tell you what will come out at the bottom.

Now we ask him what will you get if you insert a box marked *t p t*? We might get some wild guesses, or a refusal, or the reaction, "Will you allow me to try it first, so I can see what I will get?" But in all probability we will not get the answer: *f*. In fact, there is no possibility for a reasonable judgment or prediction of this kind.

Now, suppose that instead of the empty lettered boxes, we have boxes made up in such a way that in the box marked *o* there is one little marble, in the box marked *t* there are two marbles, in the box marked *th* three marbles, and in the box marked *f* four marbles. And *p* means, put the contents of the little boxes together into another box; the answer is what you get when you turn over the box, or what you see in the box when it opens and you can see all the marbles. All is changed; you will easily get the prediction, *f*.

In short, if you deal not with items and blind connections between items, but with the contents and the results of the operations, the results are in inner relation with the contents and operations. Or, if the child learns arithmetic not by drill, but by understanding the reasonable inner relations between operations and results, he need not be blind.

Are there mysterious, magic powers involved here? Or innate *a priori* propositions? No. Experience may teach us in these matters— and teach us very concretely—that the results of actions are reasonably related with the actions done, and with the contents used.

To put it extremely: nature—or our machine—certainly could be of such a character that events within it are governed by other rules, such as for example the rule that if you add anything to some item, the result will always increase by 1 $(a+x=a+1)$. And then the sum of two plus two would be 3 (by logical derivation out of the general rule, it would *have* to be 3), and the prediction, for $t\ p\ t$, of f would be factually wrong. A magical world could show such results, and not by sheer accident, but by law, by "necessity." In a magical world, the addition of two concrete items to one another could always give two as the result, the rule being : $a+b=2$. For a machine or a magical world, this is a possible rule. But one can see at once that there is a discrepancy between the equal sign, or the real equivalence on the one hand, and the inner relatedness between left and right sides of the equation on the other; the equal sign no longer means what it generally means, that the whole equation is broken in half, with the two halves sensibly equivalent to one another, one on the right and one on the left.

Fortunately experience with the real world we live in teaches us the kind of inner relatedness which is outstandingly reasonable because of the p-relation, the fitting together of requirement and result.

If we compare the first situation (the senseless letters) with the second (knowing the meaning of the letters), we have to state that there are schools in which the learning is similar to the first procedure, or in which children are forced to use the first rather than the second. No doubt there is some advantage in getting some operations down mechanically in order to free the person to deal with more difficult problems. But though it may be necessary for such a purpose, the procedure is at the same time dangerous. Because instead of opening the mind, instead of giving experience with reasonable dealings with situations, it mechanizes the mind and uses procedures that change the free and sensible manner of children.

The procedure would be even more dangerous if most children did not, fortunately, maintain an inner resistance to such influences. It is true that there are children who react as products of such an education when in the school atmosphere, but fortunately, even many of these are elastic enough to shed this mechanical attitude outside of school.

To repeat: we must differentiate, and very strongly so, between blind associations, blind habits, blind experiences, on the one hand, and the actuality of thinking, of grasping the inner relation between operations and their reasonable results.

The possibility of understanding ρ-relations in mathematics is probably the reason why, since long ago, educators have emphasized the value of mathematics in education—not because of its practical usefulness for certain jobs in life, for buying and selling, etc., but because in mathematics we have a material in which it is possible to work in a marvellously pure way, by getting directly at the inner consistency of materials and operations. The assumption of these old educators was that in dealing with such materials, in experiencing such matters himself, in developing the abilities to deal with them, abilities and attitudes are developed which will enable the pupil in other situations to look for, to be led by, to grasp the reasonableness and inner consistency of situations.

Certainly the psychologists who base everything on associations, on S-R bonds or connections, are in reality not blind to the virtues of the second procedure, since they themselves deal with it very intelligently. But it looks as if they forget it in principle when they want to be "scientific," or as if they hide it by using such terms as "appropriate," "satisfactory," etc. They clearly have recognized it in the classification they use for these second cases, terms such as "organization" and "subtle." And perhaps they will say that basically there is only a difference in emphasis. But to place the primary emphasis on the first, on drill, and to make it primary in school, may simply put the educator and his methods in opposition to the genuine direction of children, who seem naturally to be guided by reasonable considerations. One may then develop children who will react like mechanized slaves, not only in arithmetic, but in life problems too, following prestige blindly, following fashions, norms, political or musical opinions, looking—instead of to the merit of the situation itself—to what the "teacher" said, or to fashion or authority.

There seem to be three fundamental formulations. Either the senseless approach is basic, and the sensible is a kind of complication of the first; or, there is a basic difference between the senseless and the sensible, and the laws governing each are completely distinct; or —and I confess that I believe this to be the truest—sensible proceedings are basic, and senseless ones are just a special case, where the inner content, the inner consistency, approaches zero. Perhaps there is no natural tendency to act mechanically at all. Maybe acting mechanically is due to a kind of clutching at the last straw of inner consistency, namely constancy. That men are very often governed by habit would then not mean that habit is the basic source and character of their activities, but that it is a last resource when there is a lack of reasonable possibilities.

CHAPTER SEVEN

Two Boys Play Badminton;
A Girl Describes Her Office

IN THE previous chapters one issue played a particularly important role: the factor of reasonable reorganization, reorientation, which enables the subject to view[1] the given situation in a new[2] and more penetrating[3] perspective. It is this factor that leads to or constitutes a discovery in a deeper sense. In such cases a discovery does not merely

[1] Dislike of terms like "viewing," on the part of behaviorists and operationalists, should not blind them to the problem. Such terms are, I think, quite proper. But the main issue can also be formulated in the terms of these extremists, and it still remains essentially the same. Even if, strangely enough, one should want to disregard facts of conscious experience entirely, the consequences of reorganization show up in changes of objective behavior. In a first investigation, what really matters in the term "view" can be exactly formulated in terms that are operationally defined.

[2] For instance (Chap. One), the transition from ⟋⟋⟋⟋⟋ into ⟋⃒⃒⃒⃒⟍ from ⟋▱ into ⟋▱
e.g. (Chap. Four), the transition from ⟶ of the Gauss series as first seen to the new view ⟶ ⟵
also below (Chap. Eight), the transition from the sum of the exterior and interior angles of a polygon to the sum of the angles δ (see Fig. 142) plus two right angles, from the exterior angle to from the interior angle to
again, similar reorientations in the chapters on Galileo and Einstein.

[3] For instance (Chap. Eight), the way in which the sum of the angles in a closed figure or in a solid is conceived; the thought process last reported in Chap. Four, pp. 134-137; also the emergence of a more penetrating view in the chapters on Galileo (Chap. Nine) and Einstein (Chap. Ten).

mean that a result is reached which was not known before, that a question is somehow answered, but rather that a situation is grasped in a new and deeper fashion—whereupon the field broadens and larger possibilities come into sight. These changes of the situation as a whole imply changes in the structural meaning of part items, changes in their place, role and function, which often lead to important consequences.[4]

Before the thought process takes place, or in its early stages, one often has a certain whole-view of the situation, and so of its parts, which is somehow unsuited to the problem, superficial, or one-sided.[5] Such a first inadequate view often prevents a solution, a proper dealing with the task. If one sticks to this view, one will often be unable to solve the actual problem. On the other hand, when the change has occurred, and the problem has thereby been solved, one is sometimes astonished to see how blind one has been, how superficially one had viewed the situation.

The change in structural view according to the requirements of the problem is often of profound importance in the development of science. This holds likewise for human life in general, particularly in social phenomena.

Of course, such a change of structure is to the point only if the proper view has not been there from the start. Often the first view has only lacked adequate penetration, sufficient clarity; or some demand implied in the situation may not have been fully realized. In such instances the solution requires mainly that the situation be further clarified or crystallized, and that aspects or factors be realized which were only vaguely present in the first view.

In order to study such transitions and their consequences for the role and function of parts, I have sometimes employed specific experimental sets which bring about a sudden radical transformation from a first to a second view. Some simple examples have been mentioned

[4] For instance, in Chap. Four, p. 134, "+1" becomes the zero of the "real series," the "0" becomes "−1," etc.; also in the same chapter, p. 110, the 7, conceived first as 6+1, changes into 8−1.

[5] Cf. the examples in M. Wertheimer, "Über Schlussprozesse im produktiven Denken," *Drei Abhandlungen zur Gestalttheorie* (Erlangen, 1925) pp. 164-184; W. D. Ellis, *A source book of gestalt psychology* (New York: Harcourt, Brace, 1939) selection 23.

(cf. Chap. One, pp. 47-49 ff.).[6] Often powerful, dramatic occurrences take place when a subject experiences the change. The same sets also permit a study of what happens to the various regions of the structure when it changes: organization and grouping of the parts; changes in the location of "caesuras"; centering; shifts as to structural relevance; the appearance of gaps, of disturbances; changes as to the extent to which local conditions may be varied; changed trends in the subject's expectations, in the emergence of new whole-tendencies, and in the direction of requirements.

When such transitions occur in thinking, it is not the ease of arbitrary change as such which characterizes intelligent behavior; nor is it the ability in a given situation to produce one or another or a third structural view at will, as some seem to believe. Rather what matters here, and what is characteristic of intelligent processes, is the firm transition from a less adequate, a less proper structural view to a more sensible one. And in fact experiences seem to show that sensible persons, real thinkers who are often quite capable of making sensible transformations, also children, show little ability and even less willingness to engage in *senseless* changes of given situations.

Sometimes the transition from an unstructured and-sum to the appropriate structure is needed. But even more significant is the transition from a one-sided view, a superficial structurization or misstructurization, from a miscentered, distorted or poor view to the adequate and properly centered structure.

The main cause of unreasonable, blind behavior seems to be that a person sticks to an old view from sheer perseveration and habit, which make him ignore or even actively deny the more reasonable requirements that are clearly indicated in the situation.

In order to show more clearly how such transitions come about, I will now report on some simple examples from everyday life which I studied in various experiments.

[6] Cf. also M. Wertheimer, "Zu dem Problem der Unterscheidung von Einzelinhalt und Teil," *Zeitschrift für Psychologie*, 1933, Vol. 129, pp. 353-357 (See Appendix 1.—M. W.) and a description of further examples from my lectures in M. Scheerer, *Die Lehre von der Gestalt* (Berlin: Walter de Gruyter, 1931) pp. 209-210.

I

Two boys were playing badminton in the garden. I could hear as well as see them from my window, although they did not see me. One boy was twelve, the other ten years old. They played several sets. The younger was by far poorer; he was being beaten in all the games.

I heard some of their conversation. The loser—let us call him B —became more and more unhappy. He had no chance. A often served him so cleverly that he could not possibly return the bird. The situation grew worse. Finally B threw down his racket, sat on a tree trunk, and said, "I won't play any more." A tried to persuade him to continue. No answer from B. A sat down beside him. Both looked unhappy.

I interrupt the story here to put a question to the reader: "What do you suggest? What would you do if you were the older boy? Do you have a productive proposal?"

If in telling the story one stops at this point, some subjects clearly do some thinking. They make remarks which show that they see a considerable problem, and they venture some suggestion as to what the older boy should do.

Most subjects do not. They are dissatisfied with the interruption of the story, wait to have it continued, are puzzled because I do not go on, ask how things actually developed, what the boys did, whether they were my boys, why I told the story, why I stopped there, whether this was an experiment—whether later I would perhaps give a memory test, and so forth.[7]

Some reminisce, reflect, meditate, "Oh, such situations are very familiar to me. You know I am interested in children. This reminds me of my uncle's trouble with his two children." Or they recall a paragraph from a textbook on child psychology.

Some make nice subsumptions under general topics: "This is a case of . . ." and classify the case, then often embark on generalities, more or less needlessly, as, for instance, about social adjustment, adaptive behavior, problem children.

[7] The extreme case, of course, is when nothing at all happens. Finished? Finished. Are you going to tell more stories? What will we do now?

Some want to know more of the facts, ask a number of questions, more or less reasonable ones.[8] For instance, "Of course the older boy had had more practice?" Or: "Was the younger boy generally slower in his reactions?" Even psychoanalytic questions are asked.

For the most part these subjects do not produce any concrete, productive proposals and show some surprise if asked for one directly. It is clear that they have not thought of that possibility at all, busy as they are with recollections, classifications, or fact-gathering.

If asked directly, nearly all do suggest something. Often in the tone of "What should be done in such a situation is obvious." In most cases the answers are clearly given without any effort of thought, as sheer reproductions of things seen or heard before, as applications of some known rule of behavior, sometimes remembered from courses in educational psychology. Often they are given in a low tone of deep conviction, often with a superior air.

The proposals offered are frequently characteristic of prevailing ideas about children, about human beings in general, about morals, current social rules, and doctrines to which the subjects adhere. Often one can recognize doctrines of various schools of psychology in their far-reaching consequences.

The usual types of suggestion were as follows:

"Promise the younger boy a piece of chocolate."

"Start another kind of game, say chess, in which the younger is equal or even better. Or promise to play, alternately with badminton, some game in which he is by far the better."

"Bring him to reason by plain scolding. He should be manly, not a sissy. Can't he take it on the chin? He has to learn to take it. Use superior authority in bringing the younger boy to reason."

"Don't bother with him, he is a sissy. It will be a lesson to him."

"Offer a handicap."

"Promise the younger boy that the older boy will not make full use of his superior power and skill."

The reader may later compare these proposals with the boys' own solution, not merely with regard to fitness—some of these

[8] The extreme case was a nice young man who in this case—and in fact always —started at once asking question after question, lots of them. You could not stop him. Curiosity is not always, not in every sense of the word, a sign of intelligent thinking or of reasonable behavior.

proposals are proper, since they depend on actual conditions in the real situation—but with regard to the kind of thinking that is involved.[9]

Sometimes, as I have said, proposals are not made in a facile, casual way, by easy recall or application, but after serious thinking with a sense that the problem touches deep questions. There is earnest deliberation, productive questions are asked. Several times the thought processes contained steps similar to those which occurred in the boys.

I shall now continue with the story. In addition I shall try to describe what I think was going on in the boys' minds.

1. "What's wrong? Why don't you go ahead?" said the older boy in a sharp, angry voice. "Why do you break up the game? Do you think it's nice, to stop in this silly way?" He wanted to continue. The refusal of B made it impossible. He liked to play, he liked to win; it was even nice to be able cleverly to trick one's opponent with the service. B is the disturber, he makes it impossible for A to do what he so much wants.

2. But it was not so simple. At the same time A was not quite at ease, he did not feel nice about it. After a while, during which curious things were going on in his face—I wish you could have seen him as he frequently glanced sidewise at B, and away again—he said, but now in quite another tone, "I am sorry." Obviously a radical change had taken place—clearly A now felt sorry that the other boy was so unhappy. He had realized what was going on in B, how the situation looked to the other fellow.

Perhaps a sad, quiet look of B's had helped, as B once turned his head toward A for a brief moment. A realized—it was not a quick process, it took some time—why the younger boy was sad, why with no hope of holding his own he felt like a victim. For the first time A felt that his way of playing, his shrewd service, looked to B like a

---

[9] Also with regard to the philosophy of life implied, and the underlying psychological doctrines which often come out in discussion: e.g., the naïve pain-pleasure principle, reward and punishment psychology, submission to the idea that consent may be bought, horse-trading in an extreme form ("You be my slave now, then I'll be yours"); on the other hand, a moral appeal which often works productively but which under certain circumstances may degenerate into sugar-coating the pill.

Often these suggestions go with a kind of cynicism; or they are treated with easy superficiality as obvious, properly applied psychology.

mean trick; that B felt he was not being treated fairly, that A's actions were unfriendly to him. And A felt that B was somehow right . . .

Now he also saw himself in another light. To serve as he had done, without giving B the slightest chance to return, was something more, something other than skill.

3. "Look here," he said suddenly, "such playing *is* nonsense." It was now nonsense not only for B, but also nonsense for him, non-sense for the game itself. Thus the trouble had become of a deeper kind.

Expressed in adult language it was as if he had thought—he cer-tainly did not, he only felt his way through—"It is senseless for two to play together in such a way. The game requires some reciprocity. Such rank inequality does not suit the game. The game becomes real only if both have some hope of achievement. The game changes its whole character, becomes a bad thing for the one player, for the other, for both, if there is no such reciprocity; without it there is no longer really a game—a tyrant merely makes his victim run around."

4. Then the expression of his face changed. He looked like some-one trying with difficulty to grasp something, on whom something slowly begins to dawn, and he said: "Such a game is a queer thing. I am not really unfriendly to you . . ." A vague idea had arisen in him of what a grownup would call the "ambivalence" involved in the game: on the one hand, it is so nice to have a good time together, to be good friends; on the other hand, there is this effort to overcome your opponent, to beat him, to make his achievement impossible, which in certain circumstances may be felt as, or may actually become, plain enmity.

5. Thereupon a bold, free, and deeply consistent step occurred. He mumbled something like "Must it . . . ?" Clearly he desired to face the trouble squarely, to deal with it honestly, directly. I interpret this "Must it?" as "Is this factor of enmity necessary when it spoils all that is nice in the game?" Here the pragmatic problem arose: "How can I change it? Is it not possible to have, not one against the other, but—" His face lit up and he said: "I have an idea—let us now play this way: let's see how long we can keep the bird going between us and count how many times it goes back and forth without

falling. What score could we make? Do you think we could make it ten or twenty? We'll start with easy serves but then let us make them harder and harder . . ."

He spoke happily, like someone who had discovered something. It was a new thing to him, likewise to B.

B agreed happily: "That's a fine idea. Let's." And they began to play. The character of the game was entirely changed; they were co-operating, acting together, working hard and joyfully. A no longer showed the slightest tendency to trick B; to be sure, his moves became more difficult, but he called out, "A harder one, can you get that?" in a sensible, friendly way.

Several days later I saw them play again. B's playing was greatly improved. It was a real game. As one could see in his later behavior, it was quite an experience for A. He had discovered something, gained something that went far beyond the solution of a little problem in a game of badminton.

The solution in itself may not amount to much so long as it is seen merely from the outside. I do not know whether badminton or tennis experts would agree that it was appropriate.[10] It does not matter. This solution was not just a technical affair for this boy. It involved the transition from a superficial attempt to get rid of a trouble to facing the fundamental stuctural issue and to dealing with it in a productive way.[11]

What were the steps that led to this solution? Of course, when one interprets a single case, the factual basis, the basis for conclusions, is small. Still, let us try to formulate the essential points.

Initially A saw the whole situation, and in it B, the game, the trouble, centered on his ego (Fig. 105). They were determined, by this

[10] I know chess players who are intensely disturbed if fine constellations in a game are disrupted by some peripheral, thoughtless mistake. They hate it equally, no matter who makes the mistake. Some have the custom—*horribile dictu* for experts—of correcting such errors. Why? They like a good game; they have no interest in winning by some silly mistake of their opponents. Sometimes they even co-operate in order to make the game more perfect.

In general I think there should be more games of the co-operative, creative sort instead of merely competitive ones.

[11] This would by no means have been a reasonable proposal under all circumstances. If A had been a ruffian, seeking only his own advantage, bent upon conquering, whatever it might mean to the other fellow, proud even of the pain he inflicted on him, and if B then would have proposed it—it would have been strictly senseless behavior. In fact, the opposite would have been called for: to quit entirely or to train somewhere else for the real fight.

center, in their meaning, role, place, function both as to thinking and as to action. If this were an extreme case, *B* would be nothing but

FIG. 105

someone whom *A* needs in order to win; consequently, in refusing to play, *B* would be the "disturber." The game would be "the thing in which I display my abilities, in which I win." *B* represents a barrier which is in the way of *A*'s egocentric requirements, vectors, acts.

A did not persist in this one-sided, superficial view. He began to

FIG. 106   FIG. 107

realize how the situation looked to *B*, to *B* as the center (Fig. 106). In this recentered structure he now saw himself as a part, as a player who dealt in a not altogether nice way with the other player.

A bit later the *game* itself, its whole-qualities and requirements, became the center (Fig. 107). Neither he nor the other was now the center, both were viewed with reference to the game.

FIG. 108

Logically, A (as A views himself) differs in the three centerings (Fig. 108);[12] so do the other items, along with the dynamic requirements, the vectors, the actual situation. The game is now clearly seen as a deviation from the "good game."

But what in the structure of the game itself lies at the root of the trouble? There is a delicate functional equilibrium in the good game: on the one hand, having a nice time together, behaving as friends; on the other hand, "trying to beat him." Attitudes deeper than mere external rules of fair play make this delicate equilibrium possible, establish the differences between a good game and a ruthless fight or a ruthless competition; in short, make a game a game. The equilibrium is psychologically delicate; it may disappear—as it did in this situation.

The "against," the "trying to beat him," that functions properly in the good game had grown into an ugly feature which no longer fitted the game situation. That gave rise to the vector: "What could be done about it? And done immediately?" Here lies the trouble. "Is it not possible to get at the core of the situation?" This leads to considering structure II.

Structure Ia ⟶ ⟵ or, with these boys, rather

Structure Ib ⟶ ⟵ is transformed into

Structure II, ⋀ from competing to co-operation; from I against

You, to We. A and B, as parts, are here no longer as in Structure I, opponents, each for his own side only, but two human beings co-operating toward a common goal.

All the items change their meaning considerably. For instance, serving no longer means that B is to be overwhelmed by making a return of the bird impossible. In the first state of affairs (I), a player is happy if he scores and the other player misses; but now (II), each enjoys every good rally directly.

The steps which then follow show the transition to facing the problem situation on *its* merits rather than from the viewpoint of one side or the other, or of the mere sum of both. The solution

[12] Cf. M. Wertheimer, "On truth," *Social Research*, 1934, Vol. 1, pp. 135-146.

grows out of the realization of the structural trouble; then the trouble acquires a deeper meaning. The tension is not overcome superficially; rather, the new direction of the vectors follows from basic structural requirements which demand a genuinely good situation. You may think I read far too much into the boy's mind. I don't think so. You may have far too poor an idea of what can happen in the minds of boys.

In short we note specifically:

1) Operations of recentering: transition from a one-sided view to the centering required by the objective structure of the situation;

2) a change of meaning of the parts—and of the vectors—in accordance with their structural place, role and function;

3) a view of the situation in terms of "good structure," so that everything fits the structural requirements;

4) a trend to go straight to fundamentals, to face the issue honestly, and to draw the consequences.

I want to remark that the feature of straightness, honesty, sincerity, does not seem peripheral in such a process. Generally speaking, it is an artificial and narrow view which conceives of thinking as only an intellectual operation, and separates it entirely from questions of human attitude, feeling, and emotion—"because such topics belong to other chapters of psychology." This is especially clear in one example, in the transition from a blind egocentric view with its emotional ingredients to the later steps. But even seemingly mere intellectual processes involve a human attitude—that kind of willingness to face issues, to deal with them frankly, honestly, and sincerely. Although I have referred to this fact only briefly in other chapters, it seems essential in many cases of productive thinking, including even our problems in pure elementary geometry.

Of course it may happen that certain solutions are found when the subject assumes just the opposite attitude, when he tries to subdue the situation by a trick or to do violence to it. But here too such factors seem not merely to accompany the "intellectual operations"; rather, the very nature of the operations, their genesis, and their development seem deeply connected with the actual human attitude toward the problem and its solution. Neither slyness, nor a spirit of domineering seems to be the most advisable attitude in productive thinking, even though it may sometimes lead to practical success, and thus make for a certain quick, short-range efficiency.

Connected with these matters is a further point which seems of fundamental importance for a true understanding of productive thinking both in the theoretical and in the practical realm. This is the transition from a first stage in which the subject simply wants to reach a certain goal—in which his thought is entirely centered by this goal—to another stage in which the vectors, the operations, the actions become centered by more fundamental requirements of the situation. In a sense a subject may become virtually blind if he looks only at that goal, and is entirely governed by the urge toward *it*. Often he must first forget what he happens to wish before he can become susceptible to what the situation itself requires. And so, in better instances, his attitude will be far more similar to the attitude of a physician or a wise adviser than to that of a clever and domineering conqueror or aggressor.

This transition is one of the great moments in many genuine thought processes. The role of the merely subjective interests of the self is, I think, much overestimated in human actions. Real thinkers forget about themselves in thinking. The main vectors in genuine thought often do not refer to the I with its personal interests; rather, they represent the structural requirements of the given situation.[13] Or when such vectors do refer to an I, this is not just the I as center of subjective striving.

Of course the transition may lie also in the direction of the deeper requirements of the I itself. Sometimes there is a happy coincidence between the requirements of the situation which presents the problem and the real, the deeper needs of the I, as was the case with our boy.

This was only a modest little story. Yet some of its characteristics, as, for instance, the essential progress which occurred through a change of centering, are, I think, characteristic of profoundly important accomplishments[14] in human beings, in human society. One can sometimes observe marvelous changes in individuals, as when

13 See E. Levy, "Some aspects of the schizophrenic formal disturbance of thought," *Psychiatry*, 1943, Vol. 6, pp. 55-69.

14 M. Wertheimer, "A story of three days." In R. N. Anshen (Ed.), *Freedom: its meaning* (New York: Harcourt, Brace, 1940) pp. 555-569.

some passionately biased person becomes a member of a jury, or arbitrator, or judge, and when his actions then show the fine transition from bias to an honest effort to deal with the problems at issue in a just and objective fashion. The very development of the idea and institution of courts of justice is at issue here.

Centering—the way one views the parts, the items in a situation, their meaning and role as determined in regard to a center, a core, or radix—is a most powerful factor in thinking. The problems of centering have been neglected in traditional logic and in psychology. Strong forces are at work in centering, in envisaging—or in trying to envisage—the true center according to the nature of a situation; but they are equally strong in cases of blind, enforced or willful miscentering, so efficiently used in some kinds of political propaganda. Although there are many strong forces working against true centering, there is nevertheless in human beings a clear desire not to be structurally blind, a desire to center properly, to do justice to the situation, to center in accordance with the nature of the object, of the structural objective requirements.

As to the concept of centering, it seems to be tacitly recognized that *adequate* centering, with its consequences for objectivity and justice, is of the utmost importance. Otherwise, why should actual miscentering be the more energetically disguised as true and just centering, the less it is so in fact?

II

Quite a number of things are involved in the process of recentering as it occurred in the badminton example. Some basic points will become clearer if we now consider a simpler story.

I was visiting a family. The daughter of the house came home and was introduced to me. Her father asked how she had spent the day. She answered that there had been a good deal of work, but that she was fine. I asked, "Are you working?" "Yes," she answered, "I am working with a firm." "Is it a big place?" "Well," she said, "there are a number of people in the office. I have to do directly with a Mr. A, a Mr. B, and a Mr. C, who often come to my desk, ask questions, bring me letters, etc. There are others in the office with whom I do not have to do directly. Mr. A has dealings with a Mr. D, Mr. B with a Mr. *E*, and Mr. *C* with a Mr. *F*. *D* and *E* also have dealings with each other; so do *E* and *F*. Let me see, that makes six people in the office besides myself."

I asked, "Are you the boss?" "Oh no," she answered. "Do you give orders to anyone?" "Oh yes, I sometimes give orders to Mr. *A* and to Mr. *C*. I get orders from Mr. *B*; Mr. *D* gets them from Mr. *E*, Mr. *E* from Mr. *B*, and Mr. *F* from Mr. *E*." (She was apparently logically minded, and was trying to tell the whole story.)

I was somewhat disturbed—I guess the reader is too—and I said: "I am still in the dark about the people in your office." "Oh, but I have told you everything," she answered. Nevertheless, I was in the dark. Suddenly I said—it was a hunch—"So Mr. *B* is your boss, and you are directly below him, and so is Mr. *E*?" "Yes," she said.

As she saw her office, she had stated the relations correctly and completely, and yet she had not made the real picture clear. Most people, if asked such a question, would start with some such statement as "I am working directly under the Boss *B*; so is a Mr. *E*"; they might add, "Mr. *E* and I each have two people working under us to whom we give orders," and might continue, "Two of these sometimes have business with each other." This would have been a sensible description; it would have given a clear picture of the structure of the office setup. But this girl had enumerated the men and the relations in a bewildering succession, in fact in a way that was blind to the structure of the situation; she had centered everything about her ego —except for the last bewildering statement in the second description which did not refer to her.

This is an innocent example of a foolish attitude in life and in thinking, which often has considerable consequences for shaping one's views and one's actions.

Of course it might have been mere clumsiness in description, but from the girl's subsequent remarks and behavior it became clear that this was characteristic of her real attitudes. Some time later, when I met one of her coworkers from the office, I asked him how she was getting on. "Quite nicely," he said; "she is a fine person. But we are not certain whether her job will last very long. She has a funny way of behaving toward the others and even toward her work. She seems to relate all things to herself, as if she were always the center of the situation, even in business matters when nobody is thinking of her personally. That is not good for business."

When self-centering is extreme, it becomes a well-known symptom of a psychopathological state that often leads to a precarious situation both in social and in personal affairs.[15] Self-centering is not at all the general, the natural attitude, as some influential views of our time would have us believe.

Let us look more closely at what this girl did in her description. In a schema it may be represented as follows.

First Description

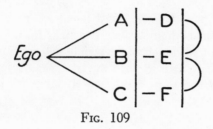

Fig. 109

This schema is quite similar to the way a logistician would write a list of relations in a relational network. He would state the relations *Ego r X*, and so forth, as follows:

$$\begin{array}{cc|c|c}
\textit{Ego} & A & AD & \\
 & & & DE \\
\textit{Ego} & B & BE & \\
 & & & EF \\
\textit{Ego} & C & CF & \\
\end{array}$$

Fig. 110

If one asks a person for a diagram that would fit the girl's descrip-

[15] Cf. M. Wertheimer, "Über Gestalttheorie," (Erlangen: Philosophische Akademie, 1925). (Editors' note: this article is translated into English under the title "Gestalt theory," *Social Research*, 1944, Vol. 11, pp. 78-99); also W. D. Ellis, *op. cit.*, selection 1; E. Levy, *op. cit.*, pp. 59-69; H. Schulte, "Versuch einer Theorie der paranoischen Eigenbeziehung und Wahnbildung," *Psychologische Forschung*, 1924, Vol. 5, pp. 1-23.

tion, a picture like this is usually given:

FIG. 111

which clearly shows the *Ego* as the center. This characteristic is usually not changed when the last two lines from *D* to *E* and from *E* to *F* are added, although some people will ask, "Is there not also a connecting line from *F* to *D*?"

FIG. 112

Second Description

In this description the girl qualified the relations by giving them directions. But the list now constitutes a veritable tangle of such directions:

$$Ego \longleftarrow \begin{matrix} A \\ B \\ C \end{matrix} \quad \begin{matrix} — D \\ — E \\ — F \end{matrix}$$

FIG. 113A

or, in the relational network of logistics:

$Ego \longrightarrow A$	$A — D$	
$Ego \longleftarrow B$	$B \longrightarrow E$	$D \longleftarrow E$
$Ego \longrightarrow C$	$C — F$	$E \longrightarrow F$

FIG. 113B

If we represent this in diagram form we obtain:

Fig. 114

At this point something usually happens to those who look at the diagram. It begins to appear as though "wrongly drawn," "distorted." It may then be changed into a form which we will give in a moment.

Third Description

Both a schema and a diagram of the adequate description look fundamentally different:

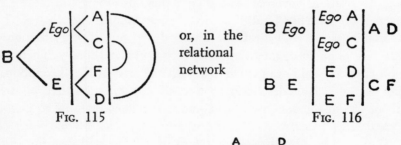

Fig. 115   or, in the relational network   Fig. 116

As a diagram one gets here:

Fig. 117

which gives quite another picture, with the clear centering about *B*.

Fourth Description

With the qualifications as to direction the schema becomes

FIG. 118A   or   FIG. 118B

and the diagram   FIG. 119

Everything is now structurally clear; there is no confusion as in the previous descriptions, schemas, and diagrams. The girl *had* stated all the relations involved, but in a rather disturbing, miscentered aggregate. The first and the second descriptions and the corresponding figures go against the objective structure of the situation: they are blind to it, they violate it, they center it wrongly. There is nothing to be said against *starting* with the *Ego* in the description, but in a reasonable description one would not center all that follows about it. On the contrary, one would see and report the *Ego* in its (secondary) place within the structure.

If the reader compares the first and the second with the third or the fourth diagram, he will see what I mean when I say that in the first and the second the succession, the grouping, the centering are done in a way that is blind to the structurally adequate picture. But let us look more closely: if we wish to characterize the place, role, and function of the various parts of the picture, we may, in a first approximation, proceed in the way in which the logicians characterize the items and the relation-lines in a relational network. The implicit definition of points by their relational places in the network, in terms of the number of relations (r) to immediately neighboring points (P_I), to secondary points (P_{II}), etc., in our example gives the following schema:

	B		Ego, E		A,D,C,F	
	r.	P.	r.	P.	r.	P.
I	2	2	3	3	2	2
II	4	4	3	3	3	3
III	2	–	2	–	1	–

In each of these three classes the individuals are "homotypes."

Fig. 120

In the third description, and at the level I, we have:

for B   for Ego   for D

Fig. 121

while the first description gives:

Fig. 122

If we characterize individuals of the three classes by the letters $\alpha \beta \gamma$ we get:

in the first description   and in the third description

Fig. 123   Fig. 124

With regard to the relations, we get:

in the first description   and in the third description

$$
\begin{array}{c|c|c}
1 & 2 & 3 \\
\beta\gamma & \gamma\ \gamma & \gamma\ \beta \\
\beta\alpha & \alpha\ \beta & \\
\beta\gamma & \gamma\ \gamma & \gamma\ \beta
\end{array}
$$

FIG. 125

$$
\begin{array}{c|c|c}
1 & 2 & 3 \\
\alpha\beta & \begin{array}{cc} \beta & \gamma \\ \beta & \gamma \end{array} & \gamma\ \gamma \\
\alpha\beta & \begin{array}{cc} \beta & \gamma \\ \beta & \gamma \end{array} & \gamma\ \gamma
\end{array}
$$

FIG. 126

The result is similar if we take into account the directed character of the relations in the second and fourth descriptions.

We find that in this example there are three kinds of people; we may call them boss, secretaries, clerks. Centered about the *Ego*, they are considerably mixed up in the groupings of the first and second descriptions. In the corresponding schemas we find, as members of one group, two clerks and one boss; and as members of another group, two clerks and one secretary; one secretary, the girl, is a single item on the left side, whereas the other secretary is one member of a triplet on the right side. Similarly with the relations: on the left side of the relational schema (pp. 183-184) we have two relations between secretary and clerks, one between secretary and boss; further to the right two relations between clerks, one between boss and secretary; to the extreme right two relations between secretary and clerks.

In contrast, everything is in clear, surveyable, flawless order when we turn to the third and fourth descriptions and schemas (p. 185). The starting point is the boss, then come the two secretaries, and finally the four clerks. The first two relations are the relations between boss and secretaries, then follow the relations between secretaries and clerks, and finally the relations between the clerks.

In short: viewed piecemeal, the first and second descriptions are in a way correct, and complete in all details, but they introduce a centering, a grouping that is blind to, and in violation of, the logical hierarchy in the situation. They put together things which are different in nature and let things appear as structurally different which are not. Seen from the girl's subjective point of view, i.e., without taking her secondary position into account, the description distorts the structure; it fails to do justice to the structural meanings of the parts.

What we have just said concerning the difference between mis-centered description and structurally appropriate description applies even if the situation is characterized in terms of implicit definitions, relation-numbers, and so forth. (Nevertheless, the question of clearness of classes as expressed in such terms is not the real heart of the matter. The reader will be aware of the fact that we must exercise caution when we use this logistical method.)

Suppose the owner of the business were to come into the picture. The relational network would be:

Fig. 127

In terms of relational numbers, B may then easily appear as homotype with *Ego* and with E, since all three have the same implicit characterization.

	B		*Ego,* E	
	r	P	r	P
I	3,	3	3,	3
II	4,	4	4,	4
III	2,	–	2,	–

Fig. 128

These numbers do not tell the whole story. For instance, under II there is a difference in the meaning which the number 4 has in the various cases: for B it means 2 + 2, for *Ego* and E, 1 + 2 + 1.

In cases such as this, it is decisive how the directions of the relations are distributed. What of a situation in which there were a boss, two secretaries, and one clerk?

FIG. 129

Without taking into account the directedness of the relations, *Ego* and *B* would be real homotypes:

FIG. 130

Here we see the decisive point: the arrows *start* from B, go on the left side *through Ego* and end in A. B is at the source of the arrows, the center in this sense; *Ego* is not. *Ego* has to be viewed in its place within the pattern of the *arrows*. No characterization suffices which is in terms of the number of undirected relations to immediate neighbor points (P_I), to secondary points (P_{II}), and to all points in terms of numbers, of relations, etc.

The deeper meaning of being the center does not rest on the fact that what is single is outstanding; it is more important that the center is the source of the arrows, that it is the heart of the matter. There could be, for instance, two bosses, partners, and one secretary, and still this secretary, *Ego*, would not be the center in terms of the

FIG. 131

business structure. (It could be, of course, in certain conditions, as, if the behavior of both bosses were determined by the wish to marry her.)

Centering, then, is not a matter merely of the distribution of numbers of relations; it is a matter of the inner structure of the whole picture, which emerges only if the direction of the relations within the whole pattern is given, and thus the functional meaning of each term.

How do people react to inadequate descriptions? The girl's first description led to the impression that she was the center. "Are you the boss?" I had asked. This question assumed that the arrows were in line with her description.

The second description was at first puzzling because the distribution of arrows did not fit the conceived structure (p. 185). In terms of the arrow distribution *Ego* no longer appears unperturbed as center.

Fig. 132

At the same time *B* becomes conspicuous as being at the source of the vectors.

If a subject looks at this diagram, a process of the following kind often develops: "This looks funny. How complicated in the center (*Ego*), with those arrows! What funny places for the lines without arrows!" Then some subjects suddenly center on *B*, saying: "The picture is distorted. Referred to the line which passes through *B*, the diagram looks like two wings which need some adjustment . . . ,"

Fig. 133

and a new diagram is drawn. Others discover first that "the funny complicated constellation of arrows in *Ego*—'two out, one in'—is structurally repeated in *E*," and in this way reach the view of our last diagram.

The preceding diagram clearly appears as something funny, something that is not in order, something that must be improved. Then a strong dynamic process follows which changes that diagram into the structurally clear view of the last diagram.

Some subjects—fewer in number—already show similar reactions when they are confronted with the diagram of the first description,

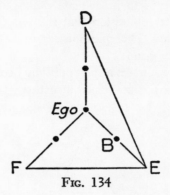

FIG. 134

and when they receive a negative answer to their question whether there is not a line *FD*. On remembering that the length of lines in relational networks is indeterminate, they sometimes get the "two-wing" view and thus reorganize the picture as in Fig. 133.

In experiments without diagrams, when only the girl's second description or the symbolic list of directed relations is used, reactions are not so strong, not so clear, but sometimes positive nevertheless. Looking for the person who gives orders and does not receive orders, the subjects focus on *B*, and thus recognize the girl's intermediate position.

Often in these cases, too, the transition appears to be a process of restructuring, although this is not so clear as it is with the diagrams: at first *Ego* is conceived as center with most other items in peripheral shadow; then *B* is focused, and *Ego* gets its secondary place, while the other items still do not occupy very clear places in the structure.

Especially in the last mentioned cases the "new idea" has the appearance of a "hunch" because of the initial lack of clearness to which too many details greatly contribute. The reasons for the guess are often not explicit but have merely the form of a direction of centering. In the experiments with the diagrams, too, there is at first an unclear state of affairs, then "some vague idea" emerges which involves directions of recentering, until suddenly the picture crystallizes into the complete new structure.

CHAPTER EIGHT

Finding the Sum of the Angles of a Polygon

1. DURING a conversation at lunch about ornaments, the discussion touched on closed geometric figures such as triangles, rectangles,

FIG. 135

hexagons, and other polygons. At one point a friend, an artist, remarked: "The sum of the angles of all such figures must of course be the same in every case." Everyone laughed. I found myself in a remarkable situation. I said, "Of course the sum of the angles is *not* the same. For the triangle it is 180°, for the rectangle, 360°, for the hexagon, 720°. But I feel the assertion must be right somehow, it touches an essential point." This feeling continued strong in me. On the one hand, it was clear that the sum of the angles was not the same in the various polygons; on the other hand, I had the feeling that I could not let the matter rest; it had to be cleared up, there had to be a way of seeing through it. There was a beautiful point in it but I did not know how to get at it. It was impossible to understand or even to express just where the problem lay. The compulsion remained: "There must be a solution. What on earth is the matter?"

For the others taking part in the conversation, there was no trouble. The matter was settled when they saw that the assertion was obviously false.

In the hours that followed, in which I had other things to do, the problem continued to be active. After several hours it had developed to this stage: "There is, on the one hand, the sum of the angles (A) in a figure; on the other hand, there is the closed completeness (B) of the figure. Between A and B there is only an 'and,' a simple con-

FIG. 136

junction. There is the one, here is the other. This *and*-relationship between them is somehow blind. What is really behind it all? What is the trouble? The two must have something to do with each other." It was not a feeling of two contradictory propositions. I was directed toward the positive problem, "How can I comprehend?"

2. The following day, while I was engaged in other work, this idea suddenly came to me, vague, indefinite and uncertain, something

FIG. 137

like this: Here is a *point*. Around a *point* there is a complete "angular space" of 360° (one whole angle). Must there not be something

FIG. 138

similar to this in the case of the closed figure? But this most hazy notion could not be further clarified at the time.

Three days passed. Whatever I did, there was always present this same strong feeling, the feeling of something unfinished, of being directed toward something I could not grasp. I felt repeatedly that I could almost tell where the trouble lay, upon what it depended, in what direction the solution would develop, but it was all in a colloidal, indefinite state so that I could not formulate it concretely. Many times it seemed so clear that "I need only write it down," but when I attempted it, I could not, the ideas could not really be formulated.

(I have found a similar course of development in many truly great intellectual accomplishments: this same feeling of directed tension with the real situation hazy, colloidal. Somehow the form the solution will take, is in its essentials on the tip of one's tongue, but it cannot be concretely grasped. It is a condition which may often last for months with many days of depression during which little success is evident; yet one cannot drop the matter.)

3. Again after two days the following question arose: "If I have a point, there is a complete angle around it. If I have a *straight line*, there is also an angular space around it. Now, if I have such a

FIG. 139

straight line, *how must I proceed to obtain a closed figure*? Simply by continuing the straight line? Not at all. I must *break* the line at some point, if it is ever to form a closed figure." This led quickly to

FIG. 140

the idea: "Let me look first at the sum of the exterior angles." And what happened? In breaking, the straight angle broke into two "side angles," each of them a right angle and between them arose a delta (δ), an "angle of rotation." It is the δ's, the rotation, that are the

FIG. 141   FIG. 142

important thing. And in the whole figure, as it closes, the sum of the δ's must be . . . a complete revolution, an angle of 360°, no matter how many side angles the figure has!

Every side has two exterior right angles, one at each end. There can be as many sides, therefore as many such angles, as one wishes; but in every figure the δ's, the angles of rotation, must make a complete revolution. This was an "intuition." I was very happy at this moment. I had the feeling: "Now I see through the matter."

What actually happened? I started with the usual notion of the angles, and the completion or closure. In trying to see how the closure comes about, the total exterior angle of a corner became two right angles plus δ; the two right angles became peripheral to the issue; the δ was envisaged with the other δ's as forming a complete rotation. With this conception of the angles, there was suddenly an interlocking of the δ's, the significant angles, with the closure of the figure. The and-relationship of A (the sum of the angles) and B (the closed completeness) had changed into a coherent, comprehensible, lucid togetherness. A and B were no longer just pieces set up alongside one another, they were now parts of an inner togetherness. Closing the figure required the δ's to complete 360°. This process of integration served as the solution: what had been just an obscure and unsatisfactory sum now assumed well-defined shape.

The idea that the sum of the δ's is 360° came into existence not as some assumed proposition, general statement, or belief, but as an "intuition": seeing in a structured view of the figure the inner relatedness between closedness and all the δ's.

Quickly this crystallized into ways of proceeding:

1) There was the realization of what happens—what reasonably

must happen—if I go around the figure step by step from the first side of a first δ: to close the figure, I must reach the starting line again, complete a full turn. This had been realized in one view at first;[1] then, proceeding, it was followed up: In the first δ the side

FIG. 143

of the angle turns by a certain amount into the position of the other side, 2, moves to 3—with *no* turn, as 2 and 3 are parallel; turns from 3 to 4—and so on. In going around, in closure, in reaching position 1 again, the side must have made altogether the full turn of 360°.

2) Just after that came: Let the side lines of the figure shrink in size,

FIG. 144.

[1] Long afterward I found in a book a remark, made by the physicist Ernst Mach, which showed a somewhat similar step in breaking the line. In this way, too, the complete 360° of the sum of the δ's is reached. The view is somewhat different: here, the angle is not divided into R, δ, R but into 2R, δ which makes the con-

FIG. 145

ditions for envisaging the completeness of the turn somewhat different psychologically.

to zero length. What happens? The distance between neighboring parallel sides of the side angles decreases, these lines fall into identity, so do the corner points—and I have just the picture shown below: the point with the angular space of 360° around it, built up out of the δ's!

FIG. 146

3) Here the following question came up: What about figures in which a corner is indented, so that the angle does not show the clear structure of the side angles with the δ between? In putting the ques-

FIG. 147

tion the answer was clear: it does not matter at all; if the side of the angle turns back it has to make up for this and altogether the δ's must complete the 360°.

4) The usual method of finding the formula for the sum of the external angles of a polygon now looked strange indeed: "The sum of all the internal *and* external angles is $n \cdot 4R \ldots \Sigma i + \Sigma e = n \cdot 4R$." Therefore, the sum of the exterior angles is $n \cdot 4R$ minus the sum of the interior angles. Since the sum of the interior angles is known to be $n \cdot 2R - 4R$ on the basis of the usual proof with the triangles,[2]

[2] The sum of the angles of a triangle, 180° or 2R (two right angles), is usually

FIG. 148

we reach the formula $\Sigma e = n \cdot 4R - (n \cdot 2R - 4R)$. Carrying out the subtraction, we get: $n \cdot 4R - n \cdot 2R + 4R = n \cdot 2R + 4R$.

In this formula the $n \cdot 2R$ is the outcome of subtracting the $n \cdot 2R$ of the triangles from the $n \cdot 4R$; the 4R is the outcome of a second negation of the negative 4R in the formula for the internal angles. The terms are understood in a roundabout way with no direct relation to how the figure is closed by the angles of the polygon.[3] But meanwhile I have seen what $n \cdot 2R + 4R$ really represents, viz., the sum of the side angles, i.e., the two right angles attached to each side, $n \cdot 2R$, plus the complete revolution, 4R, the closure, accomplished by the δ's.

5) At this moment there came a curious thought: Why do we call a triangle just a triangle? Why don't we call it, for example, a quad-

Fig. 150

rangle or a hexagon? We certainly could, because in point of fact there is an angle at every point in the sides. These are not counted. Why? Is this an arbitrary matter? No. Now it is clear: at these points in the sides there are no δ's. These places contribute nothing to the breaking of the line that bounds the figure and to the return

---

derived with no reference to the triangle's being a closed figure. The usual proof of the sum of the interior angles of a polygon is the following: Inside the polygon construct n triangles, each side of the polygon forming the base of one triangle. The sum of the angles of all the triangles is $n \cdot 2R$. To get the sum of the internal

Fig. 149

angles of the polygon, subtract from $n \cdot 2R$ the contiguous angles of the triangles which lie around the middle point. The latter are 4R. Therefore $\Sigma i = n \cdot 2R - 4R$.

[3] It is true that the 4R in the formula for the internal angles is directly related to closure in the sense of the fitting together of the triangle tops; but the inner relatedness between the sum of the angles of the triangle itself and its closedness is not equally clear.

to its beginning, to the closing of the polygon by the rotation of the δ's.

6) But how about the internal angles? When I faced this question now, I had again no notion how it could be answered directly. Again a vague idea developed first: There is a complete angle of 360° around a point; also around a figure. On the *inside*, the figure is . . . a "hole"! Quickly this became clear: There must be a complete *negative* angle of 360°: internally *the side angles overlap*. The amount

Fig. 151

of this overlap represents a negative angle of rotation, − δ. The sum of these angles, when the figure closes, must be equal to a complete negative angle of 360°.

Here the reader might well ask what came out of all this. Exactly the same formula as was known before, but in a new light: the terms of the formula acquired a direct functional meaning.

And this understanding led at once to the joyful insight: If the side angles and the particular number of them are peripheral, if only the rotation of the δ's is relevant, then the same applies to any closed *curve* in a plane, to the closure of a circle, an ellipse, etc.—(I omit the derivation).

7) But the problem was still unfinished. As the solution became clear, a requirement became urgent: If this line of thought really goes to the heart of the matter, then it should also hold for *any* closed figure. It should hold for three-dimensional solids, for four-dimensional, *n*-dimensional, indeed for all closed figures . . . with the necessary changes for non-Euclidean space.

In six weeks of hard work I succeeded in actually understanding three-dimensional figures. (A year later I heard that a mathematician had found the formula for solids years ago, yet I would not have liked to miss these experiences which led to real insight.) During these weeks the problem was constantly active, it continued to work. I studied concrete solids like the cube, parts of the cube, certain pyramids, etc.; the nature of the solid angles with regard to the way, together, they are parts of a complete solid angle. During this time I developed considerable ability to visualize solid angles and to fit them together in imagination. There was no trial and error with regard to formulas, no trying of hypotheses; there was rather the realization of what happens if the solid angles of an imagined, concrete solid are put together at one point; for instance, how the angles of a cube, viewed together in the center of a sphere, make one complete solid angle;[4] what sums the angles of other solids give —parts of the cube, pyramids, parallelepipedons, etc.

There were very dramatic moments as, for instance, when a friend said, "Stop worrying so much about this. The problem is insoluble, for the sum of the angles of a pyramid varies if you alter the altitude. To be sure, it varies continuously."

8) But the process went right on. After a great deal of effort, the solution for three-dimensional solids came in a half-waking moment during the night. Although I could not recall having written anything, in the morning I found the following formula on a slip of paper:

$\Sigma e = \Sigma$ plane angles $+ \Sigma$ edge angles $+ \Sigma \delta$ $(= 1)$, where e stands for an external solid angle. Take a plane (a); break it along a straight line (b); erect normal planes to each plane (c). Between the normal "plane angles" (corresponding to the side angles, R, of

---

[4] Just as, in two dimensions, a square angle gives one-fourth of the whole angular space, all four completing it, or the angle of a regular hexagon one-third, three

FIG. 152

completing it. In general, teaching what an angle is should bring the view of the angle as part of the whole angle, or of the complete rotation together with the remainder (see Chap. Four, p. 127).

the two-dimensional figures), you have an "edge angle" (c); break this at one point (d), and you get the δ. For closure of the solid the

Fig. 153

sum of the δ's must be one complete solid angle! It was soon seen that what holds in this special case of "breaking the plane" holds generally for solid corners. If all the corners are seen as the center of a sphere, the δ's the "polar angles," must fill up the sphere. This was followed up. The corresponding solution was then reached for the sum of the inner angles, involving the solid "hole," the −1 of the sum of the δ's.

The following days were devoted to exact demonstrations, including spheres, etc.

I shall not follow up the line of my further thinking. I shall stop here in the report, with this joyful moment in which the inner relation between closure and the sum of angles became translucid in solids as in plane figures.

Summarizing:

1. The feeling of a significant interrelatedness between the structure of closed figures and the sum of their angles, and the need to grasp it in a clear fashion.

2. A primitive whole-idea of closedness and "angular space." Here was a changing of the goal: instead of looking for the internal angles, the quest for the sum of the external angles was faced, in a hazy feeling that this was structurally the simpler question. (Later this feeling found its clear justification in the process.)

3. Emphasis on a necessary step in the procedure of closing a figure brought a radical change in the meaning of an angle, the creation of the "rotating angle," the δ, through separation of what is structurally relevant to achieving closure from what is not.

4. With the view of the δ's as a real whole, the intuition was reached of the inner relation between angles and closedness. In contrast to the and-sum of the usual angles, the whole of the δ's gives the complete shape, the closure, in the uniqueness of the 360°. Here regrouping is involved.

The δ parts, separated from the side angles, were viewed as a whole. But even if one were shown the angles with the dividing lines already drawn, so that each angle consisted of three parts, one could remain structure-blind, group in the usual way (the three angles in each usual angle belonging together, and the sum of the angles still consisting of the usual angles). Here the actual grouping

Fig. 154

(the separation of the δ's from the structurally peripheral side angles which do not contribute anything to the closing) was directed by the requirement to understand the closedness of the figure. Focusing on the δ's and viewing them as a whole emphasized the structural transposability of this factor (see p. 196) with regard to the structurally peripheral number of side angles, of usual angles, of lines and corners.

5. In order to secure the envisaged result, the matter was followed up in its details, and detailed proof was given. By decreasing the sides to zero, the direct connection of the external angles with the first view of the "angular space" around a point was concretely realized.

6. A difficulty arose and was cleared up; the principle was found

to apply also to the special case in which a corner of the polygon is indented (cf. p. 198).

7. The insight reached now gave the actual reason for a customary procedure, which in itself falls short of understanding. The customary formula appeared in a new and deeper sense: the terms found a direct, clear, functional meaning.

8. Now the question of the internal angles was faced. Again a global whole-idea arose first: the idea of the complete "hole," the 360° of the sum of the negative δ's.

9. The applicability of this view broadened; it was found to encompass any closed curve in a plane. In consequence of the insight reached, a limitation in the usual view fell away.

10. The need was felt to follow the matter up: If the insight was fundamental, the relation should also be true in three-dimensional figures, etc. Orientation was first sought in solid angle sums. The material was studied in comparatively simple cases of solids. In spite of complexities, the angles were fitted together and their sums found in imagination. At first no possibility was seen of a radical, general solution.

11. The solution appeared one night—structurally clear, as in the very much simpler case of the two-dimensional figures.

The essential thing in the process was clearly the drive to get at the inner structure of the task. Again we see the working of the whole-view, reorganization, regrouping, getting at the functional meaning of parts in the whole, etc., all in the light of the structural requirements.

Each step was a step in a consistent line of thinking; there were no arbitrary steps, no blind trial and error.

That there were several steps in the procedure, that the process did not proceed easily, seems clearly to have been caused by the fact that the process had to overcome customary, in themselves clear, strong, structural factors; and that later, in three dimensions, mastery of a structurally highly complex situation had to be achieved.

CHAPTER NINE

A Discovery by Galileo

How DID Galileo make the discovery that led to the law of inertia and thus to the beginning of modern physics?

There have been numerous discussions as to how Galileo actually proceeded. The question is not entirely cleared up even now. Historically, in its details, it is a complex question. The situation in which Galileo found himself was burdened with highly complex concepts and speculations as to the nature of movements.[1] Historical interpretations differ on several points, including the extent to which the old concepts played a role in Galileo's thinking process.[2]

Discussions centered on such points as: Was Galileo's thinking governed by induction? Or by abstraction? By empirical observation and experiment or by *a priori* presuppositions? Was it his principal merit to have made qualitative observations quantitative?

If one studies the literature—the ancient treatises on physics and those of Galileo's time—one finds that one of the great features in Galileo's thinking was his ability to get such a clear, clean structural insight against the highly complex and sophisticated background.

[1] "Natural" and coerced movements were distinguished in a specific way. There was the concept of the—necessarily declining—"vis impressa" (imposed force), and speculations about the role of the medium in delaying a body's coming to rest. There were the ideas about the "natural" circular movements at constant speed, etc.

[2] Readers who are interested in the historical development may read: von E. Wohlwill, "Die Entdeckung des Beharrungsgestzes," *Zeitschrift für Völkerpsychologie und Sprachwissenschaft*, 1883, Vol. XIV, pp. 365-410; 1884, Vol. XV, pp. 70-135; Ernst Mach, *Die Mechanik in ihrer Entwicklung* (Leipzig: F. A. Brockhaus, 1908); Alexander Koyré's beautiful studies, *Etudes Galiléennes* (I, II, III) (Paris: Hermann, 1939); and, of course, first of all, the writings of Galileo himself.

I shall not attempt here a historical reconstruction. This would require a thorough discussion of much source material—and I am no historian. Besides, the printed historical material would not be enough for the psychologist, who is interested in characteristics of the growing process of thought which is not usually put down in writing. Unfortunately we cannot question Galileo himself about the actual development of the process. I should have loved to ask him about certain points in particular.

I shall try to tell the story briefly, in a way that may show some factors which seem to me essential, some lines of the beautiful process. The story that follows is, in certain respects, merely a psychological hypothesis with no claim to historical correctness, but one from which, I think, something may be learned for our problems.

I propose that the reader not only read what I am going to tell, but that he also try to think with me.

I

Here is the situation:

1. If you hold a stone in your hand and let it go, it will fall down. Heavy bodies do. The old physics said: "Heavy bodies tend toward their home, the earth."

2. If I give a push to a body, say a carriage, or if I roll a ball straight ahead on a horizontal plane, it will move, will continue moving for a while, will then come to rest—sooner if I push it gently, somewhat later if I push it hard.

This is the simplest meaning of the old *vis impressa*. "The moving body sooner or later comes to a standstill if the force which is pushing it no longer acts."

Isn't that true? It is obvious.

3. And there are, of course, several additional factors to be considered in connection with questions of movement: e.g., the size of the object, its form, the surface along which the body is moved, the presence or absence of obstacles, etc.

So we know a great many facts about movement. They are familiar to us. Do we understand them? It appears so. Do we really know how movement comes about? Do we see the principles at work?

Galileo was not satisfied with this knowledge. He asked himself:

"Do we know *how* such movements really proceed?" Driven by a desire to get at an understanding of the fundamentals, to get at the inner laws involved, Galileo said to himself: "We know that a heavy body falls, but *how* does it fall? In falling it acquires speed. The speed is greater if the distance it falls is greater. What happens to the speed as the body is falling?"

Common experience gives only a vague picture. Galileo started to make observations and experiments in the hope of finding out what happens to the speed, and whether it is governed by principles we can understand. His experimental setups were very crude compared with those that physicists developed later, but in making these observations and experiments he tried to form and to test an hypothesis. First he made a wrong guess, then he found the formula for the acceleration of a falling body. Since the speed of falling is so great that exact values are not easy to determine, Galileo, desirous of studying the question more thoroughly, had taken counsel with himself: "Could I not study this in a more convenient way? Spheres roll down an inclined surface. I shall study them. Isn't free falling simply a special case, the case of falling at an incline of 90° instead of a lesser angle?"

Studying the acceleration in the various cases he saw that acceleration decreases consistently with the angle of inclination: the order of the angle corresponds with the order of declining acceleration.

FIG. 155

The acceleration became the foremost and the central fact as he realized the principle connecting the decline of acceleration with the size of the angle.

II

Then suddenly he asked himself: "Is this not just half the picture? Is not what happens when one throws a body upward, when one pushes a sphere in the uphill direction, the symmetrical other part of the picture which repeats, like a reflection in a mirror, what we already have, and which completes the picture?"

Throw — decrease of negative acceleration (of retardation)

Fall — decrease of acceleration

FIG. 156

When a body is thrown up, we have not positive but negative acceleration. The body slows down in the course of its upward movement. But again, symmetrically with the positive acceleration of a falling body, this negative acceleration decreases as the angle of inclination diminishes from 90°, giving a closed, consistent picture.[3]

[3] Galileo had envisaged and concretely used an idea of structural dynamic symmetry in opposite events, viz., that a body rolling down an inclined plane will

FIG. 157

FIG. 158

III

But does this complete the picture? No. There is a gap. What happens when the plane is horizontal, when the angle is zero, and the body is in motion? In all cases we may start with a given velocity. What *must* consistently happen in accordance with the structure?

The positive acceleration below and the negative acceleration above decrease from the vertical cases to . . . no positive or negative acceleration, that is . . . constant movement?! If a body moves horizontally in a given direction, it will continue to move at constant velocity—for all eternity, if no external force changes its state of motion.

This is in direct contradiction to the old statement in point 2 above (p. 206). A body moving at constant velocity will never come to rest if no external hindrances are at work, regardless of whether the forces which brought about the movement were weak or strong. What an amazing conclusion! Apparently it contradicts all familiar experience, yet is required by the consistency of the structure.

Of course we cannot perform the experiment. Even if we could eliminate all external hindrances, which we cannot, observation for eternity is out of the question. On the other hand, the decreases in the change of acceleration clearly indicate a zero amount of change for this case.

Galileo's views were confirmed and provided the basis for the development of modern physics.

The modern reader is, of course, acquainted with these views. I shall illustrate with a simple familiar example. The biggest task in moving a train is at the beginning, in accelerating it from rest. Once in motion, provided tracks and wheels are smooth, less power is required of the engine to maintain the speed; the train goes almost by itself. If we now smooth the wheels and the track more and more, and study the decreasing amount of power necessary to run the train, our curves will indicate to our surprise that with the wheels

---

have to rise to the same height on an opposite inclined plane, its velocity decreasing in the same way that it had increased in rolling down. He had first envisaged such dynamic symmetry in the oscillations of the swinging lamp observed in a church at Pisa.

and track ideally smooth, offering no friction, it would require large counterforces to stop the train, to bring it to rest.[4]

What are the essentials of this process?

First: the desire to clear up, to find out what happens when a body is falling or rolling down; the desire to see whether there is an inner principle in these events; a desire to view them comprehensively at the various angles of inclination.

This centered thought on what happens to acceleration. Experimental setups came into existence through the guess that centering on the question of acceleration might bring structural clarification.

The various cases appear as parts in a well-ordered structure, showing the relation between the angles of inclination and the amount of acceleration. Each of the cases has its place in the group, and what happens in each case is understood as required by this place.

Secondly, this structure is now seen as part of a broader context: There is another complementary part, understood as symmetrical to the first, forming a whole, in which the two halves are the two big corresponding subgroups, with positive acceleration in the one, negative acceleration in the other. The whole-qualities of the two halves complete each other. They are seen in one view, in their structural symmetry, in their consistent whole-structure.

Thirdly, it appears that there is a critical place in the structure—the place of horizontal movement. The structural principle of the whole provides clear requirements for just this place. In view of these requirements it appears as the case in which no acceleration and no retardation occur—constant velocity.

Rest, then, becomes a special case of constant velocity, a case of the absence of positive or negative acceleration. Rest and constant rectilinear movement in the horizontal direction appear as structurally equivalent.

Of course operations of traditional logic are involved, such as induction, inference, formulating theorems, derivation—and obser-

[4] Compare the much more simplified description of Galileo's thought process given by Einstein and Infeld in *The evolution of physics* (New York: Simon and Schuster, 1938) pp. 5 ff.

vation and ingenious experimentation. (One of the great features in Galileo's thinking was the way he combined strict reasoning, mathematical procedure, with the use of experiment to test the theoretical idea or to answer a theoretical problem.) But all these operations function in their place in the whole process. The process itself is governed by the recentering which originates in the desire to get comprehensive insight. It brings transformation, seeing things as parts of a new, clear structure.

Fundamental changes in concepts were involved in the transition from the old view to the new. The meanings of the concepts about motion were radically changed in their place, role, and function. The inner connections were viewed in an entirely new structure; a new grouping and dividing took place.[5]

For example, previously, rest and certain "natural" circular movements were fundamentally separated from, opposed to, the other movements. Now rest and constant rectilinear movement are seen together, as structurally equivalent, and separate from, opposed to positively or negatively accelerated movements.

Rising and falling of bodies are viewed together as cases of acceleration in the symmetrical division of the whole picture. Free falling and free rising are viewed as special cases of the whole group of movements in any straight direction.

The end of a movement is no longer seen as the necessary outcome of the diminishing, disappearing effects of *vis impressa* (imposed force). It is now seen in a basically different way: the movement is stopped externally by friction.

Friction is no longer just one of several factors to be considered in movement; it now has a role opposite to that of inertia. While previously the assumption had been that rectilinear motion comes to an end with or without friction, due to the natural extinction of *vis impressa*, the new view looks at friction as the fundamental cause of the limitation of motion.

[5] For the sake of brevity I shall use some formulations that were made only later in their full generality, but that were somehow implied or already foreseen in Galileo's views. Galileo himself was extremely cautious in his formulations.

Galileo's formulation concerns movement in the horizontal. He also applied the principle to movements in other directions. He did not generalize it in the form we now know as the law of inertia, but others did so promptly. We are not sure whether he realized the generality of the principle.

Force appears essentially as something determining acceleration. Everything gets its new meaning by virtue of its role and function in the new structure.

The new concepts opened up a most marvelous vista for understanding a huge number of phenomena. They made possible an entirely new understanding of the celestial movements. Newton subsequently could view these movements as generated by inertia, on the one hand, tending toward rectilinear movement, and by gravitation, on the other.

Productive processes are often of this nature: In the desire to get at real understanding, requestioning and investigation start. A certain region in the field becomes crucial, is focused; but it does not become isolated. A new, a deeper structural view of the situation develops, involving changes in the functional meaning, the grouping, etc., of the items. Directed by what is required by the structure of a situation for a crucial region, one is led to a reasonable prediction, which —like the other parts of the structure—calls for verification, direct or indirect.

Two directions are involved: getting a whole consistent picture, and seeing what the structure of the whole requires for the parts.

Telling the story this way, I often had delightful experiences, seeing what vivid, genuine interest was aroused, watching dramatic things happen to the class, seeing how, at the critical point, some students exclaimed: "Now I see!" For them it was a change from knowing a number of things to having their eyes really opened to a deeper understanding in a comprehensive view.

CHAPTER TEN

Einstein: The Thinking That Led to the Theory of Relativity

WHAT were the decisive steps in the development of Einstein's theory of relativity? Although this is quite a task, I shall try to make them clear to the reader. A number of issues, such as the question of the ether, the relations to the principles of Galilean "relativity," will be excluded from this discussion. The field which Einstein faced in this gigantic process of thought was very large, since it involved most of the fundamental topics of modern physics, difficult issues unfamiliar to those not acquainted with the complexity of modern physics. Although the following sketch will of necessity be condensed, I hope the reader will gain an insight into the nature of the decisive steps.

Those were wonderful days, beginning in 1916, when for hours and hours I was fortunate enough to sit with Einstein, alone in his study, and hear from him the story of the dramatic developments which culminated in the theory of relativity. During those long discussions I questioned Einstein in great detail about the concrete events in his thought. He described them to me, not in generalities, but in a discussion of the genesis of each question.

Einstein's original papers give his results. They do not tell the story of his thinking. In the course of one of his books he did report some steps in the process. I have quoted him in the proper places in this chapter.

The drama developed in a number of acts.

Act I. The Beginning of the Problem

The problem started when Einstein was sixteen years old, a pupil in the Gymnasium (Aarau, Kantonschule). He was not an especially good student, unless he did productive work on his own account. This he did in physics and mathematics, and consequently he knew more about these subjects than his classmates. It was then that the great problem really started to trouble him. He was intensely concerned with it for seven years; from the moment, however, that he came to question the customary concept of time (see Act VII), it took him only five weeks to write his paper on relativity—although at this time he was doing a full day's work at the Patent Office.

The process started in a way that was not very clear, and is therefore difficult to describe—in a certain state of being puzzled. First came such questions as: What if one were to run after a ray of light? What if one were riding on the beam? If one were to run after a ray of light as it travels, would its velocity thereby be decreased? If one were to run fast enough, would it no longer move at all? . . . To young Einstein this seemed strange.

The same light ray, for another man, would have another velocity. What *is* "the velocity of light"? If I have it in relation to something, this value does not hold in relation to something else which is itself in motion. (Puzzling to think that under certain conditions light should go more quickly in one direction than another.) If this is correct, then consequences would also have to be drawn with reference to the earth, which is moving. There would then be a way of finding out by experiments with light whether one is in a moving system! Einstein's interest was captured by this; he tried to find methods by which it would be possible to establish or to measure the movement of the earth—and he learned only later that physicists had already made such experiments. His wish to design such experiments was always accompanied by some doubt that the thing was really so; in any case, he felt that he must try to decide.

He said to himself: "I know what the velocity of a light ray is in relation to a system. What the situation is if another system is taken into account seems to be clear, but the consequences are very puzzling."

Act II. *Light Determines a State of Absolute Rest?*

Would operations with light lead to conclusions different in this respect from conclusions from mechanical operations?[1] From the point of view of mechanics there seems to be no absolute rest; from the point of view of light there does seem to be. What of the velocity of light? One must relate it to something. Here the trouble starts. Light determines a state of absolute rest? However, one does not know whether or not one is in a moving system. Young Einstein had reached some kind of conviction that one cannot notice whether or not one is in a moving system; it seemed to him deeply founded in nature that there is no "absolute movement." The central point here became the conflict between the view that light velocity seems to presuppose a state of "absolute rest" and the absence of this possibility in the other physical processes.

Back of all this there had to be something that was not yet grasped, not yet understood. Uneasiness about this characterized young Einstein's state of mind at this time.

When I asked him whether, during this period, he had already had some idea of the constancy of light velocity, independent of the movement of the reference system, Einstein answered decidedly: "No, it was just curiosity. That the velocity of light could differ depending upon the movement of the observer was somehow characterized by doubt. Later developments increased that doubt." Light did not seem to answer when one put such questions. Also light, just as mechanical processes, seemed to know nothing of a state of absolute movement or of absolute rest. This was interesting, exciting.

Light was to Einstein something very fundamental. At the time of his studies at the Gymnasium, the ether was no longer being thought of as something mechanical, but as "the mere carrier of electrical phenomena."

[1] Cf. below, Act IX.
The layman, not acquainted with modern physics, will not be able to follow the topics under II and III in my brief formulations. While these topics were important in the process, it does not seem absolutely necessary to understand them fully in order to follow the later steps within the positive solution. The lay reader may therefore pass on to Act IV.

Act III. Work on the One Alternative

Serious work started. In the Maxwell equations of the electromagnetic field, the velocity of light plays an important role; and it is constant. If the Maxwell equations are valid with regard to one system, they are not valid in another. They would have to be changed. When one tries to do so in such a way that the velocity of light is not assumed to be constant, the matter becomes very complicated. For years Einstein tried to clarify the problem by studying and trying to change the Maxwell equations. He did not succeed in formulating these equations in such a way as to meet the difficulties satisfactorily. He tried hard to see clearly the relation between the velocity of light and the facts of movement in mechanics. But in whatever way he tried to unify the question of mechanical movement with the electromagnetic phenomena, he got into difficulties. One of his questions was: What would happen to the Maxwell equations and to their agreement with the facts if one were to assume that the velocity of light depends on the motion of the source of the light?

The conviction grew that in these respects the situation with regard to light could not be different from the situation with regard to mechanical processes (no absolute movement, no absolute rest). What took him so much time was this: he could not doubt that the velocity of light is constant and at the same time get a satisfactory theory of electromagnetic phenomena.

Act IV. Michelson's Result and Einstein

The famous Michelson experiment confronted physicists with a disconcerting result. If you are running away from a body that is rushing toward you, you will expect it to hit you somewhat later than if you are standing still. If you run toward it, it will hit you earlier. Michelson did just this in measurements of the velocity of light. He compared the time light takes to travel in two pipes if these pipes meet at right angles to each other, and if one lies in the direction of the movement of the earth, while the other is vertical to it. Since the first pipe, in its lengthwise direction, is moving with the movement of the earth, the light traveling in it ought to reach the receding end of this pipe later than the light in the other pipe reaches *its* end.

FIG. 159

The arrows above indicate the directions in which the
light is travelling. The movement of the earth, and so of
the whole apparatus, is toward the right.

Actually the arrangement was more intricate. There was at the vertex
angle of the two pipes a common mirror, and there were mirrors at
the ends. In both pipes light rays from a common source were moving
backward and forward, reflected by the mirrors. The difference in time
was to be measured by means of an interference effect at the common
mirror. (The reader may be inclined to assume that, with the light
rays moving backward and forward, the difference introduced by the
movement of the earth would be canceled. This is not the case, as
some mathematical deliberation will show.) The difference could not
escape observation because the measurement by interference was suffi-
ciently delicate to reveal the amount as established by mathematical
analysis.

No difference was found. The experiment was repeated, and the
negative result was clearly confirmed.

The result of the Michelson experiment in no way fitted the fundamental ideas of the physicists. In fact the result contradicted all their
reasonable expectations.

For Einstein, Michelson's result was not a fact for itself. It had its
place within his thoughts as they had thus far developed. Therefore,
when Einstein read about these crucial experiments made by physicists, and the finest ones made by Michelson, their results were no
surprise to him, although very important and decisive. They seemed
to confirm rather than to undermine his ideas. But the matter was not
yet entirely cleared up. Precisely how does this result come about?

The problem was an obsession with Einstein although he saw no way to a positive solution.

Act V. The Lorentz Solution

Not only Einstein was troubled; many physicists were. Lorentz, the famous Dutch physicist, had developed a theory which formulated mathematically what had occurred in the Michelson experiment. In order to explain this fact it seemed necessary to him, as it had to Fitzgerald, to introduce an auxiliary hypothesis: he assumed that the entire apparatus used in the measurement underwent a small contraction in the direction of the earth's motion. According to this theory, the pipe in the direction of the movement of the earth was changed in length, while the other pipe suffered only a change in width and the length remained unaffected. The contraction had to be assumed to be just the amount needed to compensate for the effect of the earth's motion on the traveling of the light. This was an ingenious hypothesis.

There was now a fine, positive formula, determining the Michelson results mathematically, and an auxiliary hypothesis, the contraction. The difficulty was "removed." But for Einstein the situation was no less troublesome than before; he felt the auxiliary hypothesis to be a hypothesis *ad hoc*, which did not go to the heart of the matter.

Act VI. Re-examination of the Theoretical Situation

Einstein said to himself: "Except for that result, the whole situation in the Michelson experiment seems absolutely clear; all the factors involved and their interplay seem clear. But *are* they really clear? Do I really understand the structure of the whole situation, especially in relation to the crucial result?" During this time he was often depressed, sometimes in despair, but driven by the strongest vectors.

In his passionate desire to understand or, better, to see whether the situation was really clear to him, he faced the essentials in the Michelson situation again and again, especially the central point: the measurement of the speed of light under conditions of movement of the whole set in the crucial direction.

This simply would not become clear. He felt a gap somewhere without being able to clarify it, or even to formulate it. He felt that the trouble went deeper than the contradiction between Michelson's actual and the expected result.

He felt that a certain region in the structure of the whole situation was in reality not as clear to him as it should be, although it had hitherto been accepted without question by everyone, including himself. His proceeding was somewhat as follows: There is a time measurement while the crucial movement is taking place. "Do I see clearly," he asked himself, "the relation, the inner connection between the two, between the measurement of time and that of movement? Is it clear to me how the measurement of time works in such a situation?" And for him this was not a problem with regard to the Michelson experiment only, but a problem in which more basic principles were at stake.

Act VII. *Positive Steps toward Clarification*

It occurred to Einstein that time measurement involves simultaneity. What of simultaneity in such a movement as this? To begin with, what of simultaneity of events in different places?

He said to himself: "If two events occur in one place, I understand clearly what simultaneity means. For example, I see these two balls hit the identical goal at the same time. But . . . am I really clear about what simultaneity means when it refers to events in two different places? What does it mean to say that this event occurred in my room at the same time as another event in some distant place? Surely I can use the concept of simultaneity for different places in the same way as for one and the same place—but can I? Is it as clear to me in the former as it is in the latter case? . . . It is not!"

For what now followed in Einstein's thinking we can fortunately report paragraphs from his own writing.[2] He wrote them in the form of a discussion with the reader. What Einstein here says to the reader is similar to the way his thinking proceeded: "Lightning strikes in two distant places. I assert that both bolts struck simultaneously. If now I ask you, dear reader, whether this assertion makes sense, you will answer, 'Yes, certainly'. But if I urge you to explain to me more clearly

[2] A. Einstein, *Über die spezielle und die allgemeine Relativitätstheorie* (Braunschweig, 1916) pp. 14 ff. (Editors' note. The passages from Einstein quoted in this chapter were translated by Max Wertheimer.)

the meaning of this assertion, you will find after some deliberation that answering this question is not as simple as it at first appears.

"After a time you will perhaps think of the following answer: 'The meaning of the assertion is in itself clear and needs no further clarification. It would need some figuring out, to be sure, if you were to put me to the task of deciding by observation whether in a concrete case the two effects were actually simultaneous or not.' "

I now insert an illustration which Einstein offered in a discussion. Suppose somebody uses the word "hunchback." If this concept is to have any clear meaning, there must be some way of finding out whether or not a man has a hunched back. If I could conceive of no possibility of reaching such a decision, the word would have no real meaning for me.

"Similarly," Einstein continued, "with the concept of simultaneity. The concept really exists for the physicist only when in a concrete case there is some possibility of deciding whether the concept is or is not applicable. Such a definition of simultaneity is required, therefore, as would provide a method for deciding. As long as this requirement is not fulfilled, I am deluding myself as physicist (to be sure, as non-physicist too!) if I believe that the assertion of simultaneity has a real meaning. (Until you have truly agreed to this, dear reader, do not read any further.)

"After some deliberation you may make the following proposal to prove whether the two shafts of lightning struck simultaneously. Put a set of two mirrors, at an angle of 90° to each other ($\diagdown\diagup$), at the exact halfway mark between the two light effects, station yourself in front of them, and observe whether or not the light effects strike the mirrors simultaneously."

Simultaneity in distant places here gets its meaning by being based on clear simultaneity in an identical place.[3]

All these steps came not by way of isolated clarification of this special question, but as part of the attempt to understand the inner connection that was mentioned above, the problem of the measurement of speed during the crucial movement. In the mirror situation

[3] This involves other problems which we shall here ignore. The reader is referred to Einstein, *Über die spezielle und allgemeine Relativitätstheorie*, pp. 15-16.

this means simply: What happens if, in the time during which the light rays approach my mirrors, I move with them, away from one source of light and toward the other? Obviously, if the two events appeared simultaneous to a man at rest they would not then appear so to me, who am moving with my mirrors. His statement and mine must differ. We see then that our statements about simultaneity *involve essentially reference to movement of the observer*. If simultaneity in distant places is to have real meaning, I must explicitly take into account the question of movement, and in comparing my judgments with those of another observer, I have to take into account the relative movement between him and me. When dealing with "simultaneity in different places" I must refer to the relative movement of the observer.

I repeat: suppose that I with my mirrors am traveling in a train going in a straight line at a constant velocity. Two shafts of lightning strike in the distance, one near the engine, the other near the rear end of the train, my double mirror being right in the middle between the two. As a passenger I use the train as my frame of reference, I relate these events to the train. Let us assume that just at the critical moment when the lightning strikes, a man is standing beside the tracks, likewise with double mirrors, and that his place at that moment coincides with mine. What would my observations be and what would his be?

"If we say that the bolts of lightning are simultaneous with regard to the tracks, *this now means*: the rays of light coming from two equidistant points meet simultaneously at the mirrors of the man on the track. But if the place of my moving mirrors coincides with his mirrors at the moment the lightning strikes, the rays will not meet exactly simultaneously in my mirrors because of my movement.

"Events which are simultaneous in relation to the track are not simultaneous in relation to the train, and vice versa. Each frame of reference, each system of coordinates therefore has *its special time*; a statement about a time has real meaning only when the frame of reference is stated, to which the assertion of time refers."[4]

It has always seemed simple and clear that a statement about the "time difference" between two events is a "fact," independent of

[4] A. Einstein, *op. cit.*, pp. 31-32.

other factors, such as movement of the system. But, in actual fact, is not the thesis that "the time difference between two events is independent of the movement of the system" an arbitrary assumption? It did not hold, as we saw, for simultaneity in different places, and therefore it cannot hold even for the length of a second. To measure a time interval, we must use a clock or the equivalent of a clock, and look for certain coincidences at the beginning and at the end of the interval. Therefore the trouble with simultaneity is involved. We cannot dogmatically assume that the time which a certain event takes in relation to the train is the same as the time in relation to the track.

This applies also to the measurement of distances in space! If I try to measure exactly the length of a car by marking its end points on the roadbed, I must take care, when I have made my mark at one end, that the car does not move before I come to the other end! Unless I have explicitly given attention to this possibility, my measurements will be misleading.

I must therefore conclude that in every such measurement reference must be made to the movement of the system. For the observer within the moving system will get results which differ from those of an observer in another frame of reference. "Every system has its special time and space values. A time or space judgment has sense only if we know the system with reference to which the judgment was made." We must change the old view: the measurements of time intervals and of distances in space are *not* independent of the conditions of movement of the system in relation to the observer.

The old view had been a time-honored "truth." Einstein, seeing that it was questionable, came to the conclusion that space and time measurements depend on the movement of the system.

Act VIII. *Invariants and Transformation*

What followed was determined by two vectors which simultaneously tended toward the same question.

1. The system of reference may vary; it can be chosen arbitrarily. But in order to reach physical realities, I have to get rid of such arbitrariness. The basic laws must be independent of arbitrarily chosen co-ordinates. If one wants to get a description of physical events, the basic laws of physics must be invariant with regard to such changes.

Here it becomes clear that one might adequately call Einstein's theory of relativity just the opposite, an absolute theory.

2. Insight into the interdependence of time measurement and movement is certainly not enough in itself. What is now needed is a transformation formula that answers this question: "How does one find the place and time values of an event in relation to one moving system, if one knows the places and times as measured in another? Or better, how does one find the transformation from one system to another when they move in relation to each other?"

What would be the direct way? In order to proceed realistically, I would have to base the transformation on an assumption with regard to some physical realities which could be used as invariants.

The reader may think back to an old historical situation. Physicists in past ages tried to construct a *perpetuum mobile*. After many attempts which did not succeed, the question suddenly arose: how would physics look if nature were basically such as to make a *perpetuum mobile* impossible? This involved an enormous change, which recentered the whole field.

Similarly there arose in Einstein the following question, which was inspired by his early ideas mentioned in Acts II and III. How would physics look if, by nature, measurements of the velocity of light would under all conditions have to lead to the identical value? Here is the needed invariant! (Thesis of the basic constancy of the velocity of light.)

In terms of the desired transformation, this means: "Can a relation between the place and time of events in systems which move linearly to each other be so conceived that the velocity of light becomes a constant?"

Eventually Einstein reached the answer: "Yes!" The answer consisted of concrete and definite transformation formulas for distances in time and space, formulas that differed characteristically from the old Galilean transformation formulas.

3. In the discussions I had with Einstein in 1916 I put this question to him: "How did you come to choose just the velocity of light as a constant? Was this not arbitrary?"

Of course it was clear that one important consideration was the empirical experiments which showed no variation in the velocity of light. "But did you choose this arbitrarily," I asked, "simply to fit in with these experiments and with the Lorentz transformation?" Einstein's first reply was that we are entirely free in choosing axioms. "There is no such difference as you just implied," he said, "between reasonable and arbitrary axioms. The only virtue of axioms is to furnish fundamental propositions from which one can derive conclusions that fit the facts." This is a formulation that plays a great role in present theoretical discussions, and about which most theorists seem to be in agreement. But then Einstein himself smilingly proceeded to give me a very nice example of an unreasonable axiom: "One could of course choose, say, the velocity of sound instead of light. It would be reasonable, however, to select not the velocity of just 'any' process, but of an 'outstanding' process. . . ." Questions like the following had occurred to Einstein: Is the speed of light perhaps the fastest possible? Is it perhaps impossible to accelerate any movement beyond the speed of light? As velocity increases, progressively greater forces are required to increase it still further. Perhaps the force required to increase a velocity beyond the velocity of light is infinite?

It was marvelous to hear in Einstein's descriptions how these bold questions and expectations had taken shape in him. It was new, unthought of before, that the velocity of light might be the greatest possible velocity, that an attempt to go beyond that limit would require forces infinitely great.

If these assumptions brought clarity into the system, and if they were proved by experiment, then it would make good sense to take the velocity of light as the basic constant. (Cf. the absolute zero of temperature which is reached when the molecular movements in an ideal gas approach zero.)

4. The derivations which Einstein reached from his transformation formulas showed mathematical coincidence with the Lorentz transformation. The contraction hypothesis had therefore been in the right direction, only now it was no longer an arbitrary auxiliary hypothesis, but the outcome of improved insight, a logically necessary derivation from the improved view of fundamental physical entities. The contraction was not an absolute event, but a result of the relativity of measurements. It was not determined by a "movement in itself which possesses no real sense for us, but only by a movement with reference to the chosen observation system."

Act IX. On Movement, on Space, a Thought Experiment

The last statement throws new light on the changes in thinking which were already involved in the earlier steps. "By the motion of a body we always mean its change of position in relation to a second body," to a framework, or a system. If there is one body alone, it makes no sense to ask or to try to state whether it is moving or not. If there are two, we can state only whether they are approaching or moving away from each other, but, so long as there are only two, it makes no sense to ask, or to try to state, whether one is turning around the other; the essential in movement is change of position in relation to another object, a framework, or a system.

But is there not *one* outstanding system in regard to which there is *absolute* movement of a body, "the" space (Newtonian space, the space of the ether), the box in which all movement takes place?

Here I may mention something that happened not just at this point in the development of the process, but may illustrate what was really going on. It transcends the problems of the special theory of relativity: Is there no proof of the reality of such an outstanding system? A famous experiment of Newton's had been used as proof: When a sphere of oil rotates it becomes flattened. This is a real, physical, observable fact, apparently caused by an "absolute" movement.

But is this really a demonstration of such an absolute movement? It seems so certainly; but is it actually, if we think it through? In reality we have not a body moving alone in absolute space, but a body that moves within our fixed-star firmament. Is the flattening of that sphere perhaps an outcome of the movement of the sphere relative to the surrounding stars? What would happen if we took a very huge iron wheel, with a small hole at the center, if we suspended in this hole a little sphere of oil, and then rotated the wheel? Perhaps the little sphere would again become flattened. Then the flattening would have nothing to do with the rotation in an absolute space box; rather it would be determined by the systems moving in relation to each other, the big wheel or the firmament on the one hand and the little sphere of oil on the other.

Of course rotation already transcends the region of the so-called special relativity of Einstein. It became basic in the problem of the general theory of relativity.

Act X. *Questions for Observation and Experiment*

Einstein was at heart a physicist. Thus all these developments aimed at real, concrete, experimental problems. As soon as he reached clarification he concentrated on the point: "Is it possible to find crucial physical questions to be answered in experiments that will decide whether these new theses are 'true'; whether they fit facts better, give better predictions of physical events than the old theses?"

He found a number of such crucial experiments, some of which physicists could and later did carry out.

II

In actual fact, the problem leads on: it led in Einstein's mind to the problems of the general theory of relativity. But let us stop with the story here and ask ourselves: What were the decisive characteristics of this thinking?

The physicist is interested in the relation of Einstein's theory to established facts, in experimental proof, in the consequences for further development, in the mathematical formulas which follow from the theory of relativity in the various parts of physics.

The theorist of knowledge is interested in the ideas of space, time, and matter, in the "relativistic" character of the theory (with all the wrong consequences in the direction of philosophical, sociological, or ethical relativism drawn by others), in the problem of "testability" which played such an important role in Einstein's dealing with simultaneity (and later in the developments of operationalism).

The psychologist, who is concerned with the problems of thinking, wants to realize what went on psychologically.

If we were to describe the process in the way of traditional logic, we would state numerous operations, like making abstractions, stating syllogisms, formulating axioms and general formulas, stating contradictions, deriving consequences by combining axioms, confronting facts with these consequences, and so forth.

Such a procedure is certainly good if one wishes to test each of the steps with regard to its logical correctness. Einstein himself was passionately interested in logical correctness, logical validity.

But what do we get if we follow such a procedure? We get an aggregate, a concatenation of a large number of operations, syllogisms, etc. Is this aggregate an adequate picture of what has happened? What many logicians do, the way they think, is somehow like this: A man facing a work of architecture, a fine building, focuses, in order to understand it, on the single bricks and also on the way in which they are cemented by the mortar. What he has at the end is not the building at all but a survey of the bricks and of their connections.[5]

In order to get at the real picture, we have to ask: How did the operations arise, how did they enter into the situation, what was their function within the actual process? Did they just drop in? Was the process a chain of happy accidents? Was the solution a consequence of trial and error, of mathematical guesswork? Why just these operations? No doubt there were other possibilities at some points. Why was Einstein moving in just this direction? How did it come about that after he made one step, he followed with just that other step?

I shall mention one specific point: How did the new axioms arise? Did Einstein just try any axioms of which certain ones then actually happened to work? Did he formulate some propositions, put them together, and observe what happened until eventually he was fortunate enough to find a proper set? Did such propositions leap into the picture accidentally, and did the changes in the role, place, and function of the items, did their new interrelatedness appear merely as derived consequences?

The technique of axioms is a very useful tool. It is one of the most efficient techniques so far invented in logic and mathematics; a few general propositions provide all that is needed in order to derive the details. One can deal with a gigantic sum of facts, with huge numbers of propositions, by substituting for them a few sentences which in a formal sense are equivalent to all that knowledge. Some great discoveries in modern mathematics became possible only because this extremely simplifying technique was at hand. Einstein, too, used this tool in the accounts which he gave of his theory of relativity.

[5] "I am not sure," Einstein said once in this context, "whether there can be a way of really understanding the miracle of thinking. Certainly you are right in trying to get at a deeper understanding of what really goes on in a thinking process. . . ."

But, to repeat, the question for the psychologist is: Were these axioms introduced before the structural requirements,[6] the structural changes of the situation were envisaged? Was it not the other way around? Surely, Einstein's thought did not put ready-made axioms or mathematical formulas together. The axioms were not the beginning but the outcome of what was going on. Before they came into the picture as formulated propositions, the situation as to the velocity of light and related topics had for a long time been structurally questionable to him, had in certain respects become inadequate, was in a state of transition. The axioms were only a matter of later formulation —after the real thing, the main discovery, had happened.[7]

When we proceed with an analysis in the sense of traditional logic, we easily forget that actually all the operations were parts of a unitary and beautifully consistent picture, that they developed as parts within one line of thinking; that they arose, functioned, and had their meaning within the whole process as the situation, its structure, its needs and demands were faced. In trying to grasp the structure of this great

[6] In our discussions Einstein focused on the material content of the steps. He did not use the terms of the preceding sentences of the text, terms which follow from the structural approach of this book.

[7] In this respect I wish to report some characteristic remarks of Einstein himself. Before the discovery that the crucial point, the solution, lay in the concept of time, more particularly in that of simultaneity, axioms played no role in the thought process—of this Einstein is sure. (The very moment he saw the gap, and realized the relevance of simultaneity, he knew this to be the crucial point for the solution.) But even afterward, in the final five weeks, it was not the axioms that came first. "No really productive man thinks in such a paper fashion," said Einstein. "The way the two triple sets of axioms are contrasted in the Einstein-Infeld book is not at all the way things happened in the process of actual thinking. This was merely a later formulation of the subject matter, just a question of how the thing could afterwards best be written. The axioms express essentials in a condensed form. Once one has found such things one enjoys formulating them in that way; but in this process they did not grow out of any manipulation of axioms."

He added, "These thoughts did not come in any verbal formulation. I very rarely think in words at all. A thought comes, and I may try to express it in words afterward." When I remarked that many report that their thinking is always in words, he only laughed. I once told Einstein of my impression that "direction" is an important factor in thought processes. To this he said, "Such things were very strongly present. During all those years there was a feeling of direction, of going straight toward something concrete. It is, of course, very hard to express that feeling in words; but it was decidedly the case, and clearly to be distinguished from later considerations about the rational form of the solution. Of course, behind such a direction there is always something logical; but I have it in a kind of survey, in a way visually."

line of thinking, the reader may find himself at a loss in view of the wealth of events, of the breadth of the situation. What, then, were the decisive steps?

Let us recapitulate briefly.

First there was what we may call the foreperiod. Einstein was puzzled by the question, first, of the velocity of light when the observer is in motion. He considered, secondly, the consequences as to the question of "absolute rest." Thirdly, he then tried to make one alternative workable (is the velocity of light in Maxwell's equations a variable?), and obtained a negative result. There was, fourth, the Michelson experiment which confirmed the other alternative—and, fifth, the Lorentz-Fitzgerald hypothesis, which did not seem to go to the root of the trouble.

So far everything, including the meaning and structural role of time, space, measurement, light, etc., was understood in terms of traditional physics—structure I.

In this troubled situation the question arose: Is this structure itself, in which the Michelson result seems contradictory, really clear to me? This was the revolutionary moment. Einstein felt that the contradiction should be viewed without prejudice, that the time-honored structure should be requestioned. Was this structure I adequate? Was it clear just with regard to the critical point—the question of light in relation to the question of movement? Was it clear in the situation of the Michelson experiment? All these questions were asked in a passionate effort to understand. And then the procedure became more specific in one step after another.

How was the velocity of light to be measured in a moving system?

How was time to be measured under these circumstances?

What does simultaneity mean in such a system?

But, then, what does simultaneity mean if the term is referred to different places?

The meaning of simultaneity was clear if two events occur in the same place. But Einstein was suddenly struck by the fact that it was *not* equally clear for events in distant places. Here was a gap in any real understanding. He saw: It is blind simply to apply the customary meaning of simultaneity to these other cases. If simultaneity is to have a real meaning, we must raise the question of its factual recognition so that in concrete cases we can tell whether or not the term applies. (Clearly, this was a fundamental logical problem.)

The meaning of simultaneity in general had to be based on the clear simultaneity in the case of spatial coincidence. But this required that in every case of different location of two events the relative movement be taken into account. Thus the meaning, the structural role of simultaneity in its relation to movement, underwent a radical change.

Immediately, corresponding requirements follow for the measurement of time in general, for the meaning, say, of a second, and for the measurement of space, since they must now depend upon relative movement. As a result, the concepts of time-flow, of space, and of the measurement both of time and space changed their meaning radically.

At this point the introduction of the observer and his system of co-ordinates seemed to introduce a fundamentally arbitrary or subjective factor. "But the reality," Einstein felt, "cannot be so arbitrary and subjective." In his desire to get rid of this arbitrary element and, at the same time, to get a concrete transformation formula between various systems, he realized that a basic invariant was needed, some factor that remains unaffected by the transition from one system to another. Obviously, both demands went in the same direction.

This led to the decisive step—the introduction of the velocity of light as the invariant. How would physics look if recentered with this as a starting point? Bold consequences followed one after another, and a new structure of physics was the consequence.

When Einstein reached the concrete transformation formula on the basis of this invariant, the Lorentz transformation appeared as a derivation—but now it was understood in a deeper, entirely new way, as a necessary formulation within the new structure of physics. The Michelson result, too, was now seen in an entirely new light, as a necessary result when the interplay of all relative measurements within the moving system was taken into account. Not the result was troublesome—he had felt that from the very beginning—but the behavior of the various items in the situation before finding the solution. With the deeper understanding of these items the result was required.

The picture was now improved. Einstein could proceed to the question of experimental verification.

In the briefest formulation: In a passionate desire for clearness, Einstein squarely faced the relation between the velocity of light and the movement of a system, and confronted the theoretical structure of classical physics and the Michelson result.

A part-region in this field became crucial and was subjected to a radical examination.

Under this scrutiny a great gap was discovered (in the classical treatment of time).

The necessary steps for dealing with this difficulty were realized.

As a result, the meaning of all the items involved underwent a change.

When a last arbitrariness in the situation had been eliminated, a new structure of physics crystallized.

Plans were made to subject the new system to experimental test.

Radical structural changes were involved in the process, changes with regard to separateness and inner relatedness, grouping, centering, etc.; thereby deepening, changing the meaning of the items involved, their structural role, place, and function in the transition from structure I to structure II. It may be advisable to explain once more in what sense Einstein's achievement meant a change of structure.

1) In the Michelson situation—as in classical physics generally—time had been regarded as an independent variable and, therefore, as an independent tool in the business of measurement, entirely separate from, in no way functionally interdependent with the movements that were involved in that observational situation. Accordingly, the nature of time had been of no interest with regard to the apparently paradoxical result.

In Einstein's thought there arose an intimate relationship between time-values and the physical events themselves. Thus the role of time within the structure of physics was fundamentally altered.

This radical change was first clearly envisaged in the consideration of simultaneity. In a way, simultaneity split in two: the clear simultaneity of events in a given place and, related to it, but related by means of specific physical events, the simultaneity of events in different places, particularly under conditions of movement of the system.

2) As a consequence, space-values also changed their meaning and their role in the structure of physics. In the traditional view they, too,

had been entirely separated from, independent of time and of physical events. Now an intimate relation was established. Space was no longer an empty and wholly indifferent container of physical facts. Space geometry became integrated with the dimension of time in a four-dimensional system, which in turn formed a new unitary structure with actual physical occurrences.

3) The velocity of light had so far been one velocity among many. Although the highest velocity known to the physicist, it had played the same role as other velocities. It had been fundamentally unrelated to the way in which time and space are measured. Now it was considered as closely bound up with time- and space-values, and as a fundamental fact in physics as a whole. Its role changed from that of a particular fact among many to that of a central issue in the system.

Many more items could be mentioned which changed their meaning in the process, such as mass and energy, which now proved to be closely related. But it will not be necessary to discuss further particulars.

In appraising these transformations we must not forget that they took place in view of a gigantic given system. Every step had to be taken against a very strong gestalt—the traditional structure of physics, which fitted an enormous number of facts, apparently so flawless, so clear that any local change was bound to meet with the resistance of the whole strong and well-articulated structure. This was probably the reason why it took so long a time—seven years—until the crucial advance was made.

One could imagine that some of the necessary changes occurred to Einstein by chance, in a procedure of trial and error.[8] Scrutiny of Einstein's thought always showed that when a step was taken this happened because it was required. Quite generally, if one knows how Einstein thought, one knows that any blind and fortuitous procedure was foreign to his mind.

The only point at which there could have been some doubt in this respect was the introduction of the constancy of light velocity in Einstein's general transformation formulas. In a thinker of lesser

[8] In Act III, when Einstein examined whether a particular alternative would work, he actually did try several procedures. But although these attempts did not lead to a solution, they were by no means blind. At that stage it was wholly reasonable to test such possibilities.

stature this could have happened through mere tentative generalization of the Lorentz formula. But actually the essential step was not reached in this fashion; there was no mathematical guesswork in it.

In late years Einstein often told me about the problems on which he was working at the time. There was never a blind step. When he dropped any direction, it was only because he realized that it would introduce ununderstandable, arbitrary factors. Sometimes it happened that Einstein was faced with the difficulty that the mathematical tools were not far enough developed to allow a real clarification; nonetheless he would not lose sight of his problem and would often succeed in finding a way eventually, in which the seemingly insuperable difficulties could be surmounted.

Dynamics and Logic of Productive Thinking

I SHOULD love to go on telling of this exploratory trip, reporting further examples and the discussions to which they gave rise. But here I must come to a stop. I think that the few examples discussed may suffice for a first introduction. In these examples, in the concrete way of dealing with them, the reader will have seen some steps toward clarification, methods for deepening the problem, and the main lines of a new approach. Some points may be summarized briefly.

First, we have found what, in contrast to other processes, we may call genuine, fine, clean, direct, productive processes—better than some might have expected. It seems not to be true that men do not like or are generally unable to think that way. This is a result that may be deeply appreciated. Of course there are often strong external factors working against those processes as, e.g., blind habits, certain kinds of school drill, bias, or special interests.

Second, in these processes we found factors and operations at work —essential to thinking—which had not been realized by the traditional approaches, or had been neglected by them. The very nature of these operations, e.g., of grouping, of centering, of reorganization, etc., adequate to the structure of the situation (see Table III, pp. 235-236) is alien to the gist of the traditional approaches and to the operations which they consider.

Third, the features and operations described are of a characteristic nature: they are not piecemeal, they are related to whole-characteristics, they function with reference to such characteristics, determined by structural requirements for a sensible situation. In the context the items, data, relations, etc., arise and function as parts in their place and role within the whole, under the same dynamic requirements.

Fourth, while it is true that operations considered in the traditional interpretations are involved in the process (see Tables I, Ia and II, Introduction, pp. 6-9), they likewise function in relation to whole-characteristics. This is essential for the way in which they come into the picture.

Fifth, such processes are, on the whole, not of the character of an and-summative aggregation, of a succession of piecemeal, chance happenings in which items, associations, operations just occur. They are not arbitrary in nature: in spite of difficulties, in spite of some deviations and, often, of dramatic developments, thought processes show a consistency of development.

Sixth, in their development they often lead to sensible expectations, assumptions. These, as well as the other steps within the procedure, call for an honest attitude, for verification: in the absence of sincerity in one's attitude toward truth, there is the danger of dilettantism, of cheap plausibility. But the situation calls not merely for piecemeal factual truth, it calls for "structural truth."[1]

It is the features of points 2 to 6 that provide the concrete possibility for genuine, sensible, productive processes. (For other types of processes see p. 242 ff.)

TABLE III

Thinking consists in
   envisaging, realizing structural features and structural requirements; proceeding in accordance with, and determined by, these requirements; thereby changing the situation in the direction of structural improvements, which involves:

   that gaps, trouble-regions, disturbances, superficialities, etc., be viewed and dealt with structurally;

   that inner structural relations—fitting or not fitting—be sought among such disturbances and the given situation as a whole and among its various parts;

   that there be operations of structural grouping and segregation, of centering, etc.;

[1] M. Wertheimer, "On truth," *Social Research*, 1934, Vol. 1, pp. 135-146.

that operations be viewed and treated in their structural place, role, dynamic meaning, including realization of the changes which this involves;

realizing structural transposability, structural hierarchy, and separating structurally peripheral from fundamental features—a special case of grouping;
looking for structural rather than piecemeal truth.

In human terms there is at bottom the desire, the craving to face the true issue, the structural core, the radix of the situation; to go on from an unclear, inadequate relation to a clear, transparent, direct confrontation—straight from the heart of the thinker to the heart of his object, of his problem. All the items hold also for real attitudes and for action, just as they do for thinking processes. And thinking processes of this type themselves involve real attitudes.

Here again I have used such terms as "viewing," "looking for," "envisaging," etc., and I think they are appropriate and actually required. But many of the features in the table can, if desired, be expressed in objective or behavioral terms, as indicated in earlier chapters, i.e., by substituting "responses," "actions determined by structural features in the situation," etc.

To be sure, these terms are difficult. They are loaded, I think, with productive problems for research. Three groups of problems are involved in them which have to be envisaged and studied:

1. The features, laws, rules governing the neglected or barely investigated operations of segregation, grouping, centering, and structural transposability.

2. Problems as to the relation between parts and their wholes, etc., involving operations as to the place, role, function of a part in its whole.[2]

3. Problems in regard to "outstanding wholes," the good gestalten, the ρ-relations.

Gestalt theory started scientific study of these problems in the search for theoretical clarification, for the laws involved, and tried to develop appropriate scientific tools for dealing with them in many

[2] Logistics has made contributions to these problems in a way neutral to 3.

experimental investigations. Without real knowledge of this literature the terms in the table are not easily understood; indeed they are
easily misunderstood. It may suffice here that the reader regard the
items as arrows pointing toward the concrete issues discussed in the
various chapters.

Let us face the theoretical situation straight. Association theory,
Approach II, and in many respects traditional logic, Approach I,
show the following characteristics in their concrete operations, in
the way they approach and center the picture:

In their aim to get at the elements of thinking they cut to pieces
living thinking processes, deal with them blind to structure, assuming
that the process is an aggregate, a sum of those elements. In dealing
with processes of our type they can do nothing but dissect them, and
thus show a dead picture stripped of all that is alive in them. Steps,
operations come into the picture externally: on the basis of recall,
of some previous knowledge, general or analogical, of associations in
connection with some items in the situation (or even with the sum
of them all), or again, of mere chance. The items, the connections
used, are blind or neutral to questions of their specific structural function in the process. Such are the classical associations between an *a*
and some *b*, the blind connections between means and end; such is
the way in which traditional logic deals with propositions of the form
"all *S* are *P*," or "if *A* then *B*." The connections, the items, data, operations are structure-blind or structure-neutral, blind to their structural
dynamic function within the whole, and blind to the structural requirements.

All this makes direct grasp of productive processes of the type
described impossible.

Dynamically, then, little more is given for theoretical understanding
than the drive, the wish to get at the solution of a problem, and
chance happenings, recall in terms of association, the assumption
that what happened or what is true in many or in "all" cases will
happen in this case too. Of course there is, besides, in traditional logic,
the will to truth and to systematic knowledge.

The situation in the A-examples, given in the earlier chapters of this book (see Chap. One), clearly called for a theory of thinking that goes directly to the structural nature of these processes. It called for a theoretical approach in which what happens in such a process comes into the picture on the basis of vectors determined by the structural dynamics of the situation.

Generally speaking, there is first a situation
  S_1, the situation in which the actual thought process starts, and then, after a number of steps,
  S_2, in which the process ends, the problem is solved.

Let us consider the nature of situation 1 and situation 2 by comparing them, and let us then consider what goes on between, how and why. Clearly the process is a transition, a change from S_1 into S_2. S_1, as compared with S_2, is structurally incomplete, involves a gap or a structural trouble, whereas S_2 is in these respects structurally better, the gap is filled adequately, the structural trouble has disappeared; it is sensibly complete as against S_1.

When the problem is realized, S_1 contains structural strains and stresses that are resolved in S_2. The thesis is that the very character of the steps, of the operations, of the changes between S_1 and S_2 springs from the nature of the vectors set up in these structural troubles in the direction of helping the situation, of straightening it out structurally. This is quite in contrast to processes in which some steps, some operations coming from various sources and going in various directions, may lead to the solution in a fortuitous, zigzag way.

It is interesting to compare the psychological situation in cases in which, after the problem is put and seen, and the subject does not know how to proceed, someone arrives with the ready-made solution. The subject may or may not understand it, may or may not realize that this is the solution; in any case, it was not reached by him, it did not come into existence in the realization of the steps which are structurally required. It often gives him a shock, sometimes an unpleasant one. For real understanding one has to re-create the steps, the structural inner relatedness, the requiredness.

I repeat: The thesis is that the very structural features in S_1 with their particular, concrete nature create the vectors, in their direction, quality, intensity, that in turn lead to the steps and operations dynamically in line with the requirements. This development is determined by the so-called Prägnanz principle,[3] by the tendencies to the good gestalt, by the various gestalt laws.

Those particular cases appear here as the simplest archetype, in which S_1 is a structurally simple situation with no structural hiddenness, but with a structural gap or disturbance, and in which the change into S_2 is made by just getting things in shape. In such instances the structural requirements and the means to meet them are simply realized, and one often gets from almost all subjects a natural, easy, and forceful response. It is characteristic that these processes often occur even when no question is asked, no task is set: the problem itself arises in the structure of the given material.

In other cases, when the initial situation is not grasped either because it is too complex, too confusing, or because it appears in a simple but cheap, superficial structure, a transition is required first. The situation must be structurally understood so that the problem is grasped in its structural role as part of the given situation. Often this transformation actually explodes, revolutionizes the old view of S_1.

Here, stated briefly, is the gist of the thesis: Structural reasons become causes in the process. Connected with the principle of sufficient reason, there was historically a long discussion concerning the relation of "reasons" and "causes." There was good ground for emphasizing that they are fundamentally different in nature. They are, no doubt, if understood in terms of Approach I. But the thesis here is that, with regard to structural reasons, the two coincide in sensible processes.

In other terms: When one grasps a problem situation, its structural features and requirements set up certain strains, stresses, tensions in the thinker. What happens in real thinking is that these strains and stresses are followed up, yield vectors in the direction of improvement of the situation, and change it accordingly. S_2 is a state of affairs that is held together by inner forces as a good structure in which there is harmony in the mutual requirements, and in which the parts are determined by the structure of the whole, as the whole is by the parts.

[3] Editors' note. The principle of Prägnanz, first formulated by Wertheimer with reference to perception, asserts that the organization of the field tends to be as simple and clear as the given conditions allow.

The process does not involve merely the given parts and their trans-formations. It works in conjunction with material that is structurally relevant but is selected from past experience, from previous knowledge and orientation.

In all this, those movements, steps, are strongly preferred which change the state of affairs in S_1 along a structurally consistent line into S_2.

If this is basically the nature of the process, i.e., if the steps are structurally determined, then various questions arise, for instance, why often the process does not proceed more directly, why there are states in which no progress is made, why the development may come to a dead stop and often remain blocked for some time—how devia-tions, mistakes originate. I have mentioned some of the reasons. I may repeat that a first inadequate view of the situation will often prevent the subject from grasping the real structure of the gap and the nature of the requirements that would enable him to close it adequately. Often the subject is lacking in breadth of view. Even when he has it at the beginning, he may lose it in the process because he is busy with details or falls into a piecemeal attitude. Under these cir-cumstances closure may tend to occur in regions that are too narrow. On the other hand, of course, a subject's view may be overextended.

Often the possibility of a short-cut closure is seductive. When several part-problems are realized in a situation, the view of the whole may be lost as those partial views obtrude themselves. Often the impatient desire to find the solution focuses the eye too exclusively, too strongly, as a hungry animal separated from his food by bars, focuses on the near goal, loses the possibility of viewing the situation freely, and becomes unable to see that a simple detour would lead him to the goal.

And we must not forget that although the process $S_1 \ldots \ldots S_2$ is often a relatively closed whole, it is only relatively closed. It is a part-field, just as S_1 and S_2 are each only part of the field; and so is the whole process. It is a partial field within the general process of knowledge and insight, within the context of a broad historical devel-opment, within the social situation, and also within the subject's personal life. It is a part-field not entirely separated as to the material in the field, as to the amount and the sources of energy; conditions, factors, forces in the broader field, favorable or inimical, are of importance. Thus we have to take into account to what degree the partial field is separated, to what degree it is dynamically related to other parts in the broader field. But with regard to this broader field, structural dynamics as outlined above for the partial field seem again to be the real issue. As a consequence, a wide field opens up for research and understanding in terms of inner structural dynamics.

Here I may mention one special point. The forces in the situation may be of two kinds. In many instances it is the structural nature of the objective situation which essentially determines the vectors and the steps, while the I, the ego, and his personal interests and tendencies play only a small role, or none at all. If concrete ego-tendencies come into the picture, they are often disturbing (cf. Chap. Seven, section II). There are other cases in which personal needs are the source of the problem. Here the I plays an important role. But again (cf. Chap Seven, section I), in order really to solve the problem, a transformation is often needed first; the problem may remain insoluble so long as one focuses on one's own wish or need; it may become soluble only if, viewing one's desire as part in the situation, one realizes the objective structural requirements. In such cases one may reach the solution of one's goal sensibly, or else one may realize that the I-goal was itself blind and has to be sensibly changed, if not dropped altogether. So, even for the relation between the problem and the ego, structural features remain decisive.[4]

So far I have limited the discussion to the case of $S_1 \ldots S_2$ as characterized above—the problem situation and the steps leading to its solution. I have mentioned, however, that often the process does not start with S_1 and end with S_2, but that in

$$\ldots \ldots S_1 \ldots \ldots S_2 \ldots \ldots,$$

S_1 already is part of a development; that, moreover, S_2, the very solution, does not represent an end but that by its nature it leads to further dynamic consequences. (See Chap. Four, section V; Chap. Eight.)

[4] See E. Levy, "Some aspects of the schizophrenic formal disturbance of thought," *Psychiatry*, 1943, Vol. VI, pp. 59-69.

There are other types. There is the type

$$S_1 \ldots \ldots$$

in which the situation in S_1 does not primarily involve a problem as to an S_2, a concrete goal. Rather, the real achievement consists in realizing that the situation is not in as good order as it looks; that it should be improved. Under these circumstances the process is often a transition from an and-sum or from a superficially structured view to a more adequate one. As a consequence, the first achievement would consist in realizing that there *is* a problem. To envisage, to put the right problem, is often a far more important achievement than to solve a set task.

On the other hand, there are processes in which S_1 plays little or no role. The process starts, as in some creative processes in art and music, by envisaging some features in an S_2 that is to be created. The artist is driven toward its crystallization, concretization, or full realization. Characteristically the more or less clearly conceived structural whole-qualities of the thing to be created are determining in the process. A composer does not usually put notes together in order to get some melody; he envisages the character of a melody *in statu nascendi* and proceeds from above as he tries to concretize it in all its parts.[5] For some composers this is not an easy process; often it takes a long time. When ideas about the goal are somewhat vague, colloidal, there may be two directions at work simultaneously—one working to get the central idea clearer, the other to get at the parts. Characteristically in such cases what would and what would not fit is immediately clear; whereas what happens in instances of the type $S_1 \ldots \ldots S_2$, is structurally determined by the nature of S_1, or of S_1 in relation to S_2, here it is determined by the structural features in the envisaged S_2, even though S_2 is still incomplete, still vague. This somewhat changes the dynamic nature of the outline given above, but in sensible procedures the vectors are again determined by the nature of the inner structural requirements.

Often two mutually related directions are present in the process, one which proceeds from some parts toward the whole, and another,

---

[5] Similarly with a mathematician who envisages the idea of a formula or of an equation.

which goes from whole-qualities to the parts. This is generally the case when a good gestalt is reached in a sensible process. Such a gestalt is not willfully imposed on parts irrespective of their nature; it answers their requirements too.

The dynamic theory sketched in these pages is not a smooth theory, does not mean to offer generalities just for the sake of subsumption, of cataloguing; it involves many real problems for research—marvelous problems, I think. But I do not think that the gist of it is foreign to what natural common sense feels.

I hope that the reader will not misunderstand the philosophical meaning of this approach. When a picture is given here of the inner structural dynamics in the determination of processes, it does not mean that in this development man is merely passive. An attitude is implied on his part, a willingness to face problems straight, a readiness to follow them up courageously and sincerely, a desire for improvement, in contrast with arbitrary, wilful, or slavish attitudes. This, I think, is one of the great attributes that constitute the dignity of man.

Central to the theory is the transition from piecemeal aggregation, superficial structure, to the objectively better or adequate structure. The criteria for the structurally true view are more difficult to establish than those of piecemeal truth. In this book I have confined myself to showing in comparatively elementary cases that exact decisions about the appropriate, the true structure can be made—as against skeptical, relativistic negativism.

Sometimes the situation is structurally ambiguous, as in ambiguous figures in perception when boundary lines may belong to one area or another, so that more than one possibility of structurization exists. So it is in many cases in which no particular structure is as yet the right one because our factual knowledge is too incomplete, and because data, facts, relevant to a decision are not at hand or are not established with sufficient clearness. Various conditions, forces, factors may determine a structure for the subject—factors which often include inertia of habits, piecemeal attitudes, and the working of the very Prägnanz tendency in the direction of premature closure. The subject then falls victim to a seductive simplification.

All this does not do away with the issue of objectively proper structurization. The desire not to be structurally blind, to get true structural orientation, seems strong, and it often shows itself even in the course and the fate of mistakes. To live in a fog, in an unsurveyable manifold of factors and forces that prevent a clear decision as to action, as to the main lines of the situation, is for many people an unbearable state of affairs. There is a tendency to structural clearness, surveyability, to truth as against petty views—the desire not to deceive oneself. If this desire to reach the true structure sincerely is weak, then structural simplification in a desired direction prevails. The extreme case is that of a paranoid system, in which data are misrepresented and actual facts are violated. Superficially miscentered structures are often dynamically precarious: Although progress may be slow because the forces in the structure make the subject overlook or avoid crucial issues, and rationalize his error, there are clear-cut cases in which an item or an argument endangers a superficial structural view, and explodes it in dramatically productive proceedings.

Such issues play an enormous role in the personal, social and political field. Often in political discussions, in political views, one realizes the impact of the Prägnanz principle in the almost irresistible tendency, the strong desire to get at a simple, decisive structurization of the field, to get clear-cut orientation, to act sensibly, not to be blind, not to act fortuitously. There is a thirst for true orientation.

In political discussions it often happens that not so much the facts themselves, the contents of arguments, are the issues in disagreement, but rather the structural role they play, the function they have in the context, with all the features of "because," "but," "nevertheless," "although," and so forth. Men are unhappy if the complication of such features befogs the issue; they long for a structurally clear view in which the items find their clear place, function and role, do not disturb the main lines and the resulting direction of view and action. This may lead them astray. But one often sees, too, how this tendency to structural simplicity is deeply connected with the thirst to get at the true structure. Experiences and experiments show this strongly and clearly in spite of forces which try to maintain an existing structural view.

In several experiments which I have made on these issues, there have been striking results of this kind. Dr. S. E. Asch is now likewise at work on a broad investigation of these issues, which were so much neglected by social psychologists because they focused almost exclusively on the study of arbitrary forces. I hope that Dr. Asch will soon publish his findings.[5a]

Here lie great tasks for democracy. Critical attitudes, skepticism, do not suffice. What is needed is structural clearness. There is the hope that productive methods will be improved, not merely for gathering information about piecemeal facts, but also for gaining clear insight into the great lines, the basic structures of crucial situations.

Now, besides such processes as are discussed in the chapters of this book (type α), there are many others which to a greater or lesser degree contain features of another nature (type β). Even in processes of the kind described, some of the items needed for progress, or some of the operations, may drop in externally, by chance, by external analogy, by mere recall, or as a result of blind trying. Besides, on the borderline of the known, in developing science, there are too many situations the nature of which calls in the first instance for careful investigation of facts, for realization of factual relations, etc., because there is as yet too little known, too little understood. But those are marvelous moments when, after a long period of diligent, careful study or experimentation, a way opens for structural understanding; or when an experiment brings results which do not fit, which even contradict a given structural view, and the process then proceeds under this challenge.

The extreme at the other end (γ) are cases in which the result, the solution, is brought about by sheer chance discovery or merely by a succession of blind trials, by sheer external recall, sheer reliance on blind repetition, by blind drill or by prompting. There are many situations the nature of which fundamentally allows of nothing but blind proceeding and blind finding as, for instance, in widely used experiments with mazes, discrimination tasks, and problem boxes. Here all the factors that might furnish some clue to reasonably directed behavior are carefully excluded by the experimenter. Under

[5a] Some of these findings are now available in the psychological literature. —M.W.

these conditions no genius, however great, could at first do anything but engage in blind trials; success could occur only by chance, and then be repeated—unless meanwhile the arbitrary set is changed arbitrarily by the experimenter.

To repeat: The differences between the extreme α and γ concern not merely intellectual procedures; they involve deep differences in human attitude.

Many theorists try to center the whole picture of thinking around the characterization of type β, and thus neglect the structural features which the β processes, too, contain.

In modern psychology there is a strong trend to regard thinking basically in terms of the factors, operations, and attitudes of type γ, to be blind to the possibilities of type α, and to try by all means to interpret the types β and α as nothing but complications of factors characteristic of type γ. The study of such factors is undoubtedly needed. But one should not generalize too easily, too superficially. Even in cases in which it is possible to construct a piecemeal, blind mechanism for the "explanation" of a process, it is appropriate for the scientist to be careful lest instead of a true picture he may get a poor, only superficially adequate substitute. In this respect one should also be particularly careful because of the serious implications involved for questions of teaching and education, of life.

The situation is similar to the situation in the psychology of learning.[6] Type γ corresponds to learning by drill, by external associations, by external conditioning, by memorizing, by blind trial and error.[7] Type α focuses on developing structural insight, structural mastery, and meaningful learning in the real sense of the word. There is a widespread assumption that sensible learning, that learning of sensible material, is at bottom nothing but a complication of what is found in the rote learning of syllable series, etc., as though this latter provided *the* laws of learning. It does not seem possible that the char-

[6] See my introduction to G. Katona, *Organizing and memorizing* (New York: Columbia University Press, 1940).

[7] Editors' note. By "external" association Professor Wertheimer meant connections in memory which are supposed to be established irrespective of the content of the items involved. The term "external" conditioning is to be understood in the same way.

acteristics in α are reducible to factors and operations of this kind. Even if one should entertain such a hope, it is not founded in real investigation but often merely plays the role of a dogma.

To put it in the briefest way: If we call the thinking and the learning processes of type α "structurally sensible," if we call the characteristics of type γ "structurally blind," the situation in this traditional view is:

FIG. 160

In other words, γ is taken as basic, α "will certainly turn out to be nothing but a complication of γ factors."

The scientifically more careful procedure is first to study the distinctive character of each type of process. Only on the basis of such

FIG. 161

studies will it be possible to decide whether the two types are entirely different in nature, or whether α is to be viewed as a complication of the factors essential in γ, *or* whether α is the proper theoretical center and γ a special case.

FIG. 162

At the present time the last seems to be the theoretically more appropriate alternative: γ appears to be merely a special case in which the structural interdependence characteristic of type α approaches zero, a limit which is never reached in cases of real learning, of real thinking.

Let us relate this to a previous distinction among several approaches, which has occupied us before. If we look back to Table III (the gestalt approach) and compare it with the approaches of traditional logic (both deductive and inductive) and of association theory (see Tables I, Ia, and II, Chap. One, pp. 6-9), two ways are open to us. Either we regard the structural characterization of III as complicating additions to I and II, or we decide what an appropriate theoretical attitude may be only after the functional principles of these approaches and their mutual relations have actually been studied. To be sure, each of the items in I and II is important. But perhaps these operations themselves merely represent special cases. The items in II and to a degree in I were conceived and traditionally used as neutral or blind to structural features and requirements. Scrutinizing them, we find that each of the items in I and II is itself ambiguous, that each can be meant in a structurally sensible or a structurally blind way. Their structurally blind form and operation seems to be a limiting case of III, which is adequate only when structural coherence and interdependence approach zero.

This does not mean that regions possessing the appearance of I and II, and therefore lacking structural characteristics as to content and connections, are *altogether* bare of structural factors. Even if connections are merely factual, merely factually constant, and not understandable, the *hierarchy* of such connections still offers possibilities either of structurally sensible or structurally blind proceeding.

Let me now briefly characterize the ambiguity of the terms and operations of Tables I, Ia, and II.

The Terms of Traditional Deductive Logic: Table I (Introduction, p. 6).

Comparison and *discrimination* may mean, and are commonly supposed to mean, that two or many objects are compared with regard to just any features in them, blind to the given structure. From this point of view what matters is solely whether or not there are equalities or differences, and what they are. But equalities may mean piecemeal sameness which may mislead even if they are constant and general; or, quite in contrast, there may be structural equality, which can obtain even when the piecemeal data show no equality at all.

Analysis may mean that a field or an object is cut into and-summative parts, blind to structure, or it may mean structurally adequate division, and viewing parts in their part-nature.

Abstraction and *generalization* may mean a performance that focuses on pieces, is blind to structure, and leads to the and-summative form

$$m+x.$$

Here m represents facts common to several situations, and x other characteristics in which these situations differ (cf. p. 252). Now the existence of the common factor may mean no more than the coincidence of certain pieces or qualities, stated without any regard to their role in the given structure. The procedure may even involve divisions and cuts which violate their structure. On the other hand, abstraction and generalization may also mean operations that follow the requirements of given structures. Similarly with *class* concepts. The grouping into classes and subclasses may be done in such a way that it groups together objects and classes which are structurally foreign to each other, therefore basically different, and sharply separates objects which are structurally similar or even structurally identical (see pp. 253-254). Conversely, class concepts may refer precisely to those common structural factors which the first procedure ignores.

Propositions, for instance, of the character "all S are P," may state a factual and rigid but blind connection, a factual coexistence of facts that structurally do not in the least belong to each other; or again, they may be structurally sensible predications. A set of predicates attributed to a subject may either mean an and-sum of unstructured data; or it may refer to data that fit one another, and it may thus illuminate the very structure of S.

Similarly with *inferences, syllogisms*, etc. They may be conceived and used in terms of merely formal relations in which such empty quantifications as "all," "some," "none" play the essential role; or they may spring from structural requirements.[8]

The Terms of Traditional Inductive Logic: Table Ia (Introduction, p. 8).

[8] See the paper on syllogisms in productive thinking in which the empty though exact syllogisms were contrasted with sensible syllogisms. M. Wertheimer, "Über Schlussprozesse im produktiven Denken," *Drei Abhandlungen zur Gestalttheorie* (Erlangen: Philosophische Akademie, 1925), pp. 164-184; also W. D. Ellis, *op. cit.*, selection 23.

Induction may mean generalization on the basis of piecemeal, external coincidences in a number of cases; or it may mean a structurally reasonable hypothesis.

Experience may mean a heedless gathering of facts and of mere factual connections. Or experience may mean that structural features are vividly grasped, that orientation is gained, that data and connections are understood in their role and function within the context.

Experimentation may mean that just any piecemeal factors are heedlessly introduced and that results are viewed piecemeal, without regard to their structural meaning. This is often necessary as a first step. But more is needed lest in the end there be nothing but a sheer and-sum of structurally unrelated facts. At the other extreme lies structurally sensible experimenting, often in the form of asking nature a crucial question, of trying to decide between possible hypotheses in the structural context of knowledge.

"One variable is a function of another variable." This may mean, as some theorists consistently formulated it, that items of any two series of facts are correlated, and that a principle is given in terms of correlated changes without regard to the structural sense of the pairing. With this concept of function one does not consider how the pairing and the principle are related to the nature of the items and to the structural characteristics of the whole series. At the opposite extreme one may study what changes in a part may mean within the structure of the whole; one may thereby discover the inner laws governing the nature of the items within the whole, the way in which their changes depend upon this part-whole relation.

The Terms of Association Theory: Table II (Introduction, p. 9).

Association may mean chaining items together in an and-sum of connections that has by nature no structure, as in the usual theory of learning rote syllables. Or at the opposite extreme, it may mean the realizing of structural belonging in which items require each other as parts in a context—including the enduring effects of that realization.

Repetition may mean that the same piecemeal, blind connection occurs over and over again; or it may mean the change from an understood and sheer additive pairing to the realization of a structure in which the meaning of the items becomes that of parts in a characteristic whole.

Trial and error may mean a heedless succession of blind proceedings with random order of directions; or, again, it may mean that some sensible hypothesis is structurally tested. In the latter case, the very failure may elucidate the situation and suggest another hypothesis which fits the given structure better.

Learning on the basis of success may mean that an action is singled out because of the success that follows the action only factually, but is not understood; or it may mean that, in learning, a subject grasps why just this kind of action leads to just this effect for intrinsic structural reasons. It is the latter form of "learning by success" that enables the subject to vary his action in a structurally sensible way when the situation is no longer the same.

The essential difference between the two interpretations of all these concepts can perhaps best be illustrated if we once more return to logic and, in the first place, to the class concept which is so fundamental in the traditional form of that discipline. If we disregard the many intricacies, if we concentrate on just the concrete meaning of the operations involved and on what is really needed for correctness in traditional logic, we find the following points:

There are several objects. (The way in which they are segregated, and why just so, how an object constitutes itself in separation from other objects, is a question neglected in traditional logic, is taken for granted without real investigation.) I compare them. In their qualities or their parts I find similarities and differences. Abstracting from the differences, and concentrating on common qualities or parts in the objects, I get a general concept. The content is given by these common parts. This is the "intension." The "extension" is the manifold of objects embraced by the class concept.

If we call the common element m, and the other elements x, an exact expression for the class (or for any object as conceived under the class concept) is

$$m+x.$$

Between the m and the x is an "and." The m[9] is what is common in the contents of the objects; the x is what there is besides the m and

[9] The m itself may be an and-sum of several common elements.

may vary in the contents of the various objects. The conceived datum, m, is independent of its setting to the left and right, and apparently must be so for the sake of exact use of the concept in inference, syllogisms, etc. There is no reference to whatever else there may be in the object besides, no reference to the role which m plays in this object, no reference to its meaning as a part among the other parts of the same entity, no reference to the structure of this entity. This abstraction is subtractive; it simply isolates the m. For the m it does not matter what the x is. The x is in principle arbitrary; in other words, no question is raised as to what the x may be, and what the x may mean for the m. The rigid constancy of the m, and the independence of its nature from the nature of the x, is assumed to be basically needed for the proper performance of classification, subsumption, universal propositions, inferences, syllogisms, etc. as envisaged by traditional logic.

In many cases such a procedure is adequate and useful, as in often used classical examples of traditional logic; consider the proposition "All mailboxes in the . . . State are green." It is fully adequate in all cases in which the m and the x are just separate, additive, merely put together without any inner relation that would make them mutually dependent; in all cases in which the meaning of the m is invariant with regard to changes of the x, or vice versa.

In the historic development difficulties have arisen as to the adequacy of the procedure in certain cases (cf. the famous discussion of the Linnaean system of plants in the French Academy). The problem was whether such a procedure, although exact, does not easily combine objects which are basically different in nature and, on the other hand, sharply separate objects which belong to each other in fact. The logician seeks help in the term "essential." There always was emphasis on this point; but although for common sense the meaning of "essential" is often clear enough, unfortunately it was and has remained extremely controversial in logic. It has served to name the problem rather than to solve it. It has consequently been rejected again, excluded in newer developments of logic. A way to clarify its beautiful meaning opens up when we attend to structural features. I give an extreme example from music. Here are four objects:

Fig. 163

We classify. We realize, with regard to the pitches, that the objects A and B start with the same two notes. So do the objects C and D. A librarian may form a first class of melodies that start with the first two notes of A and B, and a second class that start with the first two notes of C and D. This may—although I wonder—be useful to him for bringing some exact order into his collection index. In terms of traditional logic the procedure is exact. But what would he have done in this procedure? He would have combined the first two melodies which are different in nature even as to these two first notes. And so in the second class. He would have sharply separated into different classes melodies which are the same, only in another key, C being a transposition of A, D of B.

On the piano the first two notes in his classification are the same in A and B, C and D, respectively, but they are not the same for somebody who grasps the melodies. For him the two notes which the classification, with its atomistic procedure, regards as identical are actually very different as to the role they play in the melody, different also as parts of it. If one were to write these "identical" notes with the same symbols—as I have done in Fig. 163—the musician would be exasperated, would call it nonsense, illogical. The second note in A is the tonic, the "identical" second note in B is far from being a tonic, it is the leading tone which asks for, drives toward the tonic which here is the third note. The first note in A is a major third in the harmony, in B it is a minor third. Even the relation between the two, viewed piecemeal as the same, is different: in A a third, in B a diminished fourth. In connection with this their dynamics, their stability is different, which shows itself even in the pitch intoned in actual singing: in B the second note is often pitched higher, as it tends toward the following tone. Their expressive character also is different. Thus the two first notes of A and B, although taken as common in that quasi-class concept, are different in nature; whereas, on the other hand, the two first notes of A and C are in all these regards, i.e., structurally, the same, likewise those of B and D. The AB/CD classification is blind as to structure; it is nonsensical in that it does not look at the melodies as wholes, but cuts off the first two notes, piecemeal, from their context, as though they were independent bits.

Examine the contrast: The structure-blind class formation gives the grouping AB/CD, the structural formation gives the grouping AC/BD.

FIG. 164

Here we have considered only strict transposition; but in sensible musical variations even the two starting notes of a melody and their interval may to a certain extent be changed with no real damage to the melody as a structure. On the other hand, a single note, when changed, may be out of place, may violate the structure. When one grasps such a melody one realizes that something is wrong, is out of shape, does not fit. Melodies which are violated in such a way, and senseless tone-aggregations generally, do not transpose psychologically as good melodies do. When there are structural violations, there is trouble. If one tries to recall senseless tone aggregations, to repeat them after a time, they are much harder actually to repeat, and various things may happen to them. There seems to be a strong tendency to change, somehow to improve such material in the direction of a sensible structure. So, far from being a matter of piecemeal equalities, the real issue is not even restricted to questions of place, role, and function in some whole; but it refers to fitting or not fitting given structural requirements.

I have chosen the example of melodies because in musiçal grasping the issues are vividly felt. Of course exact formulation of the whole-qualities, the structural requirements, is not easy here—it is what some great musicians have called the inner logic of melodies, one of the great problems in aesthetics. Yet much of what I have tried to show in these examples is of general import; it holds often for different materials, when exact formulation in these respects offers no difficulty. The same issues can, for instance, be studied in groups of, say, four objects in figural distributions, in the structure of events within physical systems, in abstract relational networks, and in sets of human traits. A broad field opens up, much broader than the issue of classification, when we consider the problems of transposability and search for the principles of structural invariance.

In regard to the question of classification the main point boils down to the old proverb,

si duo faciunt idem, non est idem,

if two do the same, it is not the same. In exact terms: Two items or two groups of items which are identical from an atomistic point of view (cf. above AB/CD), may mean very different things structurally, may in fact be different in nature. A necessary addition is the opposite sentence: If, from an atomistic point of view, two do very different things (cf. above AC/BD), their actions may nevertheless be structurally the same. In order to do the same in a changed situation one has to do it differently. In exact terms: Different items may be structurally the same.

Similar things hold for the items which are usually considered to be the most basic ones in logic: for the "and," the "not," the "if-so," the concept of relation, of identity, of truth, etc. I shall mention some points briefly. Traditionally all of them have been considered and used in blindness to the structural problems. All of them, in their traditional meaning, seem to be merely limiting cases of the broader issue. This holds even for the traditional principles of thought: the law of identity, of contradiction, the principle of sufficient reason.

In exact traditional logic *"and"* may combine any two things, or propositions, whatever they may mean to each other, whether or not they belong to each other structurally. "And" then means the one *is*, or *is true*, also the other. I use a characteristic example from the classical treatise of D. Hilbert and W. Ackermann.[10] One can exemplify the meaning of the traditional "and" by a statement such as, "Two is smaller than three *and* the snow is white." Here we see that the content of both, taken together, is nothing but their and-sum; the actual content of each means nothing to the actual content of the other; the subject matter of the two has no inner structural relation. In the and-sum each is just what it would be without the other, or with the other changed. This example may shock the reader, but it gives the exact meaning of the "and" in a structure-blind logic.

In fact, this empty "and" is merely an extreme case. In living thought "and" is for the most part not of this character. There is the "and" that combines two things which belong to each other, which require each other structurally. There is the "and" that states two things are together which should not be together, which violate each other. Both of these are different functionally from the neutral, structure-blind "and." The real "and" is often of a very serious character in that it involves dynamic consequences to which the use of the empty "and" is blind. Even in formal logic we should differentiate basically between the various kinds of "and," because the general use of the empty "and" may blind the thinker to what he really does in putting things together.

In modern logistics the "and" has been defined by a set of truth-values as to two propositions. Elegant in itself, the procedure strikingly expresses an underlying structure-blindness with regard to the "and," and to the meaning of the two propositions. It is adequate for cases in which the two propositions deal with subject matters that have no structural relation to each other, in regard to which "and" properly means nothing except that each is true independently. But there are cases in which the combination of two subject matters is not of a sheer "and"-summative character. If we then consider first each proposition alone, separately, and afterward realize what happens

[10] *Grundzuege der theoretischen Logik* (Berlin: J. Springer, 1928), p. 3.

when they are related by a real "and," we shall find that this often brings about serious changes in their meanings. To some extent this can already be shown with great exactness in regard to propositions on simple relational networks—when the changes occur in terms of the so-called implicit definitions of the logistician, and consequently with regard to the table of the truth-values itself. The form of the table of the truth-values in the mere and-summative case appears merely as a limiting case of the very much richer and deeper set which we get by considering structural features.

To summarize: The real "and" implies real relations, the existence of specific wholes and of their dynamics.

It is a serious matter, characteristic for the structure-blindness and function-blindness of traditional logic, that such terms as "but," "nevertheless," "however," were not considered in the logical system at all.

Similar things hold for the meaning of a *"relation"* as for the "and." There are cases, in which

$$|a| \quad |R| \quad |b|$$

constitutes a mere and-sum in which none of the three items really means anything to the others. A relation, R, to a b is stated for an a with no consequence at all for the a, and none for the b. Secondly, there are cases in which two things or two items are put into some real relation to each other, which is structurally inadequate to both, violates the requirements of each and yet they have to live it. This is the form of relationship in which violent structural dynamics often result. Thirdly, however, there are cases in which in the actual relation, the items complete each other in a good structure, fit together, and build a good whole.

Finally there are the cases in which the items mutually determine one another from inner necessity, and in a clear, clean way; where a and b determine c, or require their R; where a and R ask for the adequate b, and R and b for the adequate a.

Just as with "and" and with "relation," we find that the concept of negation may be taken in an empty, structure-blind sense. But, again, this is a limiting case of negation, applicable only in special instances. On the other hand, negating something may mean that this something is appropriately not the case, the negation being just what is required by the structural nature of the situation. But there is still another "not," which states the lack of something that would in fact be structurally required by the situation. Both are in contrast to the case of an empty negation, which has no structural meaning whatsoever. The case of the negation that states a structural lack is actually the *negatio privativa* of classical logic; but it is essential that its structural nature be clearly understood. Between the empty negation and the other forms of "not" there lies a manifold of forms.

Similar distinctions hold for the *"if-so"* form which is so fundamental in logic. The one extreme is the structure-blind, merely formal *"if* two is smaller than three, *then* snow is white."[11] For formal purposes it is important to study this most empty, structure-blind type also. We sometimes have to deal with arbitrary connections of this kind in actual life, sometimes even in the initial phases of productive processes. But in sensible thinking "if-so" is rarely, or at least almost never *remains*, of this empty kind. Common sense is right in feeling shocked by such examples as the one just given. "If-so" for the most part involves some structural justification. It does not simply mean an "if-so" with regard to structurally unrelated subject matter. The sensible "if-so" calls for some kind of inner coherence, some kind of intrinsic structural relatedness. Thus the empty type appears merely as an extreme in which all structural relatedness disappears and only an external form remains, which is indifferent to the issues under "if" and under "so."

Or take the principle of identity. The case of full identity is banal and, in actual thinking, hardly ever an issue. The real problem refers to the discovery of "identity" in spite of some apparent differences, and here it becomes a fundamental task to discriminate between piecemeal identity that ignores structure, and structural identity. It has been possible to study these differences in psychological experiments. The investigation, which referred to concrete subject matter, led to the clear-cut consequence that piecemeal identity is merely a special case, appropriate only when structural conditions allow.[12]

---

[11] This example is not my invention. It has been used for positive characterization (D. Hilbert and W. Ackermann, *op. cit.*, p. 4).

[12] J. Ternus, "Experimentelle Untersuchungen über phänomenale Identität," *Psychologische Forschung*, 1926, Vol. 7, pp. 81-136.

It is same with *truth* itself. Study of the problem of truth gave rise to the scheme of a four-valuate logic with the terms: true or false, each to be taken either in an atomistic or in a structural sense.[13] Here again structure-blind procedure leads to the special case of the merely two-valued Aristotelian logic.

———————————

All these issues play an important role in productive thinking. But in this connection they ought to be considered as parts of the great issue of the *dynamics* of thinking. Whereas traditional logic focused on the problems of validity, on static features, the doctrine of general logic has to deal with the logical features and rules of dynamic events, and these again are structural.

For instance, our statement that identity has often to be understood in a structural sense does not entirely suffice. Traditional logic regards it as a very basic rule that the items of discourse—concepts, propositions, and so on—have to remain rigidly identical if repeated. Important as this rule is for certain questions of validity, it does not generally fit real thinking. In real thinking processes, items often do not remain rigidly identical; and as a matter of fact, precisely their change, their improvement is required. If an item, concept or proposition, recurs in the process and appears from an atomistic point of view as identical, it very often is not really so. Its functional and structural meaning has actually, and fortunately, changed. Blindness to such a change in meaning often impedes productive processes. In real thinking the *functional* meaning of an item, of a proposition, that meaning which changes as thinking advances, is of the utmost importance—without it thinking gets sterile; without realization of that change one does not grasp the line of progress. For statements, etc., have a *direction* in their context. It is here that a basic feature of traditional logic comes to the fore: its disregard of the intense directedness of live thought processes as they improve a given situation.

[13] M. Wertheimer. "On truth," *Social Research*, 1934, Vol. 1. pp. 135-146.

On the Problem of the Distinction Between Arbitrary Component and Necessary Part*

THE distinction between arbitrary component (Einzelinhalt) and necessary part (Teil) has become important in many ways; it has been treated in many psychological works of the last decades; much is still awaiting exact formulation; there is a need for a demonstration with simple contrasting examples. Some examples are chosen here in which several features can be readily shown and studied.

1. Draw the groups of dots I (*a bcd e*) on the board, and expose them simultaneously.

•   •   •   •   •

After a short time, erase dots *c* and *e* (II).

•   •   •

The dots that now remain were already there before, but how different they look now.[1] Let us examine some aspects of this:

What dot *d* was on the right, in I, is what dot *b* was on the left; in II, *b* is the "middle"; *a* is now, at the left, what *d* is on the right.

---

* This appendix appears for the first time in this edition. It is a translation by Michael Wertheimer (by permission of the editor of the *Zeitschrift für Psychologie*, Kurt Gottschaldt) of "Zu dem Problem der Unterscheidung von Einzelinhalt und Teil," *Zeitschrift für Psychologie*, 1933, vol. 129, pp. 353-357. This translation is included here because the paper is frequently referred to in the text—as including examples demonstrating that what may be an arbitrary component in one whole may be a structural, intrinsic part in another. Also, because of the examples included in it, it seemed to be a paper that should be made available in English.—M. W.

[1] Such restructuring is typical when good viewing conditions are observed, the distances between the dots are not too great, and no special procedures are used which make for disintegration. The same holds true for the further examples.

In the language of relational networks, in which every arbitrary element is defined implicitly by its location in the network: b^I and d^I had (if one disregards the right-left distinction) the same implicit meaning; they were "homotypic." But b^{II} is a single central dot (like c^I before); d^{II} is not homotypic with b^{II}, but with a^{II}. If I designate "homotypic" with "$\sim$", and "not homotypic" with "$\not\sim$", in I $b \sim d$; $d \not\sim a$; in II, $b \not\sim d$; $d \sim a$.

In examining the implicit relations in the comparison, one cannot correctly even write the same letters for the dots in I and II (one must distinguish between b^I and b^{II}, etc.): the contents are *different ones* in II and in I.

(In this examination of the implicit relations, the gestalt characteristics are by no means fully presented; something is still lacking; but what is intended here can be readily represented in the same way.)

There are also differences in *relations*. Just notice this: in II, the equality of ab and bd is not only an equality of two distances, but involves symmetry; symmetry, however, not only signifies equality of distances, but contains essential characteristics of relations within the whole.

When viewing the figures, the objective equality of the distances ab and bd is not present in I in the same way in which it is in II. Often it is not even evident in the perception of I (often reproductions of the figure from memory show this characteristic—typically the equality of the distances ab and de is intended, but that of distances ab and bd is not).

The equality of distances ab and bd is much more *sensitive* in II than in I; for example if in I dot a is displaced a bit to the left (and to maintain the symmetry, dot e correspondingly to the right), nothing essential seems changed; but in II, a striking asymmetry results. (Similar findings occur with other changes—intensity, heights, etc.)

It can be seen that place and role in the whole is important for the meaning of *relations*.

2.

	·	·		a	d
I:	·	·		b	e
	·	·		c	f

Erase *c* and *d* (II). Among other things, the spatial orientation of the figure changes—(the figure is tipped); *ae* and *bf*, as parallels, determine the figure; in the normal impression of the first figure they typically do not occur. In I, *be* lay in the main spatial orientation of the figure; this is not so in II; in II, the line is often not even perceptually present; if it is, it is seen as a diagonal, homotypic with *af* (which would be atypical in I); but to be a diagonal is something different from being a line of symmetry, as in I.

In I, *a* ⸦ *b*, *f* ⸦ *e*, *be* ⸦ *af*; in II, *a* ∼ *b*, *f* ∼ *e*, *be* ∼ *af*.

3.

I: II:

FIG. 165   FIG. 166

Lengthen both ends[2] of C in I and you get II. In I, A and C were "pendants," B the line of symmetry; in II ("angle AB stands on a slanting diagonal"), A and B are "pendants." (In I, A ∼ C, A ⸦ B: in II A∼B.) In I, B is the single line of symmetry in the main spatial orientation of the figure; in II the long slanting line provides the main spatial orientation (and the line—not "given" as an ele-ment—which symmetrically bisects angle AB is at right angles to the slanting diagonal).

While in I the figure is sensitive to changes in the equality of the length of A and C, but not to changes in the length of B, II is sensi-tive to changes in precisely this equality of B and A; now B = A plays the same role that C = A played before.

If the value of 40° (instead of 60°, as above) is used for the angles, the transition to II is often especially strong, not only as regards optical characteristics: "The thing's crooked," "It's tipping over!" "That looks awful!" And under appropriate conditions, there are often

[2] Lengthen the ends more than is indicated in the diagram.

strong motivations, a need to get into the situation and "set the thing right."

4.

I.   II.

FIG. 167   FIG. 168

If one adds line D, it often appears as a senseless addition; its presence, length, angular location "accidental," "arbitrary." (That D=A, that the angles A and D make with B are equal, is often not even quite noticed—as evidenced in reproductions from memory.) In III, things are different: in the slanting trapezoid, B is a slanting side

III.

FIG. 169

of the trapezoid, as is A. In I, B ~ C, in III B ⫫ C; in II A ⫫ D, in III A ~ D. In I, B and C are the sides of the isosceles triangle; in III, B is the base, C a diagonal; this is a considerable difference.

In I, the equality B=C, and the equality of the angles B and C make with A, are important (sensitive); in III, neither of these is true; here the equality of the diagonals, and the equality of the angles A and D make with B, are important.

5.

```
                    6                          .
                  6  6                        .  .
                2  5  3                      .  .  .
              1  1  5  4                     .  .  .  .
   . .      2  1     4  4                  .  .     .  .
    .       1  1  3  4                     .  .  .  .
   . .        2  5  6                        .  .  .
              6  6                           .  .
                3                              .
```

First present only the dots designated "1"; after a short time, add the dots designated "2", then after a short time those designated "3", etc. When the dots designated "2" are added, typically the function of the "middle dot" remains as in I, etc.; but meantime: "A dot is missing on the right!" (expectation, need, requirement). The "3" dots appear as a surprisingly "senseless" slanting line when added on the right. With the addition of the "4" dots: "There's another little diamond on the right."

When the "5" dots—and especially the "6" dots—are added, a strong recentering typically follows: what was here before is sharply changed. The group at the left has exploded (its center is no longer the center . . .), the characteristic of the figures being "next to each other" is no longer present—all dots have ordered themselves into *one* united figure, now are there *as part of this figure*. (It is easy to enumerate the changes for the individual dots, etc.)

The process often exhibits—in the existence of concrete "demands," and their fate—strong dynamic properties.

6. Given:

FIG. I

FIG. II

In these two melodies, three notes and their intervals are, as "arbitrary components," identical; for the listener (and the singer) they are very different. In connection with our point, observe just this:

e, in I, is tonic	(*f flat!*) in II raising of the tonic
d sharp, in I, is leading tone	(*e flat!*) in II is tonic
g, in I, is minor third	in II is major third.

Musical logic requires a different notation for the two tones: in II, the notation *e, d sharp*, would be wrong (and vice versa).

And the interval between the second and the third note is, in I, a diminished fourth, but in II an augmented third! Functional differences are very characteristically shown in variability (changes in the height of a note, etc., during singing).

The essential differences between the two melodies also indicate some entirely different fine characteristics, but we will not go into them further here.

(Similar in form to the first examples: first play the following motif:

FIG. III

A second time, add a *b* after the first note, and an *e* at the end. Instead of *b flat, a sharp* must then be written, and in place of *e flat, d sharp*; here the first note is musically no longer the dominant, but a retardation of the dominant; the lowest note is no longer tonic, but a leading tone; the interval which leads to it is no longer a third, but a diminished fourth.)

The Altar Window*

I MADE some experiments with the following task with many subjects. Some children behaved very nicely, and got the solution, sometimes after only one minute or so of deliberation; some needed a little help. Some grown-ups, even highly intelligent and educated people, followed most amusing procedures, and experienced great difficulties in getting at the simple solution.

I propose that the reader try it.

Painters are at work, painting and decorating the inner walls of a church. Somewhat above the altar there is a circular window. For decoration, the painters have been asked to draw two vertical lines tangent to the circle, and of the same height as the circular window;

FIG. 170

* This appendix, which was not included in the original edition, is a slightly edited version of a fragment found among Max Wertheimer's papers.—M. W.

they were then to add half circles above and below, closing the figure. This area between the lines and the window is to be covered with gold. For every square inch, so and so much gold is needed. How much gold will be needed to cover this space (given the diameter of the circle); or, what is the area between the circle and the lines?

Before reading further, try to get the solution. (There isn't much mathematics needed for it.) After you have the solution, it may be of interest to you to hear of the kinds of reactions one gets in experiments with this task. I shall tell only a few. You may enjoy them.

An example, in the words of one highly educated subject: "Of course I must be able to do this. Let's see . . . which theorems about the computation of areas do I need here? Surely I must be able to recall them. . . . If this were only a real ellipse (pause) . . . but it isn't. . . . If I divide it, then these parts are very easy. At the bottom and at the top I have half-circles—and the area of half-circles I can easily calculate. But there are also these four funny remainders. . . . What theorems do I know about such "quasi-triangles," which have, instead of a straight side, such a circular segment? . . . I do not recall any. . . ." And then, after a while of hard thinking, he gave it up.

Another subject, similarly intelligent, and with a good deal of geometrical training, went about it in a similar way. When he came to the four strangely-shaped remainders, though, he said: "The area of these four is equal to the area of the square minus the area of the circle inscribed in the square. . . . The area of each remainder is $\dfrac{a^2 - \pi a^2}{4}$; this is equal to a^2 times $\dfrac{4 - \pi}{4}$ . . . . Or is it? . . . Is that correct?" (This took half an hour.)

A third one started by computing the area of the circle, and cried suddenly: "How blind I was! How simple this is! It is the area of the circle plus—what? Square . . . circle; it is simply the area of the square! Excellent problem!"

Fourth example: a ten-year-old child, with no geometrical training to help him, said, "Now, how can you expect me to do this? I can't. I have no idea how one does such things." He looked intently at the figure, and then said quietly: "The two half-circles must fit into the window. . . . It is—the whole square!" (He did not use the term "square," but traced the figure with his finger.) The whole thing took about one minute.

Fifth: another boy, twelve years old, without training in geometry, started boasting about how good he was in such problems, and made wild guesses with great assurance. For example: "The four remainders are a quarter of the circle." I said to him, "Don't talk nonsense. Think a bit." He was silent half a minute, and then said, "If you move both upper remainders up, and have them fit the upper semi-circle, and if you do the same with the two lower remainders, both things taken together make a square! That's it."

The School Inspector*

I REPEAT what I stressed in Chapter One (and elsewhere): there are items or features in a situation which are structurally central, and others which are not, which are structurally peripheral, variable. For example, the absolute lengths of the auxiliary lines of the parallelogram are not involved in the structural interrelatedness—not much more than the color of the parallelogram.

To see, to grasp, to realize what is structurally central and what is not, is, in most cases of thinking, of the highest importance. One very extreme example was mentioned in section 14 of Chapter One, in which an hypothesis was put forth—the succession of the numbers by one—which has nothing to do with the structure implied in the problem.

In order to illustrate the issue I shall tell a story of an entirely different kind. The events are said to have happened in a small Moravian village in the time of the old Austrian empire. An inspector from the Ministry of Education arrived one day to visit the school room. It was part of his duty to make such periodic inspections of the schools. At the end of the hour, after he had observed the class, he stood up and said: "I am glad to see that you children are doing well in your studies. You are a good class; I am satisfied with your progress. Therefore, before I go, there is one question I would like to ask: How many hairs does a horse have?" Very quickly one little nine-year-old boy raised his hand, to the astonishment of the teacher and the visitor. The boy stood up, and said: "The horse has 3,571,962

---

* This appendix, which was not included in the original edition, is a slightly edited version of a fragment found among Max Wertheimer's papers.—M. W.

hairs." The inspector wonderingly asked: "And how do you know that this is the right number?" The boy replied: "If you do not believe me, you could count them yourself." The inspector broke into loud laughter, thoroughly enjoying the boy's remark. As the teacher escorted him along the aisle to the door, still laughing heartily, he said: "What an amusing story! I must tell it to my colleagues when I return to Vienna. I can already see how they will take it; they enjoy nothing better than a good joke." And with that he took his leave.

It is a year later, the inspector is back again at the village school for his annual visit. As the teacher was walking along the aisle with him to the door, he stopped and said: "By the way, Mr. Inspector, how did your colleagues like the story of the horse and the number of his hairs?" The inspector slapped the teacher on the back. "Oh, yes," he said. "You know, I was really very anxious to tell this story —and a fine story it was—but, you see, I couldn't. When I got back to Vienna I wasn't able for the life of me to remember the number of hairs."

This is an invented story; at least I hope it is. I asked many people, after they had heard the story: "Now what is the point of the story?" One type of answer: "It's really a stupid story; this inspector was apparently thinking in a way which violates the old logical differences between essentials and unessentials." I said: "Certainly, but could you please tell me what you mean here by essential?" Most people have no way of saying this (besides feeling no need to explain this obvious thing). Some do; some in clumsy and odd ways; some use the historical proposals for the meaning of unessential, like not being constant, etc.—which begs the question, which is in reality no answer because it already presupposes the answer.

Some say, rightly: "You see, it doesn't matter what the number in the story is." I asked: "That's right, but will you please tell me why?" And then sometimes the "essential" answer develops: "The content of the number has nothing to do with the central issue of the story; there is no interdependence; or, better, there is no reasonable, inner relation between the whole story and just this number (no ρ-relation). Therefore, the item is reasonably variable." The function of the item in its place and role in the structure has nothing to do with being just such and such a number. The structure sets no functional requirement for the exact amount. What the structure requires here is fulfilled by any (large) number.

And why is this story often seen as a rather good joke? Because of the surprise at seeing the foolish determination to stick to just this one item, as if it were in its specific content a relevant item in the structure. It is funny to see how blind to the structure the Inspector's behavior is. I might add that some are a little disturbed, not being able to bring together the story and the reaction to it, and that some do not seem to think at all in the direction of clarifying what was involved in the thought operation of the Inspector, but speak in terms of probable personality traits of the Inspector.

Such personality problems are important, but a different point of view is also needed, to conceive clearly what this behavior meant structurally. Perhaps the occurrence of such a mental attitude is, in such cases, not at all a question of individual personality characteristics, but of a trend created by certain kinds of education (based on certain tendencies in theoretical psychology)—and only exaggerated in such a joke.

Suggestions for Teaching About Area*

I

WHICH procedure in teaching a proof is psychologically good and which may not be good psychologically—these are questions to be decided empirically. It is a question of comparing different ways of teaching with regard to difficulties in learning, retention, the possibility of reconstruction, and of application to other problems. The question concerns not only a mastery of certain issues, but also an orientation in the subject matter, an opening of the mind, development of abilities to think.

These are matters of experience and experimentation. But the need is not simply to compare blindly any kinds of teaching, but rather to try to study the effects of extremes with regard to our main issue: structural reasonability or structural arbitrariness in the teaching itself.

Here I shall sketch one of the possible procedures which the teacher could employ to teach a problem in a psychologically reasonable way.

It seems desirable for many children—not for all—to start with concrete, actual life situations in which the task, say finding the area of a rectangle, is reasonably required. One can do this, for example, with a story of two farmers who exchange two plots of land, or with the story of a farmer who is trying to find out how much seed he will need for a certain portion of his land—questions which sensibly demand the determination of the area.

* This appendix, which was not included in the original edition, is a slightly edited version of a fragment found among Max Wertheimer's papers.—M. W.

For such children it makes a big difference whether or not there is some real sense in putting the problem at all. For illustration I may describe the following instances.

Twenty-five years ago the parents of a nine-year old girl, friends of mine, told me that she experienced great difficulties in her school work. So much was this the case that the child's teacher had advised them to turn to a psychiatrist for advice. The parents brought the child to Professor Z, who was a famous psychiatrist and psychologist, at that time head of the psychiatric clinic. They told me sadly that he had tested her and had advised that she be taken out of school, her intelligence being too low. He proposed that she be placed in a home for the feeble-minded. He ended by warning the parents that if they failed to do this the child would become maladjusted and possibly delinquent.

The parents could not bring themselves to follow this advice. They felt that the verdict of the psychologist could not be true of their child, who very often showed excellent sense, especially in human situations, and who also had a sensitive feeling for art. But, on the other hand, there were the school difficulties, especially in arithmetic. That the intelligence test of Professor Z showed such poor results was in agreement with her failure in schoolwork.

They asked for my opinion. Knowing the child from infancy, knowing her as a fine child, I proposed to speak to her. I first asked her to tell me what questions Professor Z had put to her. There were the usual problems, including among others arithmetical tasks which required adding, subtracting, multiplying, dividing, etc. She was unable to solve these problems. I changed the topic of discussion. Then I told her of a concrete situation which, according to my story, developed in a neighboring family, in which the mother was preparing a bath for the baby, without having the right containers. The child was keenly interested in the story; and when, at the dramatic moment, I put the question, "What to do?" she reacted vividly and success-fully. And this despite the fact that I had chosen problems demanding not only operations Professor Z had tested, but also others more difficult. This child was not able to deal with problems the sense of which she did not see. On the other hand, if a problem grew out of the situation, if the solution was required by the situation, she encountered no unusual difficulty, frequently showing excellent sense.

A friend of mine, an anthropologist at Lübeck, had stayed for a long time with a tribe in Central Africa. Upon his return he showed me the fine objects he had brought back with him, adding: "But I am still waiting to get some very excellent things. Some of the tribesmen with whom I was friendly have agreed to make for me and to send along to me a complete native hut, with all the customary utensils and art decorations. I want them for an exhibit in my museum. They have agreed to construct all the objects to one-third of their usual size, because I have not sufficient space for a full-scale model. I should like to show them to you when they arrive. You will enjoy them."

After several months the objects arrived. Everything was in order, all the things had been reduced to one-third their original size. But he was puzzled about an incorrectness in certain articles. The pot for cooking and the wooden support on which one rests one's head during sleep came in their actual size.

The anthropologist wrote a letter to a friend, a missionary who lived with these people, asking him to give the tribesmen a friendly scolding, and to have them send the few incorrect articles in the proper proportions. It was a long time before the answer came. It read: "I was not able to get the men to do it. They insisted that while one might still be able to live in the reduced tent, it would be nonsense to make a cooking pot (already quite small in its original size) so small. Similarly for the wooden support." The missionary wrote that he had found no way of convincing them to do it.

Another example: An anthropologist, working on the construction of the grammar of a native language, had the assistance of a native who was able to help him with the translation of stories and sentences. One time the assistant was to translate a certain sentence, but the anthropologist was unable to get it from him. Puzzled, he tried to find out what words or grammatical inflections might be causing the trouble. It was only after some time that the native burst out, "How can I translate this sentence of yours: 'The white man shot six bears today'? This is nonsense. It is impossible that the white man could shoot six bears in one day!"

In these instances the operation, the goal itself, is viewed within the functional meaning of the whole situation, without abstracting from the function it has.

In short, as I formulated in an investigation about the thinking of primitive peoples,[1] there is a great difference between fulfilling a task if it is sensibly required in the actual life situation, or if it fits into it, and performing a task with no sensible relation to the actual situation, or which even contradicts the given situation, making sense only if one abstracts entirely from its role in actual reality.

But, as I said in that paper, it would be a mistake to conclude that such failure to abstract is evidence of a lack of ability to think. If someone refuses to perform an abstraction that is to him senseless, if he is not able and not willing to deal with such abstractions, this may be a sign that his thinking takes the situation seriously. Of course, in our scientific history abstraction from reality has been developed in various ways as a very important tool. But an inability or a refusal to perform steps *if* the real meaning of the abstraction in the scientific context cannot be realized is not bad but good thinking. Lack of abstraction in itself is no measure of thinking. The best thinkers refuse, and sometimes are not able, to perform tasks that involve really senseless abstractions; they revolt against it.

And so, some types of children need to be introduced to geometrical problems by way of actual situations in which the task itself has real meaning for them.

But there are many children—and grown-ups—who do not need such help. They easily become interested in the "theoretical" problems. They take the problem as an interesting task, as a challenge to their productive activity. And while learning geometry they are able, and even eager, to apply what they have gained of insight to other geometrical problems and to life problems. (The extreme of this is, of course, the foolish attempt to apply such learned procedures anywhere, whether they fit or not.)

It is, I think, a task of education to develop in children such a "theoretical" interest of the first kind. It opens to them a marvelous realm of crystal pureness, of inherent consistency. And I think that

[1] M. Wertheimer, "Über das Denken der Naturvölker, Zahlen und Zahlgebilde," *Zeitschrift für Psychologie*, 1912, Vol. 60, pp. 321-378; reprinted in: M. Wertheimer, *Drei Abhandlungen zur Gestalttheorie*, Erlangen: Philosophische Akademie, 1925.

the thesis of formal education was right in holding that thinking with pure materials is of importance generally for the development of thinking; one is then not so easily a victim of hazy, muddled thinking even in practical situations.

II

1. It has happened a number of times that teachers of mathematics have come to me and told me how dissatisfied they were with the traditional ways of teaching. They then went on to say that they had read or heard of my theories and had the feeling these might help to teach more reasonably. But they were at a loss to see how this could be done, how a concrete teaching procedure could be developed in the light of gestalt theory.

In fact, I should think that the main positive consequences for teaching are already implied in the preceding discussions of this book. I shall try to sketch here one way of proceeding which meets the theoretical requirements that have been developed. But I may say at once: there are good teachers who do similar things out of genuine feeling for what is required educationally. Most of what I shall propose is in no way surprisingly "new." But it is certainly in many ways different from the actual procedures in many schools.

Many good procedures are possible, and different children require sometimes different (though structurally similar) ways. It is, of course, easiest to teach one child alone. Here I shall speak of such teaching. But it is also possible, and sometimes very advisable, to employ group thinking in the classroom.

In the light of my teaching experiences it would seem best—especially at the start—to show, to "teach" as little as possible. It would seem desirable to avoid as much as possible the giving of ready-made steps. The child should be confronted with tasks with which he tries to deal himself. Let the child face problems, let him receive co-operative help as he needs it, but let him not simply copy or repeat given procedures. I would avoid as much as possible anything that might introduce a mechanical state of mind, an attitude of drill.

I shall illustrate with the problem of finding the area of a figure. What is most desirable is that the child should find his way himself after he has been in a structurally reasonable problem situation. If the child seems at a loss or declares: "I can't do it," it often suffices simply to say: "Try it; perhaps you'll find a way." And if this does not help, one can add the question: "Where is the trouble?" And only if such procedures fail should one go on to give concrete help.

2. *Sensible introduction of the concept "size of area" of the rectangle.* I would not start by teaching how the area of the rectangle is to be found, especially not with the details of determining the area of a rectangle. For the sense of the concept "size of area" may not be at all clear to the child. I would rather start with a situation in which the problem of being "bigger" or "smaller" is sensibly included.

For example, I would give two rectangles with the same base, one obviously higher than the other.

FIG. 171

And I would ask: "How can one find exactly how much bigger the second figure is than the first?" *Without*, of course, giving the auxiliary line. I would have the two rectangles cut out of cardboard and placed side by side, letting the child find the idea of placing one on top of the other, fitting them to each other, and noting the remainder.

Then I would turn to real measuring. "This figure, you see, is 9 inches wide and so is the other. Now the height of one measures 5 inches, the other 6 inches." And I would at first enjoy hearing the child say simply: "The one is bigger by one strip" or "by one strip which is 9 inches wide and 1 inch high."

2a. I may interrupt here. For many children this abstract procedure is, as was mentioned above, proper. For other children it is advisable to start instead with a problem situation in which they can feel the sense concretely. For example, I would start by telling a story: "Once upon a time" (or still better, for some children: "In the neighborhood some days ago") "there was a farmer who wanted to move away. He found a farmer in another place who was willing to exchange land with him. The two farms were alike in many ways and were about the same size. In talking over the matter, they wanted to find out exactly whether one farm was bigger than the other, and by how much. Here is a picture of the two farms.

FIG. 172

Now how could you find out which one was the bigger?"

The child may, instead of answering, ask questions, such as: "Would the farmer who had the smaller farm have enough money to pay for the difference?" But in most cases one can easily make the child face the problem of comparing the sizes.

At this point some children arrive at the idea of breaking the figure up into small squares.

2b. If this does not work, another concrete situation, involving more concrete help, may be tried. "You are sitting on the floor with another boy, and each of you is building a wall with blocks. You have used up all your blocks, while the other still has a pile of unused blocks beside him. You want very much to build your wall one block higher, and you ask the other boy for some of his blocks. He refuses to give them, and you say to him: 'I don't want many; you have a good many that you aren't using; why can't you let me have some?' The other boy snaps back: 'How many do you need?' Now, how many do you need if you want to build your wall one block higher, or two blocks higher?"

Some teachers may be aghast here at the mixing up of three-dimensional and two dimensional matters. One could, of course, have started with cardboard squares; but it does not seem to matter; in fact, I myself would prefer to use the blocks.

FIG. 173

3. *Reaching the "formula."* With such tasks, and preferably, if possible, with purely abstract tasks, I would try to have the child himself reach the formulation: "I need one more row (or two more rows, etc.). What I need is so many rows, and the number of rows has to be multiplied by the number of blocks in one row."

Then I would ask: "How many little squares are there in this whole figure?" or: "What is the whole area?" The child may then say: "One has to measure the base; one has to measure the altitude; and multiply."

4. Here I would let the child make the discovery that it clicks both ways, whether one or the other side is taken as base.

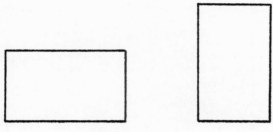

Fig. 174

It is often nice to see how the child enjoys finding that it works both ways. Under certain conditions the discovery that $ab = ba$ is a discovery, does give insight.[2]

5. *Tasks at issue.* I would not go on to the figuring out of answers to many more examples of this kind, because of the danger that the child might lose the structural character of the formula. Instead I would give at the start some interestingly different cases. And I would introduce another example to which the procedure does not apply, waiting until the child decides for himself: "I can't do it the same way here; you have to count out the little squares." I would give tasks such as determining the size of a room, or of two tables, or even the finding of the cubic volume of a room, or of a three-dimensional pile of blocks. In the problem one would focus on the number of blocks in one *square* which is to be multiplied by the altitude, and not simply on the multiplication of the three sides.

6. *The area of the parallelogram.* It seems best simply to put the

[2] Cf. M. Wertheimer, *op. cit.*

question: "What is the area of such a figure? Can you find out?" As in the case of the rectangle, some children will, after a little deliberation and encouragement, find the way themselves.

If the child makes no headway, one can ask: "What is the trouble? What makes it so hard?" To which the child might answer: "You see, the trouble is with these ends here. If the ends were like those of the rectangle, all would be well."

6a. In some cases it is helpful to give the following figure:

FIG. 175

Children sometimes respond: "Oh, everything is all right in the middle, but . . ."

6b. Or: "There is a house of blocks, the top having the shape of a rectangle. I would like to put a nice roof on it. Here I have a piece of reddish-brown cardboard. Maybe we can use it. It has the same length as the top of the house, but unfortunately it has the form of a parallelogram. Can you make the right kind of cover out of it?"

A possibly better procedure, because it gives less help, might be: "Here is this cardboard parallelogram. What can you do to make a rectangle out of it?"

6c. *Alternate procedure.* After having simply put the problem of finding the area of the parallelogram, with no result, I place an entirely different figure before the child, in which there are two structural disturbances, one clearly a not-fitting addition, the other a hole or gap.

FIG. 176

The transition from such a structurally easier task to the apparently different case of the parallelogram is, for some children, difficult or impossible without further help. But there are children who, having solved these problems, look back at the parallelogram, smile—and do it.

6d. If need be, I would introduce the problem in practical terms: "A mechanic who makes metal plates (of rectangular form) uses the following procedure to determine how much metal he will need for a certain size of rectangle. (Here follows the teaching of the area of the rectangle.) One day he is asked to make a plate of the following form.

FIG. 177

He would like to find out how much metal he will need in this case. (Or, similarly, for the question of weight, etc.)

"At first he is at a loss. 'How can I do this?' he asks. But after a short while the mechanic grins. He has found the way. How did he do it?" But I may add that I would not give a problem like this to many children. For many the thing is too obvious. They do not need the long-drawn-out story, which may be an amusing underestimation of their ability.

These figures offer considerable help toward grasping the structural character of "disturbance," "gap," "there is needed here just what is an unnecessary addition there."

At this point I would also introduce a figure to which the procedure does *not* fit, leaving it entirely to the child to see the point.

FIG. 178

6e. *Another procedure:* In some cases it may be necessary to use a figure containing one or two rows of rectangles, with the triangles at the ends.

Fig. 179

7. *Procedure in giving the auxiliary lines.* In most of the cases that I have seen, such procedures did lead to the insight: change of the parallelogram into the rectangle. Only if all these forms of help failed would I give the child concretely the steps he should have found out.

But I would not start by stating that two verticals are to be dropped. I would say first that in order to get a rectangle we have to correct the two ends. Then I would again wait to see if the child came forward himself with the next step.

Or I would ask: "How could we change it into a rectangle at one end?" If this did not help, I would start by cutting off the left end, and after waiting a moment, ask: "And what of the other side? Do we now have a rectangle at the other side?"

Should there still be no progress, I would draw all the needed lines, giving both of the following figures.

Fig. 180

If the child has not reacted to the last step, I would ask: "What about the size of the two figures?" Then: "What are the parts of the parallelogram? Of the rectangle?"

8. *After the solution: remarks on repetition and drill.* After the goal of finding the area of the parallelogram has been reached, I would give the pupil a number of figures, differing in appearance, for solution. But I would not have him repeat the solution with a great many exercises. Rather, I would give a few problems which require finding the area, making them as interestingly different as possible, and interspersing among them some tasks which cannot be solved in this way. And without any formal introduction, quite innocently, I would intersperse the task of finding the area of the trapezoid and the triangle.

Fig. 181

There are cases in which the child, without further teaching, solves these problems genuinely. If he does not, procedures similar to the above can be used.

One might suppose that to mix such varied tasks would be too much for the brain of a child. Some would say that the child should stick for a time to the area of the rectangle alone, then for a considerable time to the parallelogram alone. And they would regard the procedure of interspersing other, even "impossible," tasks as psychologically dangerous, on the ground that one should stick to a thing and give it much repetition, before turning to a new task.

According to my experience, this would be true only for certain kinds of children, for example, for those who are too timid. In such cases one needs to proceed more slowly. It is important not to go ahead before one feels that the matter has clicked for the child. (But repetition need not, of itself, make for clicking.) But with many children the desired procedure would seem to be just the opposite. To deal again and again with tasks which tiresomely repeat things the child feels he has already grasped becomes very boresome, and frequently encourages the child to work thoughtlessly. It is, I would suppose, one of the reasons why so many children, after some schooling, acquire such a hearty dislike for arithmetic and geometry. Yet with the proceedings described here, children are happy about their activities, their discoveries.

III

The Proof

1. *Basic difficulties.* The transition to the geometrical proof, to the "demonstration," should be made cautiously. The child may in all probability not catch the sense of "demonstration." It is quite a problem. And even after children have reacted positively a few times, I doubt whether they have a real understanding of the meaning of proof in the sense of the geometrician. It remains for them mostly a funny, not quite understandable, procedure of grown-ups. The interests of an axiomatically thinking grown-up are strange to them. And it does not seem really possible that they could, before acquiring a further knowledge and more "concrete" understanding of a large number of various geometrical problems, realize the aims of the mathematician which make this procedure sensible.

Nevertheless, there are sensible ways of helping children to understand the need for *some* kind of "proof," even if the traditional proofs are really understood by only a few.

2. *Introduction to proof.* The proof should not be simply imposed on the child. It might at least be introduced in terms like these: "Sometimes we cannot really 'cut up' and 'fill in.' How would you make sure in such a case that you are correct?" It might even be well to introduce a figure about which one is actually not sure, and say: "How would you make sure that the method you have used

FIG. 182

before will apply here?" To this the child may answer: "If these two oblique lines are parallel, then it must be right to do what we did before." And if the child is now asked: "Why? Why are you so sure of this?" he may reply: "What matters is that what I want to take away from the left side should fit exactly at the right side." If you then ask: "How could you prove that? What does that imply?" you may get the answer: "We have to have the two triangles equal." Question: "Could you prove that they are equal if the lines are parallel?" Answer: "Because they were made that way." Question: "Could you show in detail what was decisive in making them equal?"

And then the child may face the question of how to get at the congruence or, in his terms, at the identity of the triangles, by way of the equality of the lines and the angles.

The child may here make use of some general theorems he had learned earlier, such as the theorem concerning the equality of angles between parallel lines. If not, the child may come to these problems in this very context.

It is not intended to say that the child should always, in all cases, find the proof himself. (Though the frequent argument that this would be too time consuming seems to me factually not quite true, nor decisive.) There is nothing against having the teacher demonstrate the whole procedure. But if so, he should do it in a structurally proper way, in order to help toward a real understanding of the hierarchy of the steps.

The Balancing Stick[*]

I<small>F</small> <small>YOU</small> ask children to make a T out of blocks, standing one up vertically, and balancing a second horizontally on top of the first, it is interesting to watch developments in the subjects, to watch them come to a grasp of the structural requirement of symmetry for stability.

The same problem is involved in the task of carrying long sticks (which is interesting to study in dogs, too). First the children experiment with the stick; often they give up after some negative trials. But some persist, and most come back to it after a time. It is enlightening to see how they learn from their mistakes. Negative trials are not just negative instances. Of course, sometimes a child proceeds with blind changes, but very often we observe sensible proceedings in the changes. For example, the stick was seized at the left of center, and it falls down on the right; in the next attempt, the child may blindly repeat, grasping it at the same place—or even further to the left—but often children correct themselves sensibly; they grasp it further to the right. They may not go far enough, or they may overdo it, but then they correct sensibly again in the next attempt. Often we observe a consistent procedure in the whole behavior. There is a fundamental difference between a succession of random trials and a sensible structure in the succession of trials.

To illustrate: If somebody shoots without seeing the target, and without being able to see where his shot hit, beside the target, being told only (or experiencing somehow) that the target was not hit by his shot, he will be at a loss to change the direction of his next shot

[*] This appendix, which was not included in the original edition, is a slightly edited version of a fragment found among Max Wertheimer's papers.—M. W.

sensibly. But if he can observe the effects of his negative trial, *then* the directions in which he chooses to aim do show a difference between foolish and sensible behavior. Suppose his first shot hits at point 1, to the right of the target. To choose then, for the next shot a direction still more to the right would be foolish.

----
                          2   t   3   1

Sensibly he will aim next time so as to hit at 2 or 3, correcting his aim on the basis of the deviation, and continuing thus to come nearer to the target.

In many children, in the blocks or the long stick problem, we see very soon a considerable tendency to focus on about the middle.

If a hidden factor is introduced arbitrarily, difficulties naturally arise. But even in experimentation with such a changed stick, sensible procedures often occur (for example if a piece of lead is hidden somewhere inside the stick). But succeeding in learning what to do in such a situation may not provide for reasonable guesses in other situations, in which the location of the lead may be somewhere else again, since the place is arbitrary.

If, on the other hand, a clear asymmetry is provided in the visual appearance of the object, as for example in these drawings, the situa-

FIG. 183

tion is quite different. Here we do not observe, from the outset, a tendency to grasp just the middle, but instead, rather a trend to compensate somehow.

Now it makes a difference whether some external connection is arbitrarily introduced, or a sensible correlation is at work. The situation becomes theoretically ambiguous if a child has learned, for example, to seize the stick, in order to carry it, on a red dot which is in the middle; or if he has learned to grasp a stick, one half of which is red and the other half green, where the colors meet. But now we may introduce a variation and see what happens.

FIG. 184

Here the color conditions are the same, only the length of one end is increased. Will the children grasp at the color mark? If we introduce two procedures of learning—according to color and according to symmetry in size—then the transition from the arbitrary to the structurally sensible seems, if one is open-minded, easier than the other way around. We see again that this is not just a question of generalization, but of how—in what direction—generalization works: in a structurally sensible way, or according to blind association, blind connection. The ρ-relation between symmetry and stability seems, basically, to be outstanding.

The Sum of a Series*

I SHALL describe how a direct train of thought proceeded.[1] I shall express the series in the form

$$\frac{1}{a}+\frac{1}{a^2}+\frac{1}{a^3}+\ \cdots \qquad\qquad (a \text{ is an integer} > 1)$$

The problem is to find the sum of the continuous series.

First: How does the sum increase if the series continues? Obviously the sum in each successive step, S_{n+1}, is equal to the previous S_n plus $\frac{1}{a^{n+1}}$. The value of $\frac{1}{a^{n+1}}$ becomes smaller and smaller the farther I proceed in the series: the larger n becomes, the smaller will be the value $\frac{1}{a^{n+1}}$. Hence in later stages S_{n+1} will more and more approximate S_n— the curve of the sum will no longer rise so much, will change less and less, and will perhaps approach the horizontal.

FIG. 185

But this does not help me to see what value the sum is approaching.

Second: If I want to understand, I must realize from the begin-

---

* This Appendix was Appendix 1 in the original edition.—M. W.
[1] This report was written down during the actual thought process.

ning what the first term, $\dfrac{1}{a}$, means as part of its whole; and so with the later terms.

$\dfrac{1}{a}$ means that 1 is divided into a equal parts and that $\dfrac{1}{a}$ is one of them; e.g., ¼ means:

Remainder R_1

1/4

FIG. 186

I have divided 1, the whole, into 4 equal parts; in considering the first of these parts, ¼, I have to realize that the other parts remain, in the present case, ¾. In general, taking $\dfrac{1}{a}$ the whole 1 is divided into $\dfrac{1}{a} + (a-1)\dfrac{1}{a}$. This is the situation with the first member of my series.

What happens if I proceed to the next step, $S_2 = \dfrac{1}{a} + \dfrac{1}{a^2}$?

1 2

FIG. 187

In our case the sum is now $\frac{1}{4} + \frac{1}{16}$. This means that with the addition of $\frac{1}{16}$, the next quarter is divided into $\frac{1}{16} + \frac{3}{16}$, as the whole was divided in the first step. I have $\frac{1}{4} + \overbrace{\frac{1}{16}}^{} \; | + \overbrace{\frac{3}{16} + \frac{2}{4}}^{}$

first   second   remainder
quarter   quarter R_2

Or in general, $\dfrac{1}{a} + \underbrace{\dfrac{1}{a^2}}_{} \Big| + \underbrace{\dfrac{a-1}{a^2} + \dfrac{a-2}{a}}_{}$. R_2 must now be $(a-2)\dfrac{1}{a}$

first   second   remainder
a part a part R_2

because the first part of R_1 has been drawn upon in the $\dfrac{1}{a^2}$ division.

Again if I proceed to the next sum, $\dfrac{1}{a}+\dfrac{1}{a^2}+\dfrac{1}{a^3}$ the following happens:

FIG. 188

Here the next $\frac{1}{16}$ is divided into $\frac{1}{64}+\frac{3}{64}$; I have

$$\tfrac{1}{4}+\tfrac{1}{16}+\underbrace{\tfrac{1}{64}\;\Big|\;+\tfrac{3}{64}}_{\text{second }\frac{1}{16}}+\tfrac{2}{16}+\tfrac{2}{4}$$

$$\underbrace{\hphantom{\tfrac{1}{4}+\tfrac{1}{16}+\tfrac{1}{64}+\tfrac{3}{64}+\tfrac{2}{16}+\tfrac{2}{4}}}_{\text{second }\frac{1}{4}}$$

Or in general $\dfrac{1}{a}+\dfrac{1}{a^2}+\overbrace{\dfrac{1}{a^3}\;\Big|\;+\dfrac{a-1}{a^3}}^{\text{critical region}}+\dfrac{a-2}{a^2}+\dfrac{a-2}{a}$

Every time, in every step, the next region $\dfrac{1}{a^n}$ is divided into $\dfrac{1}{a^{n+1}}+$ $\dfrac{a-1}{a^{n+1}}$; and with that the previous $\dfrac{a-1}{a^n}$ changes into $\dfrac{a-2}{a^n}$. In this way, the critical region $\dfrac{1}{a^{n+1}}+\dfrac{a-1}{a^{n+1}}$ shifts slowly to the right, and decreases in size at the same time; the structure is

$$S_n+\overbrace{\dfrac{1}{a^{n+1}}+\dfrac{a-1}{a^{n+1}}}^{\text{critical region}}+(a-2)S_n$$

R_n in the general structure must be $(a-2)$ times S_n itself—it changes from $(a-2)\dfrac{1}{a}$ to $(a-2)(\dfrac{1}{a}+\dfrac{1}{a^2})$, to $(a-2)(\dfrac{1}{a}+\dfrac{1}{a^2}+\dfrac{1}{a^3})$, and so on.

Third: The whole, "1", is divided into S_n, the critical region and $(a-2)$ S_n, the remainder R_n. As we proceed, the critical region becomes necessarily smaller and smaller, while the sum at the left increases. If the critical region becomes exceedingly small, approaches zero, the whole appears to be divided into $S_n + (a-2) S_n$: the whole no longer appears to be divided into a equal parts, as in the beginning, but into $(a-1)$ *equal parts!* So the sum of the continuous series itself must approach the value $\frac{1}{a-1}$!

In mathematical terms: $1 = (a-1) S_n$ (+ the critical region which approaches zero). The 1 at the left means the whole, whereas in the usual derivation it is just the first member of the series $1 + a + a^2 + \cdots$; here there is the realization of what S is structurally as part of its whole, whereas in the usual derivation the value of S is reached by some algebraic operations.

Fourth: I want to formulate exactly. I had

$$1 = S_n + \text{critical region} + (a-2)S_n$$

The value of the critical region is $\frac{1}{a^{n+1}} + \frac{a-1}{a^{n+1}} = \frac{a}{a^{n+1}} = \frac{1}{a^n}$.

As we saw before it is the next $\frac{1}{a^n}$ which becomes divided in the transition from S_n to S_{n+1}. Therefore, in exact formulation

$$1 = (a-1)S_n + \frac{1}{a_n}$$

$$\text{or,} \quad S_n = \frac{1}{a-1} - \frac{1}{a^n(a-1)}.$$

$\frac{1}{a^n(a-1)}$ decreases as n increases; it never reaches, but approaches zero more and more closely.

Fifth: The whole procedure consisted in realizing the meaning of the parts in the whole structure, which led to structurization of the whole into $(a-1)$ parts plus the diminishing critical region.

The result clearly holds for whatever value $\frac{1}{a}$ may have, provided a is greater than 1. In the series starting with ½, of course, there are no $(a-2)$ parts; $a-2$ being zero, the series approaches 1. If $\frac{1}{a}$ is equal to or greater than 1, the conditions for this structurization are not given—the sum will forever increase, will not approach a limit.

But what of values between ½ and 1, e.g., ¾? There seemed at first to be no way to structural realization. The way was opened by viewing ¾ not as part of 1 but as ¼ of 3, taking 3 as "the whole":

FIG. 189

This gave the basis for understanding the fate of the critical region, etc., which is here in an interesting way more complex than in the preceding cases. But I shall not report the further steps dealing with this and other related problems.

If we look back to the usual proceeding—multiplication of the series and subtraction—this becomes clear: Although the usual procedure is so very much quicker, externally so much more elegant, though it holds equally generally for the structures first considered and for the more complex instances, it is nevertheless a trick in the sense that it gives no direct understanding of what happens structurally.

Of course such elegant external procedures, leading to quick solutions, are useful. But the longer way is needed in order really to understand the construction, to realize what happens. As for *finding* the solution, the first way is either a chance happening only, or a clever trick, the result of some valid equations, which bring the solution without giving insight into the nature of the series. To be sure, it may have started with structural insight into *one* feature of the series, viz., that it is shiftable, that if one multiplies by a or a^2, the same series appears except for the first members; but this is not sufficient to reach the solution by way of structural understanding.

Max Wertheimer: A Bibliography*

1. Psychologische Tatbestandsdiagnostik (With J. Klein). *Arch. f. Kriminalanthrop. u. Kriminalistik,* 1904, 15, 72-113.
2. Experimentelle Untersuchungen zur Tatbestandsdiagnostik. *Arch. f. d. ges. Psychol.,* 1905, 6, 59-131. Also published as a separate: (Inaugural-Dissertation) Leipzig: Engelmann, 1905, pp. 1-70.
3. Über die Assoziationsmethoden. *Arch. f. Kriminalanthrop. p. Kriminalstik,* 1906, 22, 293-319.
4. Tatbestandsdiagnostische Kombinationsversuche. (With O. Lippmann). *Zschr. f. angew. Psychol.,* 1907, 1, 119-128.
5. Musik der Wedda. *Sammelbände d. internat. Musikgesellschaft,* 1910, 11, 300-309.
6. Über das Denken der Naturvölker: 1. Zahlen und Zahlgebilde. *Zschr. f. Psychol.,* 1912, 60, 321-378. Reprinted in #28. Abridged translation in Ellis, W. D., *A sourcebook of gestalt psychology.* New York: Harcourt, Brace, 1938, pp. 265-273.
7. Experimentelle Studien über das Sehen von Bewegung. *Zschr. f. Psychol.,* 1912, 61, 161-265. Reprinted in #28. Also published as a separate: (Habilitationsschrift) Leipzig: Barth, 1912, pp. 1-105. Translation in Shipley, T. (Ed.), *Classics in modern psychology.* New York: Philosophical Library, 1959 (to appear), Ch. 31.
8. *Über Schlussprozesse im produktiven Denken.* Berlin: De Gruyter, 1920. Pp. 22. Reprinted in #28. Abridged translation in Ellis, W. D., *A sourcebook of gestalt psychology.* New York: Harcourt, Brace, 1938, pp. 274-282.
9. Über die Wahrnehmung der Schallrichtung, (With E. M. von Hornbostel). *Sitzungsber. d. preuss. Akad. d. Wiss., Berlin,* 1920, 20, 388-396.
10. Untersuchungen zur Lehre von der Gestalt: I. Prinzipielle Bemerkungen. *Psychol. Forsch.,* 1922, 1, 47-58. Abridged translation in

* This Appendix appears for the first time in this edition.—M.W.

Ellis, W. D., A *sourcebook of gestalt psychology*. New York: Harcourt, Brace, 1938, pp. 12-16.

11. Bemerkungen zu Hillebrands Theorie der stroboskopischen Bewegungen. *Psychol. Forsch.*, 1923, 3, 106-123.
12. Untersuchungen zur Lehre von der Gestalt: II. *Psychol. Forsch.*, 1923, 4, 301-350. Abridged translations in Ellis, W. D. A *sourcebook of gestalt psychology*. New York: Harcourt, Brace, 1938, pp. 71-88; and in Beardslee, D. C. and Wertheimer, M. (Eds.) *Readings in perception*. New York: Van Nostrand, 1958, pp. 115-135.
13. Über Gestalttheorie. Lecture at the Kant Society, Berlin, December 17, 1924. *Symposion: Philos. Zschr. f. Forschung u. Aussprache*, 1925, 1, 39-60. Also published as a separate: Erlangen: Philosophische Akademie, 1925, pp. 1-24. Abridged translation in Ellis, W. D. A *sourcebook of gestalt psychology*. New York: Harcourt, Brace, 1938, pp. 1-11. Complete translation in *Soc. Res.*, 1944, 11, 78-99. See item 33).
14. Zu dem Problem der Unterscheidung von Einzelinhalt und Teil. *Zschr. f. Psychol.*, 1933, 129, 353-357. Translation in the present volume (item 19, enlarged edition).
15. On truth. *Soc. Res.*, 1934, 1, 135-146.
16. Some problems in the theory of ethics. *Soc. Res.*, 1935, 2, 353-367.
17. On the concept of democracy. In Ascoli, M. and Lehmann, F. (Eds.), *Political and economic democracy*. New York: Norton, 1937. Pp. 271-283.
18. A story of three days. In Anshen, Ruth N. (Ed.), *Freedom: its meaning*. New York: Harcourt, Brace, 1940. Pp. 555-569.
19. *Productive thinking*. New York: Harper, 1945. Translated into Japanese by Tatsuro Yatabe, and published in Tokyo by Iwanami Genai Sōsho, 1952. Translated into German by Wolfgang Metzger, and published in Frankfort a/M by Waldemar Kramer, 1957. Enlarged edition, New York: Harper, 1959.

Notes, Reviews, Reprints, Abstracts, Etc.

20. Zur Tatbestandsdiagnostik: eine Feststellung. *Arch. f. d. ges. Psychol.*, 1906, 7, 139-140.
21. Über experimentell-psychologische Analyse einiger hirnpathologischer Erscheinungen. *Ber. über. d. V Kongr. f. exper. Psychol.* (Leipzig: Barth), 1912 (Abstract).
22. Review of Vera Strasser's *Psychologie der Zusammenhänge und Beziehungen*, Berlin: Springer, 1921, *Psychol. Forsch.*, 1922, 2, 384.
23. Review of P. Häberlin's *Der Gegenstand der Psychologie*, Berlin: Springer, 1921. *Psychol. Forsch.*, 1922, 2, 384-385.
24. Review of E. H. Sanders' *Over den invloed van vermoienis op de*

optische schijnbewegingen (*Nederl. Tijdschr. voor Geneeskunde*, 1921, II, #15). *Psychol. Forsch.*, 1923, 3, 175-176.

25. Review of P. Schilder's Über elementare Halluzinationen des Bewegungssehens (*Zschr. f. d. ges. Neurol. u. Psychiat.*, 1922, #80). *Psychol. Forsch.*, 1923, 3, 176-177.

26. Review of R. Thurnwald's Psychologie des primitiven Menschen, in G. Kafka (Ed.), *Handbuch der vergleichenden Psychologie*, 3 vols., Munich: Ernst Reinhardt, 1922. *Psychol. Forsch.*, 1924, 4, 207.

27. Review of H. Rotschild's Über den Einfluss der Gestalt auf das negative Nachbild ruhender visueller Figuren (*v. Gräfes Arch. f. Ophthalmol.*, 1923, 112, 1-28). *Psychol. Forsch.*, 1924, 5, 365-367.

28. *Drei Abhandlungen zur Gestalttheorie.* Erlangen: Philosophische Akademie, 1925. Pp. iv + 184. Consists of reprints of items 6, 7, and 8.

29. Zum Problem der Schwelle. *Ber. über d. VIII internat. Kongr. f. Psychol.*, 1926. (Groningen: P. Noordhoff, 1927, 447, Abstract).

30. Gestaltpsychologische Forschung. In Saupe, E. (Ed.) *Einführung in die neuere Psychologie* (Vol. 3 of *Handbücher der neueren Erziehungswissenschaft.*). Osterwieck a/H: Zickfeldt, 1st ed., 1927, pp. 46-53; 2nd and 3d ed., 1928, pp. 47-54; 4th and 5th ed., 1931, pp. 44-51.

31. Tatbestandsdiagnostik. In Abderhalden, E. (Ed.), *Handbuch der biologischen Arbeitsmethoden.* Berlin and Vienna: Urban and Schwarzenberg, Section 6, Part C2, pp. 1105-1111, 1933.

32. Foreword to Katona, G. *Organizing and memorizing.* New York: Columbia University Press, 1940. Pp. v-vii.

33. Gestalt theory. *Soc. Res.*, 1944, 11, 78-99. A translation of #13.

34. On discrimination experiments: I. Two logical structures. Late undated manuscript, edited by Lise Wertheimer. (*Psychol. Rev.*, 1959, in press.)

35. On discrimination experiments: II. A critique of Spence's approach. Unpublished late undated manuscript, edited by Lise Wertheimer.

INDEX

A-B method, 18–20, 22–24, 61–62, 65, 67–69, 99–100, 124n, 151–157, 237–238. *See also* A–responses and B–responses
A priori analysis, 158, 166, 205
A-responses and B-responses, 18–20, 22–24, 65–66, 99–100, 103–106, 116–119. *See also* A–B method
Abderhalden, E., 296
Above to below, going from, *see* Gestalt approach, Gestalt logic
Absolute movement, 215
Absolute rest, 215
Abstracting, difficulty in, 272–276
Acceleration of falling body, 206–210
Ach, N., 12
Ackermann, W., 256, 258n
Ad hoc explanation, 218
Algebra, learning of, 151–160
Altar window, problem of, 266–268
Analogies of thought processes
  mechanical, 62
  perceptual, 55–56, 73–74, 124–127, 243, 260–265
  See also Machines, Magic worlds, Musical illustrations
And in logic, 194, 255–259
Angle, nature of, 127–129
Angles of a polygon, *see* Exterior angles of a polygon, sum of
Ann Arbor, xi
Anshen, Ruth N., 180n, 295
Anthropological illustrations (of inability to abstract), 272–276
Area, problem of finding, *see* Altar window, Educational implications, Frame, Parallelogram, Rectangle, Square, Trapezoid, Triangle
Aristotle, 7

Arithmetic, learning of, 160-168. *See also* Educational implications
Arnheim, R., xv
Asch, S. E., xi, xiii, xv, 131, 131n, 245
Ascoli, M., 295
Association theory, 2–3, 5, 8–12, 42–44, 50–51, 58–65, 68–69, 75, 85, 89–96, 98–99, 120–121, 131–133, 152–154, 159–168, 234–235, 237, 245–248, 250–251
Attitudes and thinking, 2, 22n, 64, 131, 179–183, 246, 271
Aufgabe, 12
Axioms, *see* Traditional logic

Badminton, game of, problem of, 169–181
Balancing stick, problem of, 286–288
Beardslee, D. C., 53n, 63n, 93n, 125n, 295
Behavior and logic, 7n
Behaviorism, *see* Association theory
Bloomington, xi
Bohr, N., 28n
Borne, Mrs. Ray, xiii
Bridge problem, 79–96
  analysis of solution, 89–96
  blind machine for, 95–96
  gestalt logic of, 93–95
  See also Balancing stick
Brouwer, 39
Bryn Mawr College, xi
Bühler, K., 12
Buridanus, J., 10n

Celestial mechanics, 212
Centering, 176–192, 229–233. *See also* Gestalt logic
Chancourtois, de, 27n

Chess, 176n
Chicago, University of, xi
Class concepts, 6, 126, 138, 248–257
Classical logic, see Traditional logic
Commutability, principle of, 70–75
Conditioning, 8, 9, 11n. See also Association theory
Constellation theory, 11
Contiguity, 8. See also Association theory
Corners of a cube, pyramid, etc., problem of, 44n
Crystallization, problem of, in physics, 57–58
Curiosity, 1, 91–92, 173n

Deduction, see Traditional logic
Denkpsychologie, 12
Dewey, J., 11, 12
Di Piazza, Maria, xi
Distraction, effect on productive thinking of, 21, 22n
Division, structural meaning of, 132–133
Division of a sum, problem of, 129–130
Drill, 8, 22n, 30, 44, 50–51, 61–62, 68–69, 75, 99n, 115, 120–121, 131–133, 152–154, 159–168, 234–235, 245, 250–251, 283–284
Duncker, K., 131

Educational implications, 2–3, 25–26, 40n, 76–78, 127, 129–133, 151–168, 272, 275–285, et passim
Educational machines, see Machines, educational
Effect, law of, 9n, 161, 173. See also Reward
Egocentric orientation, 176–192, 241
Einstein, A., xi, 3, 169n, 210n, 213–233
Einstellung, 131–133
Elegant B, method of, 155
Elkan, Mr. and Mrs. Benno, xi
Ellis, W. D., 6n, 53n, 63n, 64n, 93n, 125n, 127n, 170n, 183n, 249n, 294–295
Environment and thinking, 63–64, 84n. See also Distraction
Excluded middle, proof by, 39
Exterior angles of a polygon, sum of, problem of, 169n, 193–204

Exterior angles of solids, sum of, problem of, 200–204

Familiarity, see Past experience
Finding solutions vs. finding questions, 141
Fitzgerald formula, 218, 229
Flight of ideas, 10, 11n
Frame, area of, 76–77
Friction, problem of, in inertia, 206–211

Galileo, G., 146n, 169n, 205–212, 223
Galvanometer problem, 143–150
Gaps in structures during thinking, 49, 126, 171, 235, 238
Gauss problem, 108–142, 169n
  extensions of, 112–142
  structural analysis of, 120–121
Generalization, 6, 22–23, 43, 111n, 150, 154, 249, 288. See also Association theory, Traditional logic
Geometry, Euclidean, xvi, 35–36
  non-Euclidean, 35–36, 200
Gestalt approach, 65, 130n, 140–142, 168–171, 212, 234, 259, et passim
  to area of parallelogram, 51–57
  to area of rectangle, 39–43
  to badminton problem, 176–181
  to bridge problem, 91–96
  to commutability, 71–75
  to description of office, 183–192
  to Gauss problem, 121
  to humor, 270–271
  to plus three, minus three problem, 146, 149
  to relativity theory, development of, 226–233
  to sum of angles problem, 202–204
  to vertical angles problem, 103–107
  See also A–B method, Educational implications, Gestalt logic, Means and ends, Whole-qualities
Gestalt logic, xvi, 212, 236–259, 260–265, et passim
  of badminton problem, 176–180
  of bridge problem, 93–94
  of plus three, minus three problem, 146–149
  of sum of angles problem, 202–204
  of vertical angles problem, 103–104
  See also And in logic, Centering, Class concepts, Gaps, Giving

"help," Homotype, Identity, *If-so* in logic, *Not* in logic, Relation, Rho relation, Truth

Giving "help," 58–61, 66, 87–90, 90*n*–91*n*

Goals in thinking, 75–78, 141, 237–243

Going from above to below, *see* Gestalt approach, Gestalt logic

Gottschaldt, K., 260*n*

Graduate Faculty of Political and Social Science (New School), xiii

Grouping, 125–126. *See also* Gestalt approach

Häberlin, P., 295

Habit, 8, 9*n*, 22*n*, 98–100, 107, 120–121, 152–154, 159–161, 167–168, 171, 234. *See also* Association theory, Drill, Repetition

Habit-family-hierarchy, 11

Hairs, of horses, number of, *see* Horse's hairs

Harvard University, xi

Hegel, G. W. F., 11

Helps, *see* Giving "help"

Henle, Mary, xv

Hilbert, D., 256, 258*n*

History of the psychology of thinking, *see* Association theory, Traditional logic, Traditional views of thinking

Homotype, 93–94, 105, 146, 187, 261–263

Hornbostel, E. M. von, 294

Horse's hairs, number of, 269–271

Hubbell, Marian B., *see* Mowatt, Marian B. H.

Hull, C. L., 11*n*

Hume, D., 8

Humor and senseless procedures, 25, 130, 269–271

Husserl, E. G., 11

Identity, principle of, 157–158, 255–259

If-so in logic, 255–259

Imposed force, *see* Vis *impressa*

Indiana, University of (Bloomington), xi

Inductive logic, 7–8, 27–29, 205, 249–250

Inertia, law of, 205–212

Infeld, L., 210*n*, 228*n*

Inner relations, *see* Gestalt approach, Gestalt logic

Insight, *see* "Seeing the light"

Intelligence, 6–7, 79ff., 272–276

Internal angles of a polygon, sum of, problem of, 199*n*, 200, 204. *See also* Exterior angles of a polygon

Jevons, W. S., 10*n*

Johnson, A., xi

Kafka, G., 296

Kant, I., 107*n*

Katona, G., 75*n*, 96*n*, 132*n*, 164*n*, 246*n*, 296

Klein, J., 294

Köhler, W., xiii, 85*n*

Kopfermann, H., 54*n*

Koyré, A., 205*n*

Krolik, W., 57*n*

Külpe, O., 12

Law of effect, *see* Effect, law of

Lehmann, F., 295

Levy, E., 64*n*, 180*n*, 183*n*, 241*n*

Lewin, K., 64*n*

Lex parsimoniae, see Parsimony, law of

Liepmann, H., 11*n*

Linnaeus, 252

Lippmann, O., 294

Locke, J., 158

Logic
  and thinking, 10, 37
  machines, 10*n*
  musical, *see* Musical illustrations
  See also And in logic, Gestalt logic, *If-so* in logic, Inductive logic, *Not* in logic, Traditional logic

Logistics, 11, 183–192, 236*n*, 256ff.

Long stick problem, *see* Balancing stick

Lorentz transformation, 218, 224, 229, 230, 233

Luchins, A., 131, 131*n*

Lullus, R., 10*n*

Mach, E., 197*n*, 205*n*

Machines
  "educational," 95–96, 158, 165–166
  for logic, 10*n*
  for obtaining area of parallelogram, 68

Machines—*Cont.*
   for obtaining area of rectangle, 30–31
   for simulating curve of thrown ball, 62
Magic trick, copying of, 87n
Magic worlds, 85, 91, 166
Maier, N. R. F., 59n, 60n, 61n, 90n, 130n, 131n
Marx, K., 11
Mathematical logic, *see* Logistics
Mathematics, *see* Algebra, Altar window, Angles, Area, Arithmetic, Corners of a cube, Division of a sum, Educational implications, Einstein, Exterior angles, Gauss, Internal angles, Parallelogram, Plus three, minus three, Products of series, Rectangle, Sides, number of, Square (area of), Square of a binomial, Sum of a series, Sum of angles, Sum of vectors, Trapezoid, Triangle, Vertical angles
Maxwell equations, 216, 229
Mayer, Clara W., xi, xiii, xv
Maze running, 122-123, 245
Means and ends, 65–69, 77. *See also* Goals of thinking
Mendeleev, D. I., 27, 27n
Mental deficiency, 6, 79ff, 272–276
Methods for studying thinking, 4–6. *See also* Operations, Research strategy
Metzger, W., 295
Michelson experiment, 216–219, 229, 231
Michigan, University of (Ann Arbor), xi
Mill, J. S., 7
Mond, Clara, xi
Moseley, H. G.-J., 28n
Motivation, 1–2, 53–57, 76–78, 88, 91–92, 133–135, 141–142, 167, 179–180, 191–194, 200–202, 218–219, 234–240, 244–246, 264, 283–284
Movement, *see* Absolute movement, Einstein
Mowatt, Marian B. H., 57n
Multiplication, 29, 33–35, 40, 43–44, 130, 160–168
Musical illustrations, 116, 242, 252–255, 264–265
Musical logic, *see* Musical illustrations

"Naturalistic approach," 12
Negation, *see* Not in logic
Negative experiences and thinking, 82, 90
Neptune, discovery of, 6
New School for Social Research, xi, xiii
Newton, I., 212, 225
Not in logic, 257–258

Operations
   of associationism, table of, 9
   of gestalt logic, table of, 235–236
   of inductive logic, table of, 8
   of traditional logic, table of, 6
   pure gestalt, xv
   structure-blind, xv
   See also Association theory, Gestalt logic, Traditional logic
Organon of Aristotle, 7

Parallelogram, area of, problem of, 13–27, 44–78, 169n, 269, 280–285
   A-B method, 18–20, 22–23, 65–69
   "blind" reactions, 17–24, 26, 50–51, 59
   experimental analysis, 15–29
   folding ruler approach, 46
   inductive formula, 27–28
   operations of traditional logic and, 69–75
   past experience and, 58–69
   proof, 14, 31–33, 70, 74–75, 284–285
   ring solution, 48–49, 52, 53, 55
   scissors solution, 47–48, 55–56
   "sensible" approach, 47–57, 65–69
   solution by infinitely thin rows, 49
   test of understanding, 15–27
   traditional teaching of, 13–15, 21, 25f., 61–62
   "ugly" procedures, 24–26, 29–33
Parsimony, law of, 37–38
Parts, arbitrary and necessary, 260–265
Past experience, 8–9, 44, 57n, 58–69, 89, 152–153, 250–251. *See also* Association theory, Drill, Habit, Repetition
Perceptual analogs, *see* Analogies of thought processes
Perpetual motion, 223

Personality and thinking, 12, 64, 176n, 180–181, 182–192, 271
Phenomenology, 11
Physics, problems in, *see* Balancing stick, Bridge problem, Crystallization, Einstein, Friction, Galileo, Galvanometer, Inertia, Plus three, minus three, Shooting at a target
Pillsbury, W. B., 9n, 12
Plus three, minus three problem, 143–150
analysis of solutions, 146–150
Political thinking, 244–245
Pragmatism, 11
Prägnanz, principle of, 238, 244
Primitive thinking, *see* Anthropological illustrations
Problems, types of, xv, 242, 245–246. *See also* Badminton, Mathematics, Physics, Social situations, Sum of vectors
Productive thinking, general nature of, 1–3, 234–259, *et passim*
Products of series, 117
Proof, 5–8, 16n, 31–33, 70, 74–75, 284–285
"blind," 26, 34–35
by excluded middle, 39
of parallelogram theorem, 14
of vertical angles theorem, 97–106
Prout, W., 27n

Reaction types, *see* Types of reactions to problems
Rectangle, area of, problem of, 29–37, 272, 276–280
association theory and, 42–44
"blind" procedures, 29–37
"sensible" procedures, 33–34, 39–42
traditional logic and, 42–44
Reenforcement, *see* Association theory, Reward
"Relations" as not crucial to productive thinking, 43, 104, 255–259
Relational networks, 11, 183–192
Relativity, theory of, 213–233
Renaissance, 7
Reorganization, *see* Gestalt approach
Repetition, 8, 11n, 22n, 115, 131–132, 250–251, 283–284. *See also* Association theory, Drill, Habit
Requirements, structural motivational force, 55–57

Requirements—*Cont.*
See also Gestalt approach, Gestalt logic, Structural approach
Research strategy in studying thinking, 3–5, 60–61, 84–85, 94–96, 234–236. *See also* A-B method, Giving "help," "Ugly" procedures
Reward, 11n, 85, 89, 92, 160–161, 173–174, 174n. *See also* Effect, law of
Rho-relations, 41, 60, 66, 83, 91, 93–94, 103, 145, 146, 158, 166–167, 236, 270, 288
Ring solution, *see* Parallelogram
Rolling body, 206–208
Rote learning, *see* Association theory, Drill, Past experience, Repetition, Trial and error
Rothschild, H., 296
Russell, B., 11
Rutherford, E., 28n

Sanders, E. H., 295
Saupe, E., 296
Scheerer, M., 171n
Schilder, P., 296
Schiller, P. von, 126n
Schulte, H., 64n, 183n
Scissors solution, *see* Parallelogram
"Seeing the light," 54, 57, 67, 88, 92, 113, 133–135, 169–171, 180, 196, 200–201, 234–237
Self-centeredness, *see* Egocentric orientation
Selz, O., 11, 12
"Sensible" procedures, *see* Gestalt approach, Gestalt logic
Shipley, T., 294
Shooting at a target, problem of, 286–287
Sides, number of, in cubes, pyramids, etc., 44n
Siemssen, Miss, 123
Simmel, G., 147n
Smith College, xi
Social situations, gestalt analysis of, 12, 169–192
Spinoza, B. de, 10n
Square, area of, 35
Square of a binomial, problem of, 153–160
"Square-sets," 124–126
Stern, Catherine, 76n, 127n, 133
Stern, W., 22n

Strasser, Vera, 295
Structural approach, 39–42, 234–259,
  et passim
  to area of parallelogram, 47–49, 51–
    55
  to area of rectangle, 39–40
  to badminton problem, 176–179
  to bridge problem, 93–95
  to Einstein problem, 226–233
  to Galileo problem, 210–212
  to Gauss problem, 121
  to plus three, minus three problem,
    146
  to social descriptions, 183–186
  to sum of a series problem, 289–
    293
  to sum of angles problem, 202–204
  to teaching about area, 272–285
  to vertical angles problem, 104
  See also Gestalt approach, Gestalt
    logic
Sum of angles of a polygon, see Exterior angles
Sum of a series problem, 38, 289–293.
  See also Gauss problem
Sum of vectors problem, 128–129
"Sums of connections," 85, 167. See
  also Association theory
Swarthmore College, xi
Symmetry, see Gestalt approach, Gestalt logic

Temperature, absolute, 224
Ternus, J., 258n
Thorndike, E. L., 9n, 100n, 151n,
  151–154, 160–161, 160n, 164
Thurnwald, R., 296
Traditional logic, 2–3, 5–8, 70, 89,
  237–238
  advantages of, 7
  behavioral implications of, 7
  deduction, 7–8
  difficulties in, 10–11, 42–44, 98,
    101, 158–160, 237–238, 247–259
  history of, 10–12
  induction, 7–8
  operations of, in Einstein problem,
    226–228
  operations of, in parallelogram prob-
    lem, 69–75
  operations of, in vertical angles
    problem, 98, 101
  syllogisms, 5–6, 7–8, 226, 248–252

Traditional views of thinking, 1–3,
  5–12, 42–44, 226–228, 237–238,
  245–259. See also Association
  theory, Traditional logic
Transfer, 35, 96, 146. See also Transposition
Transposition, 67–68, 81f, 234–236,
  253–255. See also A-B method
Trapezoid, area of, problem of, 18,
  76–77, 283
Trial and error, 9n, 11, 49–51, 68–69,
  81–82, 89, 201, 245, 251, 286–
  287. See also Association theory,
  Reward
Triangle, area of, 114n, 283
Truth, 6, 63, 235, 255, 259
Types of reactions to problems, 45,
  101–103, 110–116, 134–135, 143–
  144, 172–174

"Ugly" procedures, 24–26, 29–33, 37–
  39, 43–44, 50–51, 293
Understanding, operational definition
  of via A-B method, 23

Velocity of light, 214–226
Vertical angles, problem of, 97–107
Vis impressa, 205n, 206, 211
von Hornbostel, E.M., see Hornbostel,
  E. M. von

Wertheimer, Lise, xv, 296
Wertheimer, Max, xii, xiii, xv-xvi, 6n,
  53n, 55n, 56n, 57n, 63n, 64n,
  93n, 125n, 127n, 139n, 170n,
  171n, 178n, 180n, 183n, 219n,
  235n, 239n, 246n, 249n, 259n,
  275n, 279n, 294–296
Wertheimer, Michael, xv-xvi, 53n,
  63n, 93n, 125n, 260n, 295
Wertheimer, Valentin, xiii, xv
Whitehead, A. N., 11
Whole-qualities, 125, 136–140. See
  also Gestalt approach
Wohlwill, von E., 205n
Woodworth, R. S., 139n
Words and thinking, 228n
Würzburg school, 12

Yatabe, T., 295

Zener, K., 131